UNDAUNTED

Number Twenty:
Tarleton State University Southwestern Studies in the Humanities
William T. Pilkington, General Editor

Elise in Texas, ca. 1855. Photo courtesy of Ophelia Sparks, Denton;
copy at the University of Texas Institute of Texan Cultures at San Antonio.

UNDAUNTED

A Norwegian Woman in Frontier Texas

CHARLES H. RUSSELL

Charles H. Russell

for Andrea Davis

3/15/09

Texas A&M University Press
College Station

The paper used in this book meets the minimum requirements
of the American National Standard for Permanence
of Paper for Printed Library Materials, z39.48-1984.
Binding materials have been chosen for durability.
∞

Library of Congess Cataloging-in-Publication Data

Russell, Charles H.
    Undaunted : a Norwegian woman in frontier Texas / Charles H. Russell.
        p.   cm. — (Tarleton State University southwestern studies in the humanities ;
    no. 20)
    Includes bibliographical references and index.
    ISBN 1-58544-453-7 (cloth : alk. paper)
    1. Waerenskjold, Elise Amalie Tvede, 1815–1895. 2. Norwegian Americans—Texas—
Biography. 3. Women pioneers—Texas—Biography. 4. Frontier and pioneer life—
Texas. 5. Texas—Social life and customs—19th century. 6. Kaufman County (Tex.)—
Social life and customs—19th century. 7. Van Zandt County (Tex.)—Social life and
customs—19th century. 8. Kaufman County (Tex.)—Biography. 9. Van Zandt
County (Tex.)—Biography. I. Title. II. Series.
F395.S2R87 2005
976.4'27605'092—dc22

                                                              2005004659

For the heroes of nineteenth-century America, men as well as women, who merit William James's tribute:

"I am . . . in favor of the eternal forces of truth which always work in the individual and [in an] immediately unsuccessful way, underdogs always, till history comes, after they are long dead, and puts them on top."
Quoted by Louis Menand in *The Metaphysical Club*

CONTENTS

ILLUSTRATIONS

Acknowledgments

ELISE WAERENSKJOLD'S BIOGRAPHY could not have been written without the help of my wife, Inger Johanne Russell, a native of Kristiansund, Norway, not to be confused with the Kristiansand that is featured in this story. Because of her knowledge of her country, its language, and its history, Inger inspired the book and contributed the main translations of newly available letters and dispatches, all of them in Elise's archaic Danish-Norwegian dialect and fundamental to the narrative.

Three of the Waerenskjold descendants in Texas encouraged the effort and supplied material for the book. Sue Ann Trammel of Cleburne allowed me to photograph the paintings that Elise brought with her from Norway; Sue Ann also told me that her daughter Deanna and son-in-law Philip Lewis have named their recently born daughter Elise. Bill Van Shaw and his wife Mary Margaret graciously received Inger and me at their home in Dallas. During the visit we were shown items of Elise's possessions, some of which were later donated to the Smithsonian Institution in Washington. I was permitted to photograph Elise's embroidery portrait of Jesus and Bill's colorized photo portrait of Wilhelm Waerenskjold. In Denton I spent a pleasant two hours with Ophelia Sparks, Bill Van Shaw's sister, and was fortunate to meet her daughter Susanne and son Stephen, the fourth generation of the family, who had come from their homes in California and Michigan.

Forrest Brown, archivist of the Norwegian-American Historical Association, provided key documents from the NAHA collection at St. Olaf College, Northfield, Minnesota, and generously answered questions about Elise's life and Norwegian-American history. Judge Derwood Johnson, who resides in Waco, Texas, and is of Norwegian descent, allowed me to use his typed copy of the murderer N. T. Dickerson's trial transcript; the judge had searched out the hundred-year-old document in the dusty files in the Kaufman County Courthouse basement. John Dahle, also of Norwegian descent, my Dartmouth College classmate and now a retired attorney in Denver, made recommendations crucial to understanding the proceedings in the Dickerson trial and suggested editorial changes in an early draft of Elise's biography. His enthusiasm for the project offered constant encouragement.

Ulf Hamran, former historian for Arendal County in Norway and a specialist on the history of Elise's family, provided background on her life and was the first to disclose and translate the record of Wilhelm Waerenskjold's criminal convictions. Lisbeth Higley of Tonsberg, who has done research on Elise in Texas and published articles about her, provided an alternative translation of the same criminal records and allowed use of her photo of Elise's portrait as a fifteen-year-old girl. Translations of other letters by Elise and Norwegian Texans were made by members of the Ladies Group at the Norwegian Seamen's Church in Pasadena, Texas, among them Anne Saglokken, Astrid Mosvold, Sidsel Roemer, Randi Jahnsen, and Ingelin Saethre.

Dr. Bernard Patten, retired chief of the Neuromuscular Disease Division at Baylor College of Medicine in Houston, supplied the retrospective diagnosis of Elise's son Thorvald's illness and death. Elvis Davis of Fruitvale, Texas, sent the copy of Governor Cole's pardon for Dickerson; Elise's letter to Cole also came from Davis's files. Jeremy Hood of Higgins, Smythe, and Hood Yachts in Kemah, Texas, who has twice sailed the Atlantic from England to Texas, presented information on sailing directions and wind routes across the ocean; Janet, his wife, displayed and explained the maps of the ocean wind speeds and patterns. Alexandro De Ybañez and Roxanne Delaney, of the sailing ship *Elissa* harbored in Galveston, took me on a tour of the ship, explained sail characteristics and rigging, and described the passage from Florida to Texas. Alan Stewart, research assistant at the Maine Maritime Museum in Bath, and John G. Arrison, volunteer at the Penobscot Marine Museum in Searsport, Maine, searched out the records for the ship *New England;* Trond Austheim of the Norway-Heritage Project in Oslo did the same for the barque *Ygdrasil.* Solvi Sogner, professor of history at the University of Oslo, conveyed the information on the lack of formal divorce proceedings at the time of Elise's divorce from Sven Foyn. Betty Ann Trednick, a resident of Van Zandt County and historian of the Four Mile Prairie Lutheran Church, gave me a copy of Jensen's history of the church, the grave records, and supporting documents.

I am indebted to the following individuals for tours and other assistance with sites and sources pertaining to Elise's life in Norway and Texas: Polly Wattner and J. C. Sapp of Van Zandt County, Texas, for a visit to Elise's land and house location in Four Mile Prairie; Alvhild Gulbrandson, director of Lillesand Maritime Museum, for a tour of Elise's home and residences in Lillesand and for permission to photograph the painting of the pastor's farm at Vestre Moland; Eigil Trondsen for tours of the Sven Foyn offices, residence, church, and workers' and widows' apartment buildings and of the whaling museums in Tonsberg and Sandefjord; Doranne Stansell, former hostess at the Bosque Memorial Museum in Clifton, Texas, for a tour of the museum; Nancy Hengst, founder of the Hamilton County Genealogical Society, for a visit to Elise's grave site at the Howard Street Cemetery in Hamilton, Texas; and Peggy Fox, director of the Harold B. Simpson History Complex in Hillsboro, for assistance in finding and using records of Wilhelm Waerenskjold's Texas Confederate military service. Stale Eide, a Norwegian resident of Seabrook, Texas, found the ship's manifest for the *New England* at the New Orleans Public Library. Susan Steele of the University of Houston–Clear Lake, Texas, made invaluable contributions in solving reference problems. Mary Linn Wernet, Head Archivist, Cammie G. Henry Research Center, Northwestern Louisiana State University, Natchitoches, provided key documents on El Camino Real in Louisiana.

Copies of Elise's letters in Orm Overland's multivolume *Fra Amerika til Norge* were supplied by the National Library in Oslo, Norway. The National Archive, also in Oslo, provided copies of the boxed legal documents of Wilhelm Waerenskjold's 1842 criminal convictions. Maps and pages from various biographical dictionaries were made available at the Deichmanske Library in Oslo and by James Archer, historian at the Halden Historical Society.

The online *Handbook of Texas,* sponsored by the Texas State Historical Association and the University of Texas Libraries, proved an inexhaustible source for this book. The editors are to be thanked for their development and support of this outstanding encyclopedia.

At the invitation of Wenche Kirkebye Moe, former consul general of Norway in Houston, I gave a talk on part of the book to the annual meeting of the Norwegian-American Forum held in 2002. On the recommendation of Orm Overland and his associates, I presented at a University of Bergen Norwegian-American Historical Association–Norway conference, a paper on Elise's "bigamous" marriage to Wilhelm Waerenskjold; the paper is to be published in the forthcoming conference volume.

I am especially grateful to my brother, Dr. Anthony Russell, and to the members of a writers' critique group in the Clear Lake area—Carlos Ledson Miller, Barbara Ewing, Kay Hudson, Dick Moore, Jim Stanton, Kathy Adams, Leslie Mazina—who read the manuscript and provided valuable suggestions for revisions.

Rita Anja Huste, administrative assistant at the Royal Norwegian Consulate General in Houston, kindly made copies for me of Elise's dispatches and letters from her copy of Odd Magnar Syverson and Derwood Johnson's *Norge i Texas,* a rare book.

Financial support for research and travel in preparation of Elise's biography came exclusively from the EW Research Fund that Inger Russell and I created from our personal resources.

UNDAUNTED

CHAPTER 1

SAGA'S BEGINNING

WHAT MAKES a modern saga? Consider the life of Elise Waerenskjold (Ayleesa Varenshul in her native Norwegian), who emigrated from Norway to Texas in 1847.

Sagas tell stories of real people turned into heroes, and Elise's story fits with epic hero mythology: she answered a call to adventure, left her conventional world, went through ordeals, and in the end affirmed a truth as sweeping as it was beneficial.[1] In Elise's time women were tied to the home—children, kitchen, and church, an old saying goes—valued for their docility and domestic skills rather than for their intelligence. Her life foretold the future: women would leave the home, become wage earners, professionals, entrepreneurs, intellectuals, and strong athletes—yet, firm in their new cosmos, would still create and sustain new life as they always had.

An early feminist, reform advocate, and writer, Elise left Norway a single woman, aged thirty-two, determined to explore the possibilities for independent being in a pioneer country. In Texas she settled into hardy livestock ranching, raising cattle, sheep, and hogs. Yet through the years she maintained an enthusiastic taste for literature and a regular production of letters (many placed in print by her friends) and articles written for newspapers.

She was born into the *embets* class, the privileged caste of governing administrators who ran Norway after the country was unified with Sweden in 1815 at the close of the Napoleonic wars. Her father, the Lutheran pastor Nicolai Tvede, held his post by royal appointment and performed civic functions in the Lillesand district of southern Norway. He maintained vital public records of baptisms, marriages, and funerals, supervised religious education—the central element of the school curriculum—and exercised influence in local initiatives, among them providing relief to the poor.

Elise's residence at her father's pastorate farm, Vestre Moland outside Lillesand.
Courtesy of Lillesand Maritime Museum.

Elise was reared to be a trophy wife, as we would say today, fit for marriage within the established upper social strata. Her oil portrait painted when she was fifteen clearly shows her in debutante style, elegantly dressed in the Empire fashion, soft curls hanging to her shoulders, large doe eyes (cover photo). She studied foreign languages—German and French—read the Bible and proper books, learned artful painting and needle skills for fine embroidery. Instead of acquiescing to the implicit goal of her upbringing, however, she deliberately chose what it meant to her to be a woman, sustaining her sense of independence with lifelong faith in God's will that human beings should be free.

During her childhood and teen years her father moved through successive and increasingly important religious posts along the west coast of the wide Skagerrak that runs from the Christiania (now Oslo) fjord one hundred miles down to the North Sea. The rugged coastline there is carved into *viks* and fjords, deep water inlets that made fine harbors for towns like Lillesand, where Elise lived as a girl and young teenager (see map 1). Kristiansand, Grimstad, Dypvaag, Sandefjord, Skien, Porsgrunn, and Tonsberg are all towns readily accessible to the European mainland by sailing ship. For centuries this part of Norway had been in touch with the sophisticated civilization of nations to the south—Denmark, Germany, France, England, and even, through trade, Portugal, Spain, and Italy.[2]

CHAPTER 1

—4—

Elise's flower and vase painting, brought from Norway to Texas.
Photo by Charles H. Russell, courtesy of Sue Ann Trammel, Cleburne, Texas.

She grew up during "The Birth of the Modern," as the English historian
Paul Johnson has called the period from 1815 to 1830. The industrial revolution was just arriving in her country, and Elise witnessed it firsthand. Her
father was related to the founder of the Nes Ironworks located not far from
Lillesand, and her mother to the foundry's Danish engineer-designer, who
invented a cast-iron stove so effective that it competed with the products of
northern Europe and trebled the company's exports. Knowing these men
and their accomplishments gave Elise respect for practical work. Enterprise

Map 1. Southern Norway area known to Elise.
Map prepared by John Cotter, cartographer, courtesy of Charles H. Russell.

and invention were present to her from her earliest years; she considered them to have moral and ethical value because they brought good things to people.[3]

She shaped the opportunity of the time into her own career. Population was booming thanks to expanding industrial production and improvements in agriculture. More children were surviving to adulthood, reducing

Elise's father's last church in Holt, Norway.
His grave is marked with a cast-iron cover embossed with his name.
Photo by Charles H. Russell, courtesy of Sue Ann Trammel, Cleburne, Texas.

the need for individuals to have large families to support them in old age. As the importance of producing children and maintaining families declined, the idea that a woman might make a living without depending on a husband began to take shape. Marriage could be based on "love, happiness, and respect" rather than on the traditional "love, honor, and obey." Sensing new developments, as a young woman Elise braved the opprobrium associated with being a spinster. That status was still viewed with general contempt, but it fit right in with her rising sense of independence.

Elise's father died when she was seventeen. At nineteen, instead of following the usual pattern for well-bred young ladies coming of age, she evaded the social obligation to find a husband, give birth to children, and settle down to family life. Instead, she chose to become a schoolteacher, an occupation almost exclusively restricted to men at the time. She worked at first in Tonsberg, then moved to Lillesand, where she established her own business enterprise, a private school for girls. The school, possibly the first of its kind in Norway, stressed handicrafts and was so successful that in Texas some forty years later she wrote to her friend Thomine Dannevig back in Lillesand asking if it was still in operation; unfortunately there is no record of Thomine's reply.

While in Tonsberg Elise had met Sven Foyn, scion of a wealthy family and captain of his own merchant sailing ship. They seemed like a good match, she a lively and interesting young woman, he exceptionally competent and successful in seamanship, and both of them were animated by strong religious convictions. When her mother died in 1839 Elise, now twenty four, abandoned her spinster status and married Foyn.

Three and a half years later they separated and filed for divorce. In her old age Elise said the breakdown was "due to incompatibility—absolutely nothing else," this in a letter to the Norwegian-American historian Rasmus Anderson. Foyn, a defender of the old ways, expected Elise to be a traditional wife who would make marriage and attendance upon him the center of her existence; among other things, he objected to her running her own school. Separation and divorce at the time were so unusual that there was no established legal procedure for them, and a divorced woman became a virtual social outcast.[4]

After parting from Foyn, Elise joined a group of social thinkers who devoted themselves to progressive causes, especially to efforts on behalf of the poor. Their first initiative was directed toward the temperance movement, then less a moral crusade than an endeavor to save people from wrecking their lives by excessive indulgence in the flow of alcohol coming out of new, rapidly produced, low-cost stills that could be used to brew spirits for local sale.

To get involved in this movement Elise had to penetrate the exclusively male Lillesand Temperance Society. She considered this break in the gender barrier important enough to write about in a temperance publication: "That no women in our community had as yet become members of the society was no longer any deterrent for me but rather a potent motive for joining." Having accomplished this new intrusion into a male domain, in 1843 she issued the publication that marked the start of her career as a writer. This was a pamphlet she called *Summons to All Noble Men and Women to Unite in Temperance Societies for the Purpose of Eradicating Drunkenness and the Use of Brandy Together with a Brief Exposition of the Deleterious Effects of Brandy Drinking*—a rather overwhelming title but one that nonetheless expressed the typical rational approach Elise used in everything she wrote.[5]

Her style was lucid. Clear statements free of ambiguity conveyed unmistakable meaning. Orderly, systematic, and well structured in her thinking, she relied on rational persuasion when making a case, as in this temperance pamphlet, where she called up facts instead of denouncing drunkenness on moral grounds. Typically, she wrote straightforward declarative sentences minimally embellished with adjectives and subordinate phrases and clauses. It was a style well suited to journalism, and even the religious convictions that supported her sense of freedom to pursue an independent course in life reflected practical ideas.

In the same year that she produced her temperance pamphlet her group of socially minded thinkers took up the cause of emigration as a solution to the problems of the poor. The leader in this new path was Johan Reinert Reiersen, editor and owner of the *Christianssandsposten* (Kristiansand post) and considered to be the most effective journalist advocating progressive political and reform views in Norway. Because his father had been sexton at her father's churches, Elise had known Reiersen since her early years; like all his friends she called him Reinert. When he decided to make an exploratory trip to America in 1843–44, she became one of his financial backers as well as a deeply interested observer. In return he became her mentor regarding emigration, showing her that though some people were leaving the country to escape poverty, others more fortunate might do so because they wished to start a new life.

Reiersen's trip to America included an extensive journey through Texas, and when he returned he published a book detailing what he had discovered. The chapter on Texas praised its leading citizens' sense of equality and indifference to newcomers' personal histories and social origins. He followed publication of his book by floating *Norge og Amerika* (Norway and America), the first regularly issued emigration magazine in the country. When he left for Texas in 1845 he passed the periodical on to his brother, but his brother abandoned the project when he in turn departed for Texas the following year.[6]

At this point Elise stepped in, because, as she later told Rasmus Anderson, "No one wanted to put out such a dangerous sheet, that might lure people into migrating. To keep the paper alive, I undertook its publication." The periodical under her editorship reached Andreas Gjestvang (pronounced "Yestvang"), a prominent man who held the government license as postmaster in the Hamar area north of Christiania (present-day Oslo). Gjestvang became a subscriber, initiated correspondence with her regarding his personal interest in leaving Norway, and spread the word about Texas in his district. Hamar became a focal point for the first sizable Norwegian emigration to Texas, and today the old cemeteries where the Norwegians settled—at Brownsboro, Four Mile Prairie, Clifton, and Norse near Cranfills Gap—are well populated with the names of people who came from the area. Besides directly influencing colonization from Hamar, Elise's reputation helped draw immigrants from Lillesand, Tonsberg, and other towns along the Skagerrak coast.[7]

The Texas to which Elise was coming, with its established Hispanic, black, and southern migrants already numbering close to two hundred thousand, was attracting diverse groups—Germans, Czechs, Irish, Poles, among them Catholics and Jews as well as Protestants; Danes and Italians would come after the Civil War. For Norwegians, Texas would never attain a popularity equal to that of the northern plains states, but Elise's articles and letters, which continued to be published in Norway all her life, contributed to the image of hope for better things that would bring hundreds of thousands of her countrymen to America.

Texas in those days was unspoiled virgin territory, a hunter's paradise full of game, settled mainly in the eastern fringe bordering Louisiana and along the Gulf of Mexico. Travel was by slow ox-drawn wagon and horseback over rough trails, open space, and, to the west, Indian territory, where Comanche and other tribes trekked to Mexico on annual migrations from Colorado, Oklahoma, and Kansas. Texas had joined the Union in December, 1845, only slightly more than a year and a half before Elise came. In those first years after statehood it was getting organized politically, its huge counties being cut up into smaller and more manageable governmental units.

Within months after Elise had taken over as editor of *Norge og Amerika* in 1846, her general interest in departures from her country changed to an inspired sense that she should assemble an emigration group and herself look into the possibility of settling in Texas. Now an adult woman separated from her upper-class roots, with her mentor Reiersen established in a Norwegian Texas colony and close friends from Lillesand also there, it was time for her to make her own exploration.

She held an idealistic view: for her, Texas was a place where democracy, equality, and opportunity prevailed, where achievement meant everything and social rules and origins were unimportant and even irrelevant. Perhaps there her independent ways could take root and flourish.

She had heard the call to adventure. Over the years she would experience drama and tragedy, make choices geared to outside events, and act with feeling as well as calculated intent. In time she would become something of an icon, a person of known quality who had gone to the new western homeland. But for now the voyage ahead, seeming so rich with enticing possibilities, would prove hazardous well beyond her expectations.

CHAPTER 2

DROBAK, NORWAY, TO NEW ORLEANS

BEFORE THE TIME of steam power and steel-hulled ships, winter ice often blocked the seaward passage into Christiania harbor. People reached the city either by land or by horse-drawn sled hauled over the frozen salt water. Twenty-seven miles to the south a commanding strait narrows the long fjord leading up from the Skagerrak, and from there the way became impassable. Wooden sailing vessels could not crush through the ice or navigate the floes during spring thaws. Just below the obstructed zone, Drobak served as the winter harbor for Christiania.

At Drobak Elise Tvede, age thirty-two, promoter of emigration and former editor of the magazine *Norge og Amerika* (Norway and America), boarded ship for Texas in the spring of 1847. Well-off and traveling at her own expense, she was unmarried, an unusual state for a woman considering emigration in that era. As organizer of the Texas journey she supplied the names of enrolled voyagers to persons whom she hoped would join in the expedition. Wilhelm Waerenskjold, one of the travelers, never appeared on her lists. Even after they married in Texas and settled down on a prairie ranch, she never explained who he was or how he came to be in her group.

Her silence had a cost. People in the Texan Norwegian colony were suspicious about him. They knew Elise had a former husband, the sea captain Sven Foyn, a man on his way to becoming one of the richest people in Norway. Her marriage to Foyn had ended in separation after three wasted years. Wagging tongues clucked. It was rumored that Waerenskjold had clerked in Foyn's office and run off to America with the captain's wife.

There was no truth to the tale and its nasty hint of lewd behavior. Elise never acknowledged the gossip. She was self-assured and willing to defy convention, but she was firm in her moral outlook: love and desire come only with marriage, fully bonded. Besides, on the ocean journey she and Waeren-skjold shared quarters with two other passengers—"farmer Andersen" and "student Buch" she called them in her dispatches to *Norge og Amerika*. If any scandal hung over her relationship with Waerenskjold it concerned the lawful status of their eventual marriage, which took place months before her Norwegian divorce became final.[1]

The name of the ship they boarded at Drobak lent an epic quality to their journey. *Ygdrasil*. The word came from a mythological object of the old heathen Viking religion. In ancient Norse beliefs *Ygdrasil* was the primeval world tree, the ash standing at the center of the earth, filled with magic life-preserving powers, guarding Asgard, the home of the gods. The Norns, goddesses of destiny, sat by a spring at its base and cast the fates of men. The tree twined down around all the worlds into deepest hell. In the sea abyss a giant coiled serpent lay tearing at its roots, threatening the earth with destruction.[2]

Elise probably cared little for the myths surrounding *Ygdrasil*. Norwegians had adopted Christianity nearly one thousand years before she sailed, and her religious convictions ran deep. Among seafaring men, though, pagan memories from the Viking era lingered on. Ship owners sometimes drew on ancient mythology when choosing names for their vessels.

Contrary to her fabled name, *Ygdrasil* was a humble ship, a plain cargo carrier built to haul timber, a three-masted barque designed for capacity rather than speed. No queen of the fleet, she had a wide, rounded hull and blunt bow that battered into the seas rather than cut through them. With a broad, nearly flat underside she could sit upright like a squatting goose in harbors where low tide dropped the water level down to the mud. Her gear was planned for economy. The two forward masts carried square sails on yardarms while the third set was aligned fore-and-aft as on a yacht—fewer men could handle rigging of this type. At sea she averaged three to four knots per hour, about half the usual speed of a passenger ship under sail.[3]

Cargo carriers offered minimal service. Passengers had assigned berths in a deck cabin adjoining the master's quarters. They supplied their own food and bedding, and cooked their own meals in the galley. They chose *Ygdrasil* for economy rather than luxury. Thrift was a primary consideration for the four passengers who came aboard at Drobak to travel to the French port of Havre de Grace (present-day Le Havre) on the first leg of their journey to Texas. Thrift, however, was realized by none of them.

Elise was responsible. As editor of *Norge og Amerika* and organizer of the voyage she had negotiated the arrangements and payment for the trip. She

Ygdrasil, Elise's departure ship from Drobak.
Courtesy of Norwegian Maritime Museum, Bigdoy, Norway.

had a practical turn of mind, but her experience was limited to publishing reports from Norwegian emigrants in America. She knew little about negotiating long sea fares and less about haggling with a canny ship owner who might deceive a naïve broker. In her familiar and privileged world as the daughter of a Lutheran clergyman, people were mannerly. Trust prevailed. She expected merchants to quote fair prices and stick by their word.

She was about to enter unprotected territory.

J. G. Kock was owner of *Ygdrasil.* He met sociably with Elise, his wife present. The couple spoke nicely, seemed polite and hospitable. Elise addressed him as "Mr. Kock." At that meeting and on several later occasions she asked for the exact fare to Havre de Grace, where they would board the trans-Atlantic passenger ship for New Orleans.

Kock did not quote a specific figure. To Elise's repeated inquiries he answered pleasantly that no one would be overcharged. "In fact," she was told, "the fare would be so moderate that none of them would be dissatisfied in any way."

Content with these assurances, Elise made no effort to contact other ship owners regarding rates. That gave Kock an opportunity to play a crafty game. Ship arrivals and departures were subject to natural forces. Wind, weather, tide, fog, or plain luck determined ship availability and sailing schedules. He knew how to use these uncertainties for money-grubbing.

Elise could only use common sense in deciding when to sail for America. Avoid dangerous conditions. Leave after the winter storms in the North Sea, English Channel, and North Atlantic have passed. Go before the hurricanes and devilish humidity rise on the mid-Atlantic way and the Caribbean Sea. Try to reach New Orleans before the yellow fever–ridden summer months. She and her friends had to leave Norway in March so that they could reach New Orleans by the end of May or early June—if all went well.

Kock waited until no other cargo carriers were in the Drobak harbor to offer him any competition. Only *Ygdrasil* was ready to sail. He named an outrageous price, almost three times the usual fare to France. Elise had no alternative. She had to agree to the fare.

But she got even. From Havre de Grace she sent a sharp dispatch to *Norge og Amerika:* "I find it despicable of Mr. Kock to come forward at a time when we had to pay what he demanded. What made me feel so very uncomfortable in this matter was that my blind trust in Mr. Kock was hurting not just me but also Waerenskjold and Andersen." She made no reference to Buch because he paid his own fare.

Thus she put Kock's underhand dealings on public record and warned future emigrants to beware of cunning merchants offering sea passages—some might even seem kind and hospitable. S. T. Kirkgaard, the printer in Trondheim who had taken over publication of the magazine, immediately issued her account. A favorable report from her would have helped Kock's future travel bookings because sources of information about emigration were few. Instead, his money-grubbing scheme was exposed just when passenger travel to America was beginning to boom. Elise had her payback. She never had to mention Kock again.[4]

Captain Einersen and First Mate J. Christiansen, masters of *Ygdrasil,* proved far more honorable than the ship's owner. "Well-bred," as Elise described them. They possessed the characteristics vital for good sailing ship command. Elise would learn just how important these characteristics could be on the second stage of her journey from Havre de Grace to New Orleans. For now, the journey went nicely thanks to *Ygdrasil's* two officers.

Fog and headwinds delayed their departure to March 22. In a letter to *Norge og Amerika* Elise recorded her feelings as they were sailing away from her homeland, her words hinting at a sense of exile: "For a moment it was as if I left all the ones I love in Norway, maybe never to be seen again in this life. But whether we will gather again or not, I will remember with joy and gratitude every proof of friendship and goodwill I received. And all my warmest wishes will be for the good of my beloved Norway, the country where I spent my childhood and youth, the country that contains so many precious memories, so many beloved friends. It can never be forgotten."[5]

Her statement had more finality than she intended—she had not yet decided to stay in Texas—but once they cast off she turned her mind to the future. The freshening sea air and winds of spring swept away her melancholy. Out on the Christiania fjord spectacular scenery slipped by, low-lying mountains ground smooth by mile-deep glacier ice millennia before, now grown up with the rich, dark green boreal forests of northern lands.

In a day and a half they reached the open Skagerrak, where the waters spread two hundred and fifty miles from Kristiansand in Norway across the Kattegat to Malmö in Sweden. The Scandinavian landmass there makes a giant dragon maw, seeming ready to tear away the Danish peninsula jutting up into the Kattegat from Europe. As they passed Kristiansand, a city just a few miles from where Elise had grown up, she had a last waning glimpse of the world she had known until mature young womanhood. She would never see it again.

Ygdrasil sailed onto the North Sea, down the choppy English Channel, stopping to deliver timber in England at Deal near the white chalk cliffs of Dover. She docked on April 3 at Havre de Grace, the port at the mouth of the River Seine flowing from Paris.[6]

The entire journey took twelve days, covering some 730 miles at about 2.25 knots per hour. Passenger ships sailing direct from Christiania to Havre de Grace would normally take less than five days. In spite of her slow progress *Ygdrasil* made nearly as much speed as their next ship, *New England,* on the way from Havre de Grace to New Orleans.

In Havre de Grace Elise toured the markets to compare local prices with those in Christiania. Her goal was to publish the information in *Norge og Amerika* so that future emigrants could decide whether to purchase supplies in Norway or wait until they reached France.

Her inventory of supplies undoubtedly matched the purchases she had made in Christiania, and it may have helped create a model for commercial passenger ships going to America. Not long after her account appeared in *Norge og Amerika,* a leading shipping company issued an almost identical store of provisions that passengers were required to bring aboard for the trans-Atlantic crossing.

In bulk Elise named bread (100 pounds), peas (one barrel), and potatoes (half a barrel). By the pound she specified bacon, ham, coffee, powdered sugar, rice, butter, wheat flour, tea, prunes, and candles—amounts to be determined by the buyer. In general, prices were higher in Havre de Grace than in Christiania—except for lemons ("big, beautiful, inexpensive") and red wine ("decent quality at half a franc per bottle"). Eggs, she said, stay fresh a long time at sea, and twenty-six (a baker's two dozen) could be bought in Havre de Grace at a reasonable price.

"I am satisfied with shopping in Christiania," she declared, and then turned to the question of bringing Norwegian products into France. Readers might fear that French port officials would use overly strict inspections to prevent the transfer of supplies purchased in Norway to ships sailing from Havre de Grace. She reassured them by telling about her untroubled passage through the port: "When we got on board our clothing and food were just loosely checked by the customs officers. They did not demand that I open anything more than what I wanted to open."[7]

Besides the favorable attitude of French port officials, emigrants could count on support from their government's representative at Havre de Grace. At the time Norway was united with Sweden (Elise's American neighbors in Texas would consider her a Swede), but government officials, whether Norwegian or Swedish, held emigrants in disdain. Not so J. P. Clausen, the consul at the French port. About him she wrote: "I cannot praise his willingness to help us even though we never asked for his help. He negotiated our fares and he also helped and advised us in every possible way."[8]

Her sentiments were real, but she should have tempered her praise. The fares Clausen negotiated for them on *New England* bought quarters far inferior than they expected. Someone more suspicious than Elise might have thought Clausen was a private agent hired by the shipping company to sell *New England*'s passenger space.

Aboard *Ygdrasil* Elise and her shipmates had lived next to the officers in quarters up on the main deck. Each one of them had a berth in a private room adjoining a small parlor where they dined at a tidy mess table with the captain and first mate. On *New England* they knew they would travel on the mid-deck, the main passenger section of the ship, but they assumed Clausen's fare would buy them seclusion—a small room that locked, individual bunks, and a personal table where they could eat their meals alone. This notion turned out to be pure fantasy.

The passenger mid-deck on *New England* was an all-in-one residence, a 130-foot-long dormitory, dining hall, and living space. Narrow wood-frame berths, completely open and intended to sleep three people, ran in two tiers along the bulkheads on both sides of the ship. The common mess table, with cooking utensils hanging on hooks above and below it, stretched almost the full length of the deck. Heavy chests for personal belongings obstructed the passageways between the mess table and berths. The passengers' bread and smoked meat, supposedly enough to last for the entire journey, hung from the ship's timbers overhead. There were no rooms that locked, and passengers had no privacy whatsoever.

In later years equivalent second-rate quarters aboard steamships would be called the "steerage" because of their location next to the vessel's massive rudder control machinery. On nineteenth-century sailing ships like *New England* the mid-deck loomed low and dark, a five-foot-high cavern with air and light admitted only through two main hatchways, one at either end. Elise and her friends lodged with more than two hundred other passengers in this crammed mid-deck space.

Descriptions of quarters aboard sailing ships show that *New England's* three masts, each a foot thick, were sunk through the mess table to the keelson down below. Stagnant seep water could be heard splashing against the pillow blocks where the masts bedded, surrounded by ballast stones. At night the mid-deck's hanging lanterns cast a dim, swinging, yellow light into the dusky shadows.

At sea, whatever the time of day or night, the fore and aft entry hatches of the mid-deck were often kept closed to prevent flooding by wave-borne seawater. Always dank, the deck was filled with human odors. During windless weather when no air blew through, a vague stench rose up from the bilges. Elise was provoked to advise her *Norge og Amerika* readers: "Under all circumstances one ought to try to make a physical division between each person in the bunk because it is very hot and stifling."[9]

Consul Clausen seems not to have told Elise and her friends that growing emigration from northern Europe had caused prices to spiral. The 150-franc fare (about $950 in today's currency) they each paid would no longer buy them privacy on the mid-deck or anywhere else. Clausen's good service promised hope and comfort. A trusted adviser, he failed them.

In spite of the misunderstanding about accommodations, *New England* was a good ship. Nothing about her construction and appointments could be blamed for the ordeal that befell her passengers on the crossing from Havre de Grace to New Orleans. Her history tells the story of her good qualities.

She was built in 1836 before the days of fast clipper ships, at a time when Yankee sea merchants still favored wide vessels designed to carry large quantities of cargo. Her specifications on file at the Maritime Museum in Bath,

New England, Elise's ship from France to New Orleans.
Courtesy of Maine Maritime Museum, Bath.

Maine, show she was broad of beam like *Ygdrasil,* but she was a bigger and faster ship. At 546 tons she had a third more capacity, and with a 131-foot hull she was longer by thirty-two feet. Her main deck, over thirty feet wide, allowed passengers considerable space for open-air promenade. Built for deep harbors—her draft was fifteen feet—she probably had an underdeck where passengers could store bulky home furnishings and goods.

Her three masts were rigged with eleven square sails; when fully spread these gave her some 19,000 feet of canvas to *Ygdrasil's* 12,000 feet. Cruising with all sails set before a following wind she would have been able to travel more than twice as fast as *Ygdrasil.* In spite of her greater potential for speed she averaged only 3.5 knots per hour across the Atlantic, scarcely a knot more than *Ygdrasil* made from Drobak to Havre de Grace.

New England's design could not be blamed for her slow journey or the problems that beset the passengers on the way across the ocean. Her homeport was Bath, Maine, where the converging Androscoggin, Kennebec, and Sagadahoc river currents scoured a good harbor. During the 1840s the shipwrights in Bath sent four hundred new vessels out over Casco Bay to the Atlantic.

In 1846, the year before Elise and her friends sailed, *New England's* owners docked the ship at the Bath shipyards to have her made over from a cargo carrier to a passenger vessel. In terms of weight, humans and commodities were interchangeable: one human with baggage occupied about as much space and cost about the same to haul as a ton of commodities. When refitted for passengers *New England's* yawning cargo space made adequate, if cramped, quarters.

Compared to the later sleek clipper ships, *New England* looked tubby—her square stern and billet bow with no figurehead made her seem that way. Like those of the clippers, though, her hull must have been lined with copper sheathing so that she could sail in tropical waters without being attacked by teredo worms with their sharp, wood-boring teeth drilling into her underbody planks. A captain with a copper-sheathed ship would have had no reason to avoid taking a route through a warm sea like the Caribbean.

After the refitting, *New England's* owners sailed her in a packet line taking passengers and mail to Europe. A painting on file at the Maine Maritime Museum shows her entering the French port of Marseilles (see painting of *New England,* previous), disclosing that she must have made at least one trip to that Mediterranean city. Considering *New England's* history, the captain who took her from Havre de Grace to New Orleans in the spring of 1847 should have been a highly competent seaman.[10]

Illness broke out on his ship during the passage. Elise wrote to *Norge og Amerika* that the passengers failed to maintain personal cleanliness and that this contributed to sickness on board. Sanitation and water supply facilities aboard a sailing ship like *New England* seem impossibly crude by present-day standards, and they did little to promote personal hygiene. Beyond the primitive conditions, it was *New England's* incredibly long time at sea that caused the ordeals of the journey. Her transit from Havre de Grace to New Orleans lasted from April 20 to July 10, eighty-one days. A voyage that long was almost unthinkable—in the 1850s shippers directed passengers sailing from Norway to America to bring food for the longest imaginable trip: ten weeks, seventy days.

New England's eighty-one-day crossing requires explanation. A full-rigged ship like her sailing at a fast seven to eight knots per hour could conceivably have covered the longest route from Havre de Grace to New Orleans in less than fifty days. Simply to reach sight of the American mainland took her until June 22, sixty-three days. When Columbus became lost on the Sargasso Sea on his first trip to America in 1492, he still took only thirty-six days to sail from the Canary Islands off Africa to San Salvador in the Caribbean. *New England's* crossing went desperately wrong. Hunger, disease, and death unavoidably claimed the ship.[11]

A competent captain would have sailed on the best winds to get from Havre de Grace to New Orleans. He would have gone south on the prevailing air stream, running down along the coasts of Portugal and Africa, going far south of the Canary Islands to reach fifteen degrees north of the Equator. At that point he would have turned west on trade winds blowing a steady twenty to twenty-five knots. With *New England's* ample canvas taking this much force, he would make eight knots per hour across the Atlantic.

He would have entered the Caribbean near Antigua, where favorable winds would carry him by Jamaica. From there he would have turned up through the Yucatan Channel and into the Gulf of Mexico. In the Gulf he would have come on lighter breezes, but these, generally blowing behind him from the south, would have given him an easy trip up to the Mississippi Delta. Assuming even a six-knot average over this long 7,500-mile route, he would have reached New Orleans from Havre de Grace in sixty days or less. *New England's* journey took three weeks longer than that.[12]

Wives of sea captains often learned navigation and guided ocean ships over thousands of miles. Elise was no navigator; her dispatches to *Norge og Amerika* did not record *New England's* exact path to New Orleans. She did, however, provide enough information to deduce the ship's probable course.

The journey was uneventful. The sea remained calm and free of storms even when crossing outside the rough Bay of Biscay. A sailing ship driven by good winds would typically suffer instances of slatting, a condition in which the blowing winds suddenly die but the seas remain high. The ship would roll and pitch on the swells, her sails on the wide yardarms flapping with explosive bursts as the masts oscillated like uncontrolled metronome rods. A careful reporter, Elise would have mentioned slatting had it occurred. An uneventful journey without slatting means that the winds were poor.

Too, a ship with good winds would sail on long, fast reaches heeled over fifteen to twenty degrees, the spray flying over the gunwales, the seas occasionally washing onto the deck as waves broke over the bow, and the wind roaring in the sails. When the ship set out on a new tack she would come about sharply, leaning over at forty-five degrees, the aftermast boom shrieking as it slewed across the stern, sailors shouting; everything not securely anchored down, including people, would slide across the decks and cabins into bulkheads. Elise never mentioned spanking seas or hard, fast reaches.

They rarely had good winds, she wrote. The sailing was sluggish, the breezes nearly motionless. On the passage from Europe to America conditions like this arise east of Bermuda, an area generally avoided when ships were driven by the wind. No matter how many square feet of canvas she carried, *New England* could not make headway without power from the atmosphere. Her disastrously long voyage occurred because the captain laid a course right into some of the most stagnant air on the planet.

He clearly blundered. Elise knew him as Captain Robinson (he may have been Alfred T. Robinson, master of *New England* on later voyages) and commented that "he was not a real man." He must have turned west just south of the Canary Islands, at thirty degrees north latitude, rather than continuing south to catch the trade winds at fifteen degrees.[13]

A route along the thirtieth parallel would lead to northern Florida. It provides a logical explanation for Elise's statement that their first sighting of land on June 22 was the American continent. Had they sailed along the fifteenth parallel their first sighting would have been farther south, Cuba or a Caribbean island.

The distance from Havre de Grace to Florida at the thirtieth parallel is about 5,600 miles. The next leg around Key West and through the Gulf of Mexico to New Orleans adds another 900 miles, making a total journey of 6,500 miles. Robinson probably assumed, wrongly, that he could sail this shorter distance in less time than was required for the 7,500-mile route down the coast of Africa, across the Atlantic at fifteen degrees, and through the Caribbean. He may even have chosen the shorter route to avoid the twenty- to twenty-seven-knot trade winds at fifteen degrees above the Equator.

Whatever the reason, a turn west at the Canary Islands would lead into dull, mirror-flat seas that barely ripple or make scale patterns even when the breeze manages to get above a knot. The area has been called the "horse latitudes" because crews handling cargoes of horses in the doleful air supposedly threw the animals overboard for lack of drinking water.

At the center of this airless mass is the Sargasso Sea, where the weak "Bermuda high" pressure zone swirls the water in an endless clockwise circle, round and round, forming a vast forest of free-floating seaweed that consumes the oxygen and chokes off life except for small clinging crabs and crustaceans.

On this route the crew on Columbus's first journey came close to mutiny. In such waters a ship loses headway and may lie utterly motionless, becalmed. Winds may puff first from one compass point and then another, providing no consistent direction for a tack. The unfortunate vessel drifts on the aimless current, making almost no progress for hours or even days at a time. When she finally passes through the torpid air and tangled seaweed she ends up in the Bermuda Triangle, reputed to be a mysterious void where ships and even airplanes supposedly just vanish.[14]

Elise's account relates that the passengers were joyful and often sang on the first part of their *New England* journey. As the days dragged on they lost hope. The singing stopped. Food shortages developed. People accustomed to heavy work and the simplest foods had nothing to do, so they ate too much as long as their provisions lasted. Some went about unclean—"and helped the rest of us to lice and fleas, especially toward the end of the voyage," she wrote.

Dysentery and diarrhea spread. The disease caused intestinal bleeding with bloody stool in severe cases. Dehydration resulted. Patients needed copious rations of fresh water to replace their lost body fluids. Elise's report makes no mention of giving water to sufferers. Water may have been withheld due to a short supply or the medical illiteracy of the captain and crew. The first deaths occurred on May 11, three weeks into the journey. Two girls died, one aged two and the other fifteen. By May 20 another girl of two years and nine months and a boy seven years old had fallen victim.[15]

Then on May 29 a man twenty-one years old died. According to Elise he was a young Jew; the ship's manifest filed at New Orleans gives his name as Herman Wallenstein. He did not take care with what he ate and drank, Elise said. Language problems contributed to his death. Most of the passengers were German or German-speaking Swiss, and Wallenstein most likely spoke that language or perhaps Yiddish.

By law the captain was in charge of the ship's medicine chest and served as physician. He could not understand what Wallenstein said, but he and a passenger who "pretended to be a doctor," in Elise's words, gave the young man medicine that made his illness worse. Most likely they dosed him heavily with castor oil or mercury-based calomel, standard laxatives believed in those days to purge the body of illness. The treatment totally ravaged Wallenstein. Dehydration and secondary infections of vital organs inevitably set in. Deprived of essential fluids and power to fight the disease, his body broke down.[16]

Four more deaths followed, two girls and two boys. The girls were less than two years old. Because infants were usually breast-fed until the age of two, their mothers may have been dehydrated by diarrhea due to dysentery and may have lacked enough milk to nurse their children properly. One of the boys was sixteen, the other ten.

According to sailing ship customs, the victims had to be committed to the sea. It was an honorable burial. Reports indicate that the bodies would have been stitched into canvas shrouds with ballast stones or lead pieces added for weight. Without something to make them sink, bodies were known to float and sometimes drift along in a ship's wake.[17]

The last death occurred on June 25, three days after they sighted the American mainland. Elise noted that all those who died were young. She said nothing about funeral services, the tragedy of cherished children lost, or the young victimized by racking illness and untimely death. Her silence was not due to indifference. In the mid-1800s medical practice was primitive. People were steeled to sickness and death among the young.

When *New England* reached the American mainland on June 22 she must have arrived at a point somewhere between St. Augustine and the coastal area known today as Cape Canaveral. "Our oldest passenger, a very old German, started singing in praise and giving thanks at the sight," Elise reported. It took another eighteen days, nearly three more weeks, to reach New Orleans.

Florida's east coast was a bad place to begin a voyage around Key West to New Orleans. *New England* was heading on a southerly course, but along Florida's east coast the Gulf Stream flows north on a two-and-a-half- to three-knot current. The predominant winds likewise blow north. Against that current and contrary wind the ship would have trouble making headway; with an incompetent sailor for a captain she may even have been driven backward at times.[18] From her first sighting of the American mainland *New England* traveled about 920 miles to New Orleans. Her average speed over the distance was barely above two knots, less than *Ygdrasil's* 2.25 on the way from Christiania to Havre de Grace.

The ordeals of the journey lasted all the way to the delta of the Mississippi River. Elise and her friends managed to fend off crisis up to a point. They kept their bodies as clean as possible using the crude shipboard facilities. They drank boiled water flavored with vinegar and their small reserves of condensed fruit juices. They stretched their food supplies for nearly four months from the time they left Norway. Eight days from New Orleans they ran out—as Elise put it, "we were empty because we had shared with others who had nothing."

Outside the Mississippi Delta the passengers were able to secure victuals from nearby ships. Shortages persisted, however, because Captain Robinson handled the purchases. Elise viewed his actions with contempt; he secured too little food even though the other ships were loaded with provisions.

On the last days *New England's* cook prepared rations in batches for the passengers. Typical shipboard bulk fare consisted of meat preserved in brine, cooked as stew and dished from wooden tubs set on the deck. Possibly, too, the passengers were served fatback, strips of nearly pure lard cut from a hog carcass and dry-cured in salt; Elise warned future travelers against consuming greasy salted meat like this.

She and her fellow Norwegians never touched the batch meals no matter what was served. Instead they chose to prepare their meals for themselves using meat and bread bought from the ship's stores. It was a wise move because the amoebae that caused the dysentery were probably spread from the cooks' hands. Near the end of the journey, however, food stocks for sale ran out, and hunger drove the Norwegians to accept leftovers from meals made for the crew. The quantities were small, provoking Elise to write: "We never really starved, but we were never filled either."[19]

They entered the Mississippi Delta at Southwest Pass, probably about July 4. Elise recorded the last scene of Captain Robinson's calamitous leadership: "He fled from us onto a passing ship before we arrived in New Orleans. . . . That we had such a Captain was bad for us," she added. It was far too mild a reproach. Whether an incompetent navigator or a despot indifferent to suffering, he was in command. His passengers endured weeks of sickness, deprivation, and death.[20]

Robinson's departure ended the bad days. In the Mississippi Delta *New England*'s journey brightened. Elise was entranced with the exotic semitropical flora and the overpowering contrast with Norway's forested mountains. "Sailing up the river is superb," she wrote. "The banks of the Mississippi are flat but heavily grown with beautiful sometimes flowering trees, in between which can be seen big and small houses surrounded by fertile fields."[21]

It was a happy start for her life in America. At Pilottown a few miles inside the delta *New England* had to stop to pick up an expert pilot. He would have known how to avoid the many shoals and snags that lay along the way, how to navigate the south-flowing river currents that threatened to force the ship backward, and how to set the sails to catch the slightest breeze blowing up from the Gulf of Mexico.

After entering the delta *New England* had to travel 130 miles up the river to New Orleans. Just below the city the ship met English Turn, so named because when the Spanish ruled New Orleans in the 1700s they fooled an English sea captain into thinking that the river was impassable from that point.[22]

At English Turn the Mississippi River channel swings to the southeast around a more than ninety-degree turn. The previously favorable wind coming from the south now becomes an adversary—it blows almost directly against the sails. A good spread of canvas like *New England*'s would not have helped her at all. The pilot would have had her towed around the Turn with hawsers pulled by teams of horses from the riverbank, or he would have had to wait for the wind to change and come from the northwest. The two-mile stretch below New Orleans could delay a sailing vessel for a week or more. The skilled pilot brought *New England* in to New Orleans on July 10.[23]

At the dock Elise settled down to compose a long report for *Norge og Amerika*. The hard journey had convinced her to change her advice to emigrants radically. It was not enough to speak merely about booking fares and buying supplies. She had to emphasize illness prevention, medical remedies, and ways to cope with shipboard life. Her tone was urgent, emphatic, based on personal experience rather than secondhand knowledge garnered from the letters she had edited for *Norge og Amerika*. She was telling future emigrants how to survive.

Bring food, she said, for at least eighty days if sailing from Havre de Grace. Bring more if leaving from Norway. Take rye grain—almost no one brought any aboard *New England;* when cooked it provides wholesome nourishment for people who are ill. Use oats to make a soup for the sick. (Other women's accounts of sea journeys reported that boiled rice made a good broth for the invalids; it could also be given to nursing infants to supplement mother's milk).

Bring sugar and berry juice, Elise wrote. Include lingonberry—wild mountain cranberry, cheap in Norway. Make soup from the juices. Mix the berry juices or tea with boiled water for drinking because they taste much better than vinegar. If short of berry juice, stock up on inexpensive wine in Le Havre. Forget the half bottles—buy kegs. Get lemon acid in glass bottles at the apothecary shop. (Elise never mentioned scurvy, but the potency of fruit juice, especially citric acids, to prevent the disease was well known by the 1840s.)

Bring eggs. She put them on her list once again because now she knew exactly how long they would stay edible at sea. Bring staples—bread, flour, butter, and potatoes. For these she recommended even larger quantities than before. Hang bread and meat in a well-ventilated space; they must be aired to prevent mold. Avoid fatty bacon because it contains too much salt (used extensively as a preservative in Elise's time, salt would increase the traveler's need for water).

Cook in tall, narrow tin containers and never even think of using slow-heating iron pots. Cook early, she said, because the small daily ration of wood and coal for the galley runs out quickly. Cooking is a trial—the passengers' galleys are tiny and the stoves small—so make portions for more than one person at a time.

Tip the ship's cook occasionally to get boiled drinking water, potatoes, puddings, and freshly baked crackers. Bring two open vessels to catch rainwater and have a container to take the ship's daily ration. She provided a recipe: diced meat with a large quantity of potatoes fried with a little butter in a tin pan. Elise's only recipe, it suggests a starchy diet cooked with the simplest utensils.

Before you leave, she advised, consult with a physician to assure that your individual health requirements will be considered when you buy medicine. Otherwise bring camphor (an inhalant and unguent for chest colds as well as sore muscles). Bring a laxative and a remedy for diarrhea. As the airless passenger deck got stifling hot, she recommended making a physical division between berth occupants, typically by putting a board between them. Passengers should try to arrange for two persons to a berth rather than three. Better still would be to negotiate for one of the small rooms up on the main deck, available at a modest additional payment.[24]

However valuable her advice to future emigrants, Elise could not escape unharmed from the journey's ordeals. In New Orleans she came down with dysentery almost certainly caught from *New England*'s galley. She considered the city water atrocious and blamed it for her disease because her companions escaped the sickness. "It caused an attack of an old evil that is not in any way dangerous but is unpleasant," she reported.

The unnamed condition racked her for days and caused her greater distress than she admitted. When she tried to compose her report to *Norge og Amerika* seated at a wooden box "among a couple of hundred noisy people," intermittent pain caused her to interrupt her work repeatedly. She made an effort to struggle on foot around the city to find people she had promised friends in Norway to see, but she had to give up the search. The last day aboard *New England* she could scarcely rise to leave the ship.[25]

In New Orleans "student Buch"—forty years old, according to the ship's passenger manifest—parted company with the other Norwegians. The group had continued to share quarters and meals until the end of the journey, but somehow relations with Buch had gone sour. Not a new immigrant like the others, he was returning to America after a trip home to Norway. He had lived in Chicago; perhaps because he could speak some English he had more in common with the ship's crew than with his own countrymen. Whatever the reason, Elise scornfully omitted his name when she wrote about their departure from New Orleans: "Saying 'we,' I mean Andersen, Waerenskjold, and myself. We haven't had anything in common with the fourth Norwegian for the longest time, and I don't know where he intends to go."[26]

Her letter from New Orleans was dated July 12, two days after their arrival in the city. On that date *New England's* substitute captain filed the ship's manifest at the Port of New Orleans collector's office. Although the city had been an American port since the Louisiana purchase in 1803, the passengers' nationalities were all recorded in French: Norvege, Suisse, Baviere, Badois, France, Irland (Norway, Switzerland, Bavaria, Baden, France, Ireland). Pennsylvania was listed as their common destination even though nearly all were going to other states.

Waerenskjold, his name spelled "Wernskyol" and his age given as twenty-three, appeared as passenger eleven, Elise as twelve, Andersen as thirteen, and Buch as fourteen. They were the only Norwegians out of the 219 persons who had come aboard at Havre de Grace.

William Sprague, the new captain, signed the manifest with the title "Master or Commander of the Ship *New England.*" He solemnly swore to the names on the list and "all matters therein set forth." At the close he warranted: "I do further swear that nine passengers have died on the voyage." All but Wallenstein were children.

Scholastica Rolle, two
Francisca Leibfriet, fifteen
Barbara Schroepfer, two years, nine months
Caspar Hause, seven
Herman Wallenstein, twenty-one
Jacob Maizie, sixteen years, two months
Felicia Pourront, one year, two months
Michel Schill, ten
Theresa Biesingen, one year, seven months.[27]

CHAPTER 3

NEW ORLEANS TO
NACOGDOCHES

"I AM NOT WELL HERE," Elise wrote to *Norge og Amerika* from New Orleans. "The water, which is really bad, has had its common influence on me—that is, diarrhea." In a dispatch sent a month later from Nacogdoches she recalled her distress: "Bored to death with unclean and unkempt New Orleans, we left the city on July 15, the Thursday after our arrival. The last day I was so sick that I could not go out, so I never got to say goodbye to our friends."

They were heading for Shreveport, a town that lay on the Red River in northwest Louisiana and offered good access to their destination in Texas (see map 2). In those days it was possible to sail directly by steamboat from New Orleans to Shreveport because the Red River flowed into the Mississippi at Lettsworth in Pointe Couppe Parish. Now the journey cannot be made by water; a massive dam diverts the Red River into the Atchafalaya ("Chafalaya" to natives) to control flooding in New Orleans.[1]

In New Orleans the three companions took passage on the paddle-wheeler *St. Helena,* a modest-sized ship in the 200- to 225-ton class. They expected a routine journey broken only by transfer to a smaller ship at Alexandria, where a rock ledge, later blasted away, created falls during seasons of low water.

Thrifty as usual, they paid the lowest fare and found themselves assigned to distinctly second-rate quarters on *St. Helena's* cargo deck. Elise reported her acute discomfort there: "I cannot think of a worse way to travel as it is incredibly dirty and the engine gives off terrible steam and heat. You can imagine what it is to be sick in a place like that."

She might have been better prepared for the discomfort had she under-

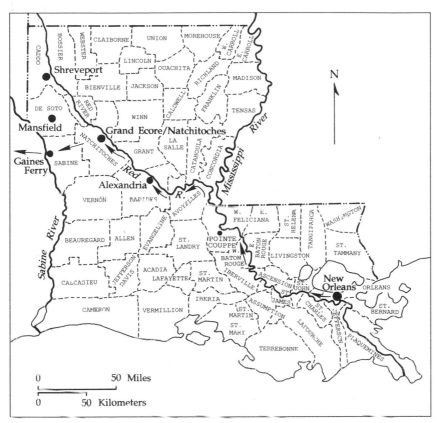

Map 2. Elise's route from New Orleans to Gaines Ferry.
Map prepared by John Cotter, cartographer, courtesy of Charles H. Russell.

stood that riverboats were built to go on strange waters and to perform odd tasks. None of the accounts sent to *Norge og Amerika* had explained that the ships went into swamps and bayous, sailed in springtime floods and drought-shrunken summer waters, and sometimes halted in midstream to load and unload. Sandbars, gravel banks, ledges, and treacherous underwater snags cropped up on even the best routes. Some of the hazards were so famous that boatmen gave them names—Big Bone, Pig's Eye, Horse Tail, Beef Slough, Shuffletown—ever menacing, whatever they were called.

Like others of her kind, *St. Helena* confronted these conditions head-on. She carried stilts that stood prominent as masts on her bow, ready to be lowered over the prow if she ran aground. When she stuck fast, ropes were run from the stilt tops through deck rings leading back to windlasses. The crew worked the windlasses and hoisted her bow up. The engineer powered on full steam, the water boiled under the paddlewheels, and she lurched forward. The stilts tumbled over and her hull splashed down. If the first attempt failed, the maneuver had to be repeated until she scratched off free.[2]

A few years before Elise and her compatriors traveled aboard *St. Helena*, Henry Miller Shreve, for whom Shreveport is named, had successfully cleared the "Great Raft." This was a vast tangle of logs and brush that blocked the Red River northward from the Grand Ecore bend just above Natchitoches ("Nakitosh," in Cajun parlance). Some accounts claim the raft stretched 180 miles; even conservative estimates are that it was 160 miles long.

For centuries floodwaters had torn trees from riverbanks as far away as New Mexico, sweeping them down the Texas-Oklahoma border through southwestern Arkansas into Louisiana, where they piled up into the Great Raft. When the French owned the Louisiana Territory in the late 1700s their cartographers called the mass Embarras d'Arbres — "blockade of trees"; a copy of their engraved map can be seen at the Watson Memorial Library at Northwestern Louisiana State University in Natchitoches.

The main boat route to Natchitoches originally ran along the Cane River, a Red River tributary that steamships could enter at Rigollette de Bon Dieu — "God's little waterway." Had the Great Raft remained in place Elise and her friends would have been able to land at Natchitoches, but when it was removed the Red flowed faster and jumped to a new channel about four miles east of the town. The Cane River now became a thirty-two-mile oxbow, a relic later renamed Cane River Lake. Natchitoches took on a quiet, haunting beauty, its handsome New Orleans Vieux Carré–style buildings sitting high on a bluff overlooking what had once been a busy river dockside. Today the town's manicured lakefront has the charm of the finest European river or canal waterfronts.

Once free of the Great Raft, the Red drove logs and brush farther downstream. Steam-powered snagboats dragged sunken obstacles away. Besides trees their burden included rafts, small boats, and even steam vessel hulks with bottoms ripped out.

To navigate the various hazards, riverboat hulls had to be modeled on the flatboats and log rafts that had been floating woodsmen down the inland waterways for two hundred years. Like these unpretentious transports, *St. Helena* had a flat bottom. She sat on top of the water rather than in it. Some of the biggest river vessels drew nine feet, but *St. Helena* was shallow — fully loaded, she probably settled no more than a foot deep. A wag once remarked that "steamboats must be so built that when the river is low and the sandbars come out for air, the first mate can tap a keg of beer and run the boat four miles on the suds."[3]

Many workhorse vessels on the backwaters and tributaries of the great western rivers had no passenger facilities at all. They hauled only cargo, some of them looking like ramshackle paddlewheel scows carrying a smokestack and abandoned two-story house on their decks. *St. Helena* was more refined—she transported passengers as well as freight, but she had the same type of underbody as her less elegant relatives. Her hull was minimal, a mere vestige compared to that of an ocean-going ship. Her keel, almost nonexistent, projected little more than an inch. With this pygmy stub, her bottom looked as if it belonged on a rowboat rather than a ship, but it allowed her to glide sideways to landings.

Elise noted that *St. Helena's* main deck "was just a bit above the water line." Flattened hulls required drastic modification to give them buoyancy. The first river ships were as wide as *New England*—she was about four times as long as she was wide (131.4 feet to 30.5 feet). By the 1840s the river steamships were long and narrow; *St. Helena* was about seven times as long she was wide (166 feet to 25 feet). Shreve, in competition with the famous Robert Fulton of New York, developed the long, shallow, narrow design so that the river ships could carry heavy tonnage at a fast four to eight knots per hour.

Elise's comment on *St. Helena's* design, "American steamers are built quite differently than ours," was equally to the point. Built for generally placid waters, the ships' underbody planks were only two inches thick. In contrast, Norwegian passenger steamers had sturdy hulls, four inches thick or more, built to thrash into heavy ocean waves and hard fjord chop. Because of their bulk, the sea-going Norwegian steamers could support an interior mid-deck where the low-fare passengers could lodge as Elise and her friends had done aboard *New England*. Only the largest American river steamboats could carry anything that resembled a deck inside their hulls, and even then, this space was below the waterline and had to be used for storage.

To provide passenger space, riverboat designers got around the shallow hull problem by adding two levels above it. As a result the floor atop the hull, called the main deck, was the lowest level. The second level, the upper-between-decks, housed the staterooms and lounge for high-fare passengers. The third, the hurricane deck, carried the pilothouse, officers' quarters, and an extensive promenade. This triple-deck construction gave the ships a lofty, top-heavy silhouette—three-quarters to four-fifths of their bulk stood above the water.

While higher-fare passengers relaxed in lounges and staterooms in the upper-between-decks, lower-fare passengers like Elise and her friends had the bare planks of the main deck for their quarters. They had no staterooms, no berths, not even benches to sit on. They traveled with the cargo, the huge steam boilers, and the paddlewheel engines; the heat and steam were oppressive.

Judging from Elise's comments in her dispatch to *Norge og Amerika*, *St. Helena* carried a new feature that river ship designers introduced at about the time of this journey. An "annex" was attached to the pilothouse and officers' cabins up on the hurricane deck. Nicknamed the "Texas," it was apparently so called to honor the annexation of the young republic by the United States in 1845.

However honorific its name, the Texas increased the contrast between high- and low-fare passenger quarters. Set above the other decks, it became the most elegant part of the ship. It was the place for the finest staterooms and a dazzling gallery known as the salon, in elegant French fashion, or the saloon in American frontier style. Originally intended simply to provide more passenger space, it developed into the crowning feature of riverboat opulence.

The lowest deck where Elise sailed remained unchanged—it was the work plant, hot, coarse, and ugly. She described the main deck accommodations in one tart sentence: "This is where one finds the engine and the deck passengers, with some few empty hammocks." The cargo—cotton bales, logs headed for sawmills, furniture, and almost any imaginable freight—lay piled up on it to the superstructure above. Stacks of cordwood fuel for the steam boilers stood there. Passengers boarded and disembarked on this deck. Stevedores tramped over it. It was the alleyway for goods, baggage, produce, galley victuals, drink, and gamblers.

To allow maximum storage, the main deck needed plenty of vertical space. On riverboats like *St. Helena* the next deck was at least eleven feet higher up; on the biggest ships that height topped out at twenty feet. *New England's* mid-deck may have been a low-roofed cavern inside the hull, but it carried only passengers and their supplies. *St. Helena's* bottom deck was a high-ceilinged engine room, cargo warehouse, and ship's vestibule, incidentally providing lodging for low-fare passengers.

Travelers on this deck were called "deckers." They had no privacy. An ordinary wooden bucket served to dip up river water for washing and toileting. Just so much baggage, another kind of load that could be stowed here and there at will, these passengers put up with the press of their fellows jammed into whatever space was left after the cargo was loaded.

Elise was assigned a hammock because of her illness, but once the hammocks were all taken, the remaining travelers had to drape themselves on the stacked cargo or sleep on the gouged and splintered plank flooring. During the day they stood, sat on boxes, or hunkered down against a bulkhead. The entire freight area at times would become crammed with passengers. At that point they would spill out onto the guards, the unsheltered fenders protecting the hull and paddlewheels.

Deckers were allowed to climb up to the unshaded hurricane deck. Elise considered this no privilege during the day. When she recovered enough to go topside, the burning sun quickly drove her below again.

She wrote that they had to purchase and cook their own food. According to other riverboat accounts, folk living at plantations and woodlots along the riverbanks sold food, and cooking was done on a single woodstove intended primarily to heat the cargo space. Elise easily coped with the food arrangements on *Ygdrasil* and *New England,* but she loathed the conditions aboard *St. Helena*—"One has to get provisions and cook oneself, which makes the journey even more unpleasant."

She contrasted the lower deck passengers' crude conditions and coarse treatment with the luxurious life above: "The cabin passengers were traveling in a grand way, having a Grand Salon for conversation and dining purposes and neat little rooms with two bunks each equipped with bed clothing and mosquito netting. Even when they go out on their deck, which is right above [our] lower deck, they have a roof that shades the sun and keeps off the rain."[4] Cabin passengers, she noted, were served excellent food, while the deckers could not even buy leftovers, which were passed out free to the servants and crew. For the cabin deck passengers the steamboat was a sumptuous palace.

In spite of their dismal accommodations, Elise and her friends had some enjoyable moments while aboard *St. Helena.* Wilhelm described the great Mississippi's solemn beauty to Elise as she lay in her hammock. Soon after the ship turned west onto the Red heading for Alexandria and Shreveport, Elise began to feel well enough to get around. During the cool evening hours she climbed to the hurricane deck to be with her friends as they gazed at the exotic flora, fields, and occasional plantations slipping by. There, in the fading light and soft breeze caused by the ship's forward motion, they saw fireflies for the first time. Enchanted, Elise wrote to *Norge og Amerika* that the flying insects were "blinking between the trees like tiny swiftly disappearing lights."

She noted, too, that American steamboats fired their boilers with wood rather than coal, like the Norwegian steamers. At night when the captain stopped the ship at riverbank woodlots to pick up fresh supplies of fuel, she and her companions watched fascinated as the crew lit their surroundings with burning firewood carried onto the shore in a great cauldron.

Alligators floating on the river surface proved intriguing, but it was the sinewy Red River itself that offered the greatest appeal. Her Norwegian correspondents had described it poorly when they sent her reports for publication in *Norge og Amerika.* The river was far more delightful than she expected. Its red hue was acquired from rust-colored loam and iron-bearing stone along its twisting thirteen-hundred-mile course. Its banks wound along ever changing—sometimes wooded, sometimes grown up with riverine plants, sometimes open to plowed fields and pastures. She never traveled the Red again, but the river had a strange significance for her life, an almost uncanny quality, as if its color, veering channel, and resolute motion forecast the experiences she would have in Texas.

Pleasing impressions during the river trip notwithstanding, the Norwegian passengers were treated to one final affront. When they reached Alexandria the ship that was to continue to Shreveport was not at the dock. Several days might pass before it would come in, so when they learned that *St. Helena* could slip by the falls and journey as far as Grand Ecore, part way to Shreveport, they decided to continue with her. They assumed there would be no additional charges because the seventy-five-dollar fare they had paid covered the entire journey to Shreveport. Farmer Andersen had also been told in New Orleans that there would be no additional baggage charge for continuing to Grand Ecore if they chose to go on with *St. Helena.*

Now they learned otherwise. Each of them would have to pay $3.50 for freight plus $2 for baggage overweight, a total of $5.50. Ten dollars a month was a common wage at the time, so the cost was exorbitant. This unexpected development recalled Mr. Kock's chicanery back in Christiania, but Elise barely winced. The journey's ordeals had dulled her fighting edge. She wrote to *Norge og Amerika* merely cautioning prospective emigrants to make very precise contracts with Americans. It was good advice: reports about steamboat travel elsewhere in the United States show that ship owners often gouged immigrants. Newcomers were entering an uncertain world.[5]

From Grand Ecore their journey would take them overland to Nacogdoches, the gateway town of East Texas. The riverside where they disembarked stood at the terminus of the Harrisonburg Road leading from Natchez, Mississippi, through Louisiana. Though Grand Ecore was only a small settlement next to the steamboat and ferry landing, it was a main crossing point for southern pioneers heading west. Cotton growers in northeast Texas also used it as a freight depot for shipping their produce down to New Orleans.[6]

During the 1860s a Confederate Civil War cartographer drew a bird's eye view of the Grand Ecore landing. He showed a dozen or so miniature black squares representing homes and warehouses standing by the riverbank. Just north of these he drew the Red River rounding a wide bend. On the west bank above Grand Ecore, he penned a series of short down-strokes that might be taken for tiny fence pickets. In fact, they represented the spectacular red clay varves that rise one hundred feet above the river, still conspicuous today. Modern geographers call this cliff the Great Bank and consider it the most impressive landform in the wooded wilderness known as the Nacogdoches Wold. In 1847 it was the landmark indicating the start of the wilderness trail that led from the Red River through western Louisiana to Nacogdoches.[7]

The trail traversed some ninety miles of dense woodlands, swamps, rivers, streams, and bayous. It was originally part of El Camino Real, the royal or king's highway that ran for hundreds of miles, connecting a string of missions and forts that began south of the Rio Grande in Mexico, passing through San Antonio and Nacogdoches and ending at Los Adaes (now Robeline), fourteen miles west of Natchitoches in Louisiana.

The section between Texas and Los Adaes was intended to be a Spanish bastion in Louisiana against expansion by the French from their base in New Orleans. By the time Elise headed along this trail to Nacogdoches the area was United States territory, part of the Louisiana Purchase bought by the United States from Napoleon in 1803. When the Mexican-American war broke out after the United States annexed Texas in 1845, American army drovers used the old El Camino Real to haul military supplies to troops invading Mexico. By then the former Spanish forts and missions were barely memories, and Texans were calling the historic way the Old San Antonio Road.

In spite of its long history, the Old San Antonio Road offered no easy crossing to tenderfoot travelers like Elise and her friends trekking from Grand Ecore to Nacogdoches. Ungraded, irregular, barely maintained, it was scarcely a road at all. It was more like what westering Americans called a wilderness trace, a path marked by notched trees, crushed underbrush, and rutted imprints left by previous travelers. Such routes were best suited for the tough muleskinners who drove the American army wagons loaded with military supplies.

Hardy settlers struggled along it, and disastrous accidents were not uncommon. Johan Reinert Reiersen, Elise's respected friend who had left her in charge of *Norge og Amerika* when he emigrated to Texas in 1845, had nearly lost his life on one of the river crossings when his flatboat capsized loaded with store goods bought in New Orleans. Total greenhorns like Elise and her associates would need to find a first-class guide to lead them on their five-day trip to Nacogdoches. To make the situation more difficult, none of them spoke more than a few words of English.[8]

In Grand Ecore they had the good fortune to meet a friendly German; Elise spoke the language, and Waerenskjold probably did also. The man took them to a drover's stable where for thirty-five dollars they rented a wagon, four horses, and a teamster-guide. Pleased by the reasonable rate, the Norwegians did not ask who would lead the way, apparently assuming it would be the drover himself. They spent the night in Grand Ecore and returned to the stable the next morning to pick up their transportation. There they met their designated guide face to face. He was a slave. Elise described him in her report to *Norge og Amerika* as a "big man, a Negro."

An unexpected meeting on both sides! The Norwegians had known only members of their own race until they reached New Orleans. Here they would be traveling with a strange man, this slave, for five days. They would be depending on him exclusively for the entire trip, yet they knew nothing about him, his customs, or his attitudes.

For his part, he knew nothing of them or their foreign ways. Though a slave he would be far more than a servant and drayman. He would be their leader and escort over a difficult road. Not hired to be their teacher, he would nevertheless be introducing them to southwestern traditions. Besides that, he would have to find ways to bridge the language barrier.[9]

The first day ended poorly. The German had assured Elise that they would find food and lodging with residents along the route, but they rarely passed any homes on the way. In the evening after an exhausting trek they came to a lone house. Their guide drove right by it. Not far beyond, he halted the wagon by a swamp. There, according to Elise, "he made signs to us that there were good beds under the trees."

Astounded by these instructions, the three Norwegians balked. Elise described their protests: "We aired our dissatisfaction as best we could, and indicated our wish to go back to the house we had just passed. The guide would not be moved. He made it clear we could go back to the house if we wanted, but we didn't dare to do so fearing he had something up his sleeve and would disappear with our belongings during the night."

Turning the horses and wagon around on the stump-filled road would anyway have been difficult, if not impossible. It was too dark to walk back. They were trapped.

Elise and Wilhelm spent the night by the swamp in alarm, filled with fears she later realized were absurd, even farcical. She opened her account of the next event with a quip: "After we had succumbed to the will of our black master . . . we lit a fire and prepared a simple evening meal, whereupon Waerenskjold and I decided to keep watch during the night. Andersen arranged himself in between all the boxes in the wagon. Waerenskjold and I spent a strange night in an agitated mood because we imagined all kinds of nonexistent dangers partly made up by fear of snakes, and partly by fear of humans. From the swamp and the trees there was an uninterrupted cacophony of sounds from frogs, turtles, and birds that disturbed the silence of the night most fearfully."

In spite of their fears, the outdoor location turned out quite tolerable; the air by the swamp was mild and dry and the ground soft. After the first night their guide obligingly took them to wayside houses. Through no fault of his, though, all but one place proved dreadful: inferior inside and out, awful food, excessive prices. In the one case where they found truly hospitable quarters Elise described their hosts as *kondisjonerte*—Norwegian for "people of 'condition'"—a term for country gentry as well as government officials and successful business people.[10]

Their guide had been right. But for the language barrier he might have become their genial mentor, a friendly adviser about everyday life. His job was to get them to Nacogdoches, and he could only show them what he knew as they went their way. Elise quietly acknowledged their guide's good judgment. She told her readers that camping by the wayside was customary on travels. "It is much smarter to sleep under the open skies when the weather and season permit," she observed.

Elise's account of their journey to Nacogdoches gains support from a book written by Frederick Law Olmsted, America's foremost nineteenth-century landscape architect, who traveled across the Nacogdoches Wold in 1853. After the Civil War Olmsted originated the plan for Yosemite National Park and designed many of the nation's outstanding urban nature landscapes, among them Central Park in New York City. When he made his trip through Louisiana into Texas as far as Mexico, he had already written successful books on travel in the southern states. His vivid descriptions of the accommodations, food, and the wilderness road to Nacogdoches amply corroborate Elise's chronicle and support a remark she made about her guide's skill—"he handled the horses . . . masterfully no matter how bad the road."

Olmsted traveled by horseback with his brother, John Olmsted, a physician suffering from tuberculosis. They were undertaking the journey, he wrote, "in hope of invigorating weakened lungs by the elastic power of a winter's saddle and tent-life." His journal, published in 1857 as *A Journey through Texas,* touches each of the subjects Elise covered.[11]

About the surrounding woodland, Elise and Olmsted agreed in general but expressed differing personal interests in specific features. She found the forest very appealing though somewhat spoiled by rampant weeds—"especially a yellow flower that is definitely not pretty." As to the trees, she saw mostly leafy varieties with some pine. Olmsted saw heavy pine growth, mentioned nothing about weeds or flowers, and exhibited the landscaper's eye that later made him famous; he named oaks, cottonwoods, willows, swamp oaks, chestnuts, magnolias, China trees (a type of fir), and evergreen Cherokee roses.

The wealth of trees made the Nacogdoches Wold a lumber center in the late 1800s, but at the time of his travels the number of deserted cabins struck Olmsted most of all. These derelict homes, he said, were left by a kind of soil-destroying slash-and-burn agriculture. The settlers cleared trees, grew commercial crops with the help of farm loans, and then after a few years abandoned the exhausted land. His comment: "If you ask, where are the people that once occupied these [homes], the universal reply is, 'gone to Texas.'"[12]

Elise was more interested in food crops and flowering plants than was Olmsted. She intended to raise garden produce if she settled down in Texas, so she looked for fruit and vegetables growing in clearings along the way. She saw figs, peaches, and watermelons that appeared much better than the greenhouse varieties grown at the fine homes she knew back in Norway. Carrots and cabbage also grew in backyard plots, but these she considered inferior to Norwegian produce. She attributed the difference to the homeowners' incompetence as gardeners.

"Of pretty flowers," she said, "I recognized only the Passion Flower that appears in several colors and has a beautiful scent." Her liking for indoor plants led to an unexpected discovery: "To my great surprise I spotted great trees of a kind that I had in pots at home—we called them Mimosa." Olmsted paid no attention to this tree and said nothing about any potted plant. Interested in economic matters, he found the forest timber and landscape resources drawing his eye.

As to housing, Elise commented on the unsatisfactory lodging along the way, and Olmsted gave facts that support her observation. He reported that the wilderness residents expected to do "inn duty" and aimed to profit by charging exorbitant prices for their efforts. The dwellings he described were commonly log cabins twenty by sixteen feet, drab, often windowless, with the door left open to admit daylight. One interior space served every purpose: living room, dining room, kitchen, and bedroom—shelter, meals, warmth, and sleep.

Typically the log timbers in cabin walls were left rough hewn so that gaps between them had to be chinked with mud and wood chips. In some homes, Olmsted said, the chinking had washed away because the timbers fit together so poorly. As a result residents inside could peer through crevices out to the surrounding forest. Victorian modesty must have kept him from mentioning that outhouses accompanied nearly every home, and he never hinted that some residents simply relieved themselves in the natural surroundings.

Several cabins where Olmsted stayed had no ceiling, merely rafters open to the roof. At one, the entryway wall topped out at the frame over the door, leaving a huge triangle open to the wilds. The wind "rushed in with a fierce swoop" he said, chilling him and his brother as they sat by the fire. They spent the night cold and sleepless even though sharing a bed.

He identified one residence as a "dog-trot" house. It consisted of two separate cabins, one room each, joined together by a long roof stretching over the in-between dirt floor. Called dog run as well as dog-trot, houses of this type took their name from the open space—the family dogs presumably loped through from the front yard to the back or slept in the dirt passageway. Log cabins often had chimneys made of mud and sticks; Olmsted commented that some of these simply leaned over against the home.

Cooking was done in chimney fireplaces, but some residences had small separate cabins that served as kitchen houses. In these the homeowners cooked on a fire set in the middle of the dirt floor. Logs were placed in a circle pointing in toward a core of burning coals, and the smoke rose up through an opening in the roof. People in homes with neither a cookhouse nor a chimney prepared their meals on the floor. Not infrequently black smoke blew back down from the roof opening, spreading a layer of greasy soot on clothing and furnishings.

Elise noted that it took considerable skill to cook on a floor fire. Back in Norway the homes she knew had cast-iron woodstoves with sturdy wall pipes that carried smoke outdoors. Those stoves had an ample surface for moving pots and pans around. Floor hearths, however, had no cooking

New Orleans to Nacogdoches

—39—

surface. Utensils sat on the open coals or were precariously hooked to tripod frames or leggy trivets set over the fire. One false move could flip a pot or frying pan over, dumping the food into the fire and scattering burning coals out onto the cook's shoes and clothing. After observing the hazards of cooking on a dirt floor fire, Elise remarked on the deficiencies of pioneer life: "Altogether, I find that people here care very little about the things that make life pleasant."

Both Elise and Olmsted mentioned that bread made of white flour and yeast was a luxury. Cornbread was the standard fare. Elise grew used to it on the way through the wilderness, but she came to hate it later in Nacogdoches while suffering a bout of illness. Little wonder; as Olmsted explained, the cornbread in many homes was actually "pone," ground corn meal mixed with no other ingredients than salt and water—no eggs, butter, or baking powder. The mixture was stirred into a thick batter, formed between the palms into ovals, and baked in a heavy iron kettle covered by red coals.

Other than mentioning the cornbread, Elise spoke only about the high price and poor quality of the food. Olmsted, however, grumbled freely and gave details that add substance to her complaints. Invariably, he said, the inn-keeping residents on the trail served cold salt pork, stale pone, lard called "butter," and a "black decoction of the South called coffee."

Both Elise and he reported that it was dangerous to drink from the Red River. She recommended that all water should be boiled. Olmsted added that natives even avoided drinking from natural springs and any sort of surface water. Mainly they used milk, claret, and whiskey. If they drank water at all it came from cisterns filled by rain runoff from their cabin roofs.

The road, according to Elise, was crude and built with minimum effort. Brush had been hacked down and thrown onto the bed, and bushes and young trees were left standing to be crushed by passing travelers. Only enough timber had been cleared to let a wagon through; stumps stood in and around the trail, some of them directly in the rutted tracks.

She stopped short of describing what happened when a wagon wheel wedged against a stump, but other accounts tell of the brute strength required to power by these. On some occasions a young tree had to be cut down for use as a lever to force the wagon along. The horses backed and heaved, their haunch muscles bulging, goaded on by the drayman's yells and lashing whip.

Olmsted considered the road "execrable," dull as well as arduous. He and his brother started out from Natchitoches where they had bought horses, a pack mule, camping equipment, and weapons for protection and hunting.

Within five minutes, he said, they were deep into the dark pine forest. It was easy to lose the way. For several hours they passed no houses or people, just deserted cabins.

Washboard roads—saplings and small logs set side by side—had been laid through wetlands, along riverbanks and creeks, and at swamp margins. Bridges had been erected only over the widest waterways; the travelers went splashing through streams, marshes, and river fords. He mentioned that Texas and Louisiana met at the Sabine River (pronounced "Sahbeen," French style) where Gaines Ferry was the well-known passage point. Today Gaines Ferry lies drowned under Toledo Bend Reservoir, but travelers crossing the river back then must have used a common ferrying setup of the time: a raftlike boat pulled slowly across the water by rope, the power provided by people, horses, or mules.

In the Red Lands of eastern Texas near Nacogdoches Elise told of trudging through red sand. It was an exhausting experience. Shoes sank and slipped back with every step, doubling the effort and number of paces needed to move forward. Olmsted also spoke of the sand at Nacogdoches, but he added that near Gaines Ferry and the Texas-Louisiana border he ran into heavy clay soil colored brick red by iron oxide. It was winter when he crossed, and wet weather had turned the clay to a quagmire; mud stuck to everything it touched. Migrating settlers toiled through it, their clothing stained maroon. On some nights he came on cotton wagons half mired in swamps, their black draymen a quarter mile apart gamely calling to one another with long musical "yo-hoi's."

From Gaines Ferry the wilderness road continued to Milam some ten miles into Texas, and then to San Augustine, once site of Misión de Nuestra Señora de Los Dolores de Los Ais, the last Texas outpost on El Camino Real. When Olmsted and his brother reached Nacogdoches they turned southwest, continuing through Austin and San Antonio down to San Fernando across the Rio Grande. By the time of Olmsted's journey, the immediacy of the Mexican War was beginning to fade; it had ended in 1848, the year after Elise reached Texas.

On their return trip the two men separated outside New Orleans, Olmsted going north on horseback and his brother going into the city and taking a ship to New York. Once back home Olmsted spent two years writing his book. His brother, a married man, fathered three children over the next six years. He died when the children were still infants—the trip had been invigorating but had not healed his lungs.

Elise and her companions reached Nacogdoches on July 25 thanks to the skill of their guide. He had succeeded in taking them and their wagonload of possessions fifteen to twenty hard miles each day, a feat that gained him so much respect as to leave Elise regretting her thought about the possibility of his stealing their belongings the first night on the trail. In her dispatch written to *Norge og Amerika* from Nacogdoches she recorded her change of mind. She proposed that fear of robbery was a European sickness, a disease caused by Old World poverty.

Americans rarely steal, she said—they know they can always make a living. They worry so little about theft as to leave their houses unlocked night and day, even while away on travels. "Our fears," she confessed, "were probably quite stupid, but they were rooted in our lack of knowledge of conditions and customs in this country. . . . I have to smile to myself," she added, "when I think there are people in Norway who believe one may starve to death here."[13]

Their guide had been his own man, a trustworthy and competent leader. She never gave his name in *Norge og Amerika,* perhaps because she did not speak enough English to ask him for it. Nor did she tell much about him besides indicating that he had introduced them to the ways of their new land. Once settled in Texas they would blend with the Norwegian colony, and it would be some years before they would have close contact with another American, whether slave or free.

She left no doubt that she considered the man an equal. Although she made no special issue of it, she would hold this attitude toward black people all her life. He parted from them at Nacogdoches, now more their companion than their "black master." They went their way and he went his. No doubt he headed back to Grand Ecore with a load of cotton bales, ready to guide others, perhaps more Europeans, across the Nacogdoches Wold.

CHAPTER 4

NACOGDOCHES TO BROWNSBORO

O N THE SURFACE Nacogdoches was a typical southern American town. The white houses in small gardens along the main street were built of sawmill lumber, framed up, neatly boarded, and plumb bob square. Fraternal organizations—Masons, Odd Fellows, Sons of Temperance—held parades at Christmas and on other occasions. There were Protestant churches, merchant stores, and an elected local government.

Appearances can be deceiving; Nacogdoches stood near the thin edge of American settlement. Fewer than five hundred people lived in the town. A community of Mexicans established there by the Spanish viceroy in El Camino Real days kept their own language, Roman Catholic religion, and distinctive customs. The Cherokee Indian War, fought in 1839 within a day's ride from the town, was still a living memory. Although the naked frontier had moved beyond Dallas and Waco, the country leading to it from Nacogdoches was barely getting organized.[1]

Before moving on to the new territory west of Nacogdoches Elise expected to stay with her friend Thomine Grogard, who had left Norway with her husband, Christian, and their ten children in 1845 with the first group of Texas-bound emigrants. They should have been well established by now, but severe misfortunes had overtaken them. Christian had died of yellow fever in Grand Ecore on a trip back from New Orleans, where he had gone to buy provisions for their new general store. Other woes followed: the supplies he bought never reached Nacogdoches, and within the year three of Thomine's children sickened and died. Elise had heard about these sad events in New Orleans and realized that Thomine might be overwhelmed. Alone, grieving, with limited means and seven surviving children to support, she might be too crushed to offer any sort of hospitality.[2]

Much to Elise's surprise she found her friend fit, managing well, and quite ready to take her in. Instead of fretting about herself, Thomine had been worrying over Elise's long delayed arrival. Six months before, she had received word that Elise would be leaving Norway for Texas, but no news had come since. Anything could have happened to her—a change of plans, shipwreck, death from disease, or calamity crossing the wilderness leading to Nacogdoches.

They were both overjoyed when they met, but Elise the more so because Thomine's success proved the case for emigration. Elise reported to *Norge og Amerika:* "Friends of Grogard will be pleased to hear that his widow is doing quite well by sewing and baking for people. With regard to the future of her numerous children, it was a blessing the family came to Texas as it will be much easier for them to make a living here than it would have been in Norway."[3]

Two of the eldest daughters were working for prosperous families who treated the girls like their own children. Three sons were in school, and two others would start work with German businessmen in the fall. All the same, she had to temper the good news. Thomine's powerful resolve, nothing less, had carried her through. Some prospective emigrants seemed to think Texas was a bucolic paradise and place for relaxed hunting and fishing. Not so. Like other new arrivals Thomine lived under Spartan conditions.

Her home outside town was a one-room cabin built frontier style: logs adzed and notched to fit together, wall openings instead of windows, rafters open to the roof, dirt floor, and barely any heat. A plank sleeping-loft accessed by a ladder stretched over half the room. A small separate cabin served as the kitchen—here Elise learned more about the hazards of cooking on a floor hearth.

Elise knew what log cabins should look like. Scandinavians had introduced them to the American wilderness in the 1600s, and she viewed Thomine's home with a critical eye: "As houses go in this country it is quite nice, but in Norway we would say it is quite poor." Besides, certain staples an emigrant might expect to find were missing or in short supply—rice, white flour, live yeast to raise bread dough, rye grain, and berry juice. Nacogdoches was a place of thin existence, borderland country.[4]

Hardships aside, Elise was eager to journey farther west where she could test a new life in an untried world. Johan Reinert Reiersen, her mentor from Norway, had established a colony in remote Henderson County near present day Tyler, about ninety miles northwest of Nacogdoches (see map 3). The county had been organized for settlement by the Texas legislature only in 1846, the year before Elise arrived. Reiersen called his colony Normandy, after the province in northwest France where Vikings had installed themselves almost a thousand years before. The new Normandy settlement would be Elise's window on pioneer life. She meant to push right on to it after a short stay with Thomine.[5]

Unexpected obstacles held her back for three long months. At first she could not find transportation. "Most horses," she explained in *Norge og Amerika,* "are kept for riding and cannot draw a carriage, so to hire a horse and carriage is almost impossible." Besides, it took time to gather the essentials for starting pioneer work; axes, mattocks, shovels, plows, and seed were expensive. The ample stocks of her everyday world were far behind in Norway.[6]

Just when she thought she had located transportation she was struck down by sickness. "A cold fever," she called it. She languished helpless in bed for fifteen days, and then recurring fever kept her confined for six more weeks. Her report to *Norge og Amerika* remained unfinished. The sickness was almost certainly malaria, or "ague," as they called it in those days. Quinine, long known to medicine, was not available in Nacogdoches.

When finally able to resume her report she described the disease and told about the old-time country treatment she had to undergo for it: "It is supposedly not dangerous since I have not heard of anyone dying of it, nor is it painful. The fever manifests itself partly by feeling cold and shivering, partly by a burning heat. This is helped by pouring cold water over people, and then there are days between attacks without any symptoms at all. Nevertheless, it is a great curse."[7]

The frequency of illness forced her to confront the problem of sickness in Texas. "Fever is catching up with people very often," she wrote. "Lots and lots of people in Nacogdoches have caught it this year." Medical science had not yet proven that insects brought the malaria and yellow fever epidemics that ravaged Texas and Louisiana, but she seemed to suspect they might be to blame. She spoke of mosquitoes, and—translating her Norwegian into equivalent English—"itsy-bitsy insects called 'ticks.'"

In New Orleans annual yellow fever epidemics killed people by the hundreds. There, she said, the mosquitoes had been terrible. But in Nacogdoches: "Those who live here pay no attention to them—I'm not even sure they know there are mosquitoes. All the same, they were bad enough for newcomers."

Ants, too, invaded people's homes. She mentioned them especially because her countrymen would find it hard to believe they could become indoor pests. In Norway the cold climate kept their numbers and foraging down. She described the ants as little yellow-brown things. They crawled about looking for food. Butter and sweets were their favorites.

She was aware that word of sickness and death was turning prospective Norwegian settlers away from Texas. The Great Plains—Iowa, Illinois, Wisconsin, even Missouri—were appealing to her countrymen and could be reached within a few days by steamboat from New Orleans. Besides, St. Louis, the major stopping point on the Mississippi, offered ready access to Missouri and the middle states. Some of the Norwegians who arrived with the second shipload for Texas in 1846 went north because they heard about the death-dealing sicknesses at their initial destination.[8]

Elise's consideration of health problems began her career as a Norwegian-language publicist for Texas. Before long she would be answering a broad attack about the state published in Norway, but in this first foray she showed her keen sense of strategy. She admitted the facts and then attacked them sidelong, on the flank. Prudent individuals, she declared, generally stay well and manage to foil death even when they do become ill. Many who had sickened and died in Texas actually caused their own demise. They simply did not use common sense.

The causes of disease were little known at the time, so she began by relating an argument she had had with a neighboring Danish farmer. He was Lindberg, a man with impeccable credentials, one whom her readers might have heard about and certainly would respect. He had moved, she said, from Wisconsin to Texas—a hint that he had made a wise decision. He was the son of a minister, a "cultured and sensible man," a knowledgeable husbandman who had owned his own farm in Denmark for twenty-four years. Besides, he had more experience than she—"I cannot say much as I have not been farther than here [Nacogdoches] and have spoken with very few." Lindberg had traveled. His ideas had to have merit.

When asking him why he had not remained in Wisconsin she innocently remarked, "I thought the climate in Texas was not healthy." He denied this immediately and emphatically. Not at all! Forget climate. Turn the fault around, he said. Individuals create their own sicknesses. Blame the Texans themselves. They gorge on lethal foods. They stuff on meat and fat at every meal and gulp strong coffee to wash them down. That is the reason they get sick and die.

Elise suggested another cause: abundant weeds in Texas produce illness.

Offending plants grow everywhere. They fill the air with noxious odors and ooze unhealthy juices.

Lindberg refused to be moved. He rejected her idea categorically. Bad diet is the cause of ill health in Texas, he insisted. Nothing more to it. Besides, he agreed with her friend Reiersen: Texas was just a better place to live than any northern state.[9]

Underneath their seeming differences Elise actually shared Lindberg's outlook. She was an individualist, a believer in personal responsibility. People were accountable for their own lives. They should guard their own good health. Many who sickened and died in Texas were victims of their own bad judgment. Quite plainly, she told *Norge og Amerika,* they brought on their own destruction.

She cited cases as proof. Germund Olsen had died the previous October after recovering from "the fever"—probably malaria, although she did not say so. Instead of resting to build up his strength, he had left his sickbed and immediately gone to visit his brother. After that he walked miles to call on an elderly Norwegian friend, and then dropped in on several neighbors. On his way home the fever returned. It gripped him hard. All at once he could go no farther. He collapsed on the wayside grass outside an American's house. He died on the spot.

Two other Norwegians had died of dysentery a few months after they arrived in the summer of 1846. They were Gregers and Jens Jensen, both from Holt, the town where Elise's father had had his last pastorate. The two men contracted the illness while traveling from New Orleans to Nacogdoches. They became sick, she said, "from a combination of river water and whiskey—a kind of liquor made from corn that acts like a laxative, especially when combined with water from the Mississippi and the Red River."

Gregers died in a few days, but Jens partially recovered. While still weak he bought land, built a temporary cabin, cut timber for a new house, and then went to another county where he helped Andersen build his home. After a few days Jens started back to his cabin. On the way he stayed overnight with an American family. There the fare turned out to be too heavy and indigestible for his weakened intestines. They served him fresh, warm milk and fatty bacon—probably fatback, judging from Elise's description. He never should have eaten what he was offered; an intense attack of diarrhea followed. His American hosts had to carry him back to his home and in a few days he died.[10]

Elise's concern with illness faded as her bouts of fever declined. In the last days of September she was able to resume work on the next stage of her journey. She had dropped her previous travel arrangements and the problem of finding transportation was once more upon her. Nacogdoches was the last outpost before the small settlement at Dallas, and it could not produce a horse-drawn rig, no matter what kind—carriage, shay, wagon, or cart.

To make matters worse, one of Thomine's American neighbors named Mr. Tom got Elise off to a false start. He was a longtime resident, so she was pleased when he offered to get her a wagon and a team of horses. But he frittered away ten days and then backed out on his offer. Annoyed by his time-consuming and futile effort, Elise summarily dismissed him like a feckless charlatan.

Following this, she located a wagon for rent and got a horse from Roeraas the blacksmith, a fellow Norwegian. Roeraas had arrived the previous fall and had only recently started to train his horse to harness and wagon. Not suspecting that the animal was only partially trained, Elise accepted it.

Waerenskjold had not appeared in her reports since the dramatic night by the swamp. He turned up now, apparently having been with her all along, and took on the seemingly routine task of getting the horse and wagon ready. He put the collar on the animal, laid the harness on its back, backed it between the wagon shafts, hitched it up, and loaded the baggage. They climbed aboard and seated themselves. Waerenskjold picked up the reins and gave them a snap to get the horse started.

The animal stood stock-still, refusing to move, absolutely unwilling to draw the wagon. Waerenskjold urged him on, doubtless with a whip. At that the animal reared up and came down kicking so hard that he threatened to wreck the whole rig. Waerenskjold got him calmed but had to unhitch him, remove the harness, and unload their baggage. After that he personally had to drag the wagon back to its owner and return the horse to Roeraas.

This misadventure suggested why Mr. Tom had failed to deliver. He had tried in a few short days to train his own horses to haul a wagon. When he found it impossible he saved face by backing out on his offer without explanation. The added failure with Roeraas taught Elise she had to make sure horses proffered for rent were actually trained to harness and wagon. Knowing this turned out to be no help, however—trained horses could not be had. If a drover in Grand Ecore could supply a team and driver to haul immigrants and their baggage to Nacogdoches, why were no rigs available to go from Nacogdoches to Normandy?

In frustration Elise explained again: "Riding is the most usual way to travel for women as well as men, and one rarely sees anyone driving [a wagon or cart] except when they are moving their home. Even more rare is it to see anyone on foot. Everybody has a horse." Horses trained to wagon were busy hauling cotton bales east to Grand Ecore rather than to risk taking settlers west into poorly settled territory where there might be no return business.

She was almost without hope: "No matter how hard we have tried we have not succeeded in getting another horse, so God knows how this will work out." When she made special mention of women as well as men riding horseback she meant to hammer home her point. In Europe women traveled in carriages or rode sidesaddle; sitting astride a horse was considered indecent.[11]

The journey to Brownsboro finally worked out when the Dane, Lindberg, came to the rescue. Their differences over the causes of illness had left no grudge between them, and he offered his oxen and cart at no charge. Even though it took oxen five days to travel as far as horses could go in three, Elise settled for them gladly. All the same she had to observe: "Oxen are not as comfortable to travel with as horses. They are lazy and hard to handle."

Elise's comment on this point presents something of a mystery because in spite of their unhurried pace, oxen at the time were widely used for hauling and plowing in Texas. It seems, however, that the oxen did not understand Norwegian. The solution was to have Lindberg's son come along to teach Elise and Waerenskjold how to shout the English commands "go," "stop," "right," and "left."

The young man made the return trip on his own, having given Elise and Waerenskjold more useful instruction than they expected. By learning the commands and how to drive oxen with a flailing whip, they were able to use the animals as their main beasts of burden when they started their own ranch. Slow they might be, but the oxen hauled everything.

It took the little group seven days to cover the ninety miles to Normandy, walking alongside the oxcart much of the time. Passing through Cherokee County they stopped overnight with a Norwegian who was opening a general store at a crossroads that later became the center of Larissa. At Rusk, about halfway, Elise began to see the sort of land she was looking for. There were breaks in the wilderness forests, the first natural open spaces they had seen since leaving Grand Ecore.

The countryside for miles was scarcely touched by human habitation. Elise described Rusk as a "little town." She exaggerated: with only one family in residence, it had recently been designated as the county capital by the state legislature. She felt increasing delight as the dense forests gave way to patches of prairie covered with luxurious stands of native grasses. "As far as I am concerned," Elise remarked, "the open spaces are the most appealing, but they say you haven't seen anything until you come to the vast prairies, which are supposed to be extremely beautiful."

There was no risk of encountering hostile Indians. The Cherokee War had ended with the resident tribes driven out or onto reservations, and it was only beyond the Dallas to Waco frontier that marauding Comanche bands were destroying other tribes and the settlers who were beginning to trickle in. The counties that Elise soon came to know best—Cherokee, Smith, Kaufman, and Van Zandt—were about to undergo an influx of land-hungry Americans and Europeans.

At the time that Elise made her way to Normandy, Van Zandt and Kaufman counties had not yet been organized. The wagon trail through Cherokee and Smith counties probably followed a trace blazed from Nacogdoches by a man named John Jordan, who had hauled two iron kettles through to start a salt works at a place now called Jordan's Saline. As Elise described it, the way through the two counties was almost as rugged as the road through the Nacogdoches Wold.

The country was more open than the Louisiana wilderness, but it had its share of obstacles. Some of the stands of trees were too extensive to be detoured, and in these the trailblazers had notched bark to mark the way through. Windfalls in the woods, heavy rainstorms, and rich carpets of prairie grass all conspired to obscure wagon tracks.

Bridges had been built only over the deepest rivers and streams, with smaller waterways to be crossed at fords. Under the flowing waters, perilously smooth rock could cause dray animals to slip and break their legs. Just as in the wilderness from Grand Ecore to Nacogdoches, trees had been cut only where absolutely necessary, and swampy stretches were made passable by logs laid on top of the wet soil. Wagons traveling on these corduroy roads bumped along, jolting the passengers' buttocks on the unkind seats. People scraped their spines, knees, and elbows against the wooden bench backs and sideboards. "With so little work," Elise observed, "roads like this in most countries would be considered impassable, but here they are quite good."[12]

The party arrived in Normandy on Sunday, October 10, for a joyful reunion with Reiersen and his family. During the days they stayed at his home Elise had time to study the community and to learn about her countrymen. Regrettably, all was not well with them.

Reiersen had warned his emigration group to avoid taking residence in swampy bottomlands, but twenty-one of them had disregarded his advice and packed together in a shabby house located in a soggy hollow. An unscrupulous landlord, a man named Cook, had lured them into the location by offering to rent them the house in return for sharecropping. Instead of paying rent in cash, he told them, they could work his land and give him half their crop.

Typically, new sharecroppers had to borrow from their landlords to buy food and clothing during their first months. After harvest time they made repayment with their share of the crop. Cook would have known that future prices would determine how much of their crop he would get. This, along with charging them an exorbitant interest rate, might yield him their entire crop. The Norwegians would end up his perpetual tenants locked in debt peonage, a common fate for sharecroppers.

Cook not only convinced them they could profit by sharecropping, but he gave them no warning about the house being located in a foul, pestilential hollow. Disease filled the place, the water was bad, and soon most of the twenty-one became sick. Four died immediately, and others only survived through Reiersen's efforts. After warning them against living in such a place, he now found he had to turn around and take care of them. He traveled miles to buy them medicine at his own expense, and thanks to him a number of them did survive to escape from peonage in Cook's clutches.[13]

Another problem Elise found in Normandy related to religious life. Like many of the first Norwegian immigrant communities in America, the people were without a pastor or a church. Most were accustomed to regular religious services because their government at home had formally established Lutheranism as the country's official religion. Churches in Norway were tax supported, built and maintained under royal authority, with pastors trained and paid at public expense. The pastors often doubled as schoolmasters, and their church records of marriages, baptisms, confirmations, and funerals served as the local sources of vital statistics. Voluntary personal contributions by members of parishes were a minor part of religious support.

In the early 1800s fervent religious movements had swept Norway and converted many people to deep spiritual piety. Sincerely devout settlers sent letters home punctuated with expressions like "God be thanked" and "the Lord keep you." No doubt the Normandy pioneers used the same terms in daily speech as well as correspondence. Elise found her countrymen severely distressed by the absence of trained religious leadership. Christian Grogard, Thomine's husband, had been expected to take care of spiritual matters. He had completed theological studies, and though never formally ordained he was designated to serve as their pastor.

He would ride a circuit of the main settlements to perform the sacred rites and sacraments, but if he were not always able to reach them all, the settlers would reverse the order and go to him. Back home many people had been accustomed to making strenuous efforts to attend religious services. They traveled long distances to get to their churches, sometimes having to oar themselves by rowboat on journeys across fjords or to rock-girdled islands more than a mile out at sea. In Texas the hardships of pioneer life would surely make them eager to travel over long distances to find comfort in religious ceremonies.

When Grogard died a year after he arrived, the residents were left without anyone who knew anything about performing essential rites. Baptisms, marriages, and funerals had to be performed by lay people, a necessary but barely suitable alternative to services by a trained pastor. Confirmations could not be performed at all.

Even more serious considering the frequent deaths, the settlers had no cemetery for burials. Family members and friends had to be interred in earth not blessed by a pastor, unconsecrated soil. People were laid to rest wherever they died, near homes or out in fields. Worse still were the lone burials far off in woodlands or patches of prairie. Strangers who came to own such properties would care nothing for the graves left on their lands, their fading markings in a foreign language. Final resting places like these would be untended, overgrown, and forgotten.[14]

Elise clung to the name Normandy for the town long after it had been changed to Brownsboro, and this may have been because a cemetery for her people was founded while she was staying there. At the time many of the settlers, not the least of them Reiersen and his family, were planning to move away to better land elsewhere. A man named Brown was one of the stalwarts who stayed behind and is buried in the cemetery. Originally his name was the Norwegian Brun, and it seems reasonable that after he had it translated to its English equivalent it became identified with the town.

Possibly he was the John ("Red") Brown who operated a toll bridge across Kickapoo Creek on the road to Tyler and was said by a local historian to be the person after whom the town was named. Whatever the truth, when the issue of a legal designation for the place came up, Brownsboro was substituted for Normandy, though apparently not to Elise's satisfaction.[15]

The Old Norwegian Cemetery in Brownsboro was at first a plain graveyard, an unhallowed plot of land for simple interment. Although more suitable a place for burying people than out by homes or fields or forests, the soil was not consecrated until the mid-1850s, when a pastor from Norway finally performed the necessary rites.

Sometime later a small church was built by the cemetery, but today the church is gone and the cemetery remains only as a historic site. No longer used for burials, it lies peacefully on two sunlit acres in a stretch of prairie surrounded by dispersed forest groves. Worn gravestones dating from the late 1840s into the twentieth century bear the names of original residents and their descendants. One row of plain brownstone markers on a grassy stretch runs along conspicuously to one side of the center.

The markers in this separate row bear no sign of inscriptions. Set up by Reiersen's father Ole (pronounced "*Oh*luh"), at his own expense, they are the burial places of unnamed individuals who were paupers or whose bodies were exhumed and brought in from lonely places. When first set up the stones must have stood a foot high. Now but jagged eight-inch stubs, they seem too insignificant to memorialize those first pioneers who came and died at Brownsboro when it was still called Normandy. Only the nationality of the persons in those graves is known, not their names.

Will Tergersen was the last person descended from those original settlers to be buried at the Old Norwegian Cemetery. His is a well-marked memorial; he died in the 1970s some 130 years after the first arrivals in the colony, the last descendant of people whom Elise knew and who were laid to rest in the ancestral cemetery.[16]

In spite of the hardships experienced by the first Norwegian settlers, Elise found more cheerful than gloomy news to report. Besides supplying advice for newcomers, she was interested in what was going on and in social and personal news. No one knew as many people as she or kept as closely in touch with who was where and what they were doing—marriages, births, deaths, visitors, arrivals, departures, enterprises, successes, and failures. In years to come, she would devote substantial parts of her letters and published accounts to these topics.

Information about thirty-seven individuals appeared in her dispatches written in Brownsboro and Nacogdoches. Some she merely identified by name and occupation—Gerhard the watchmaker, Reier Roa the wheelwright, Jens Ousel the blacksmith. About Syvert Nielsen Haavesland, however, she wrote in more detail. His story had traveled by word of mouth over more than three hundred miles from South Texas. Haavesland had enlisted in the American army and gone to join the war with Mexico. When the main fighting was done south of the border he returned from his tour of duty to live in San Antonio—she spelled it Antonia. He was now working as a blacksmith in the large community of German settlers there.

Reports about jobs and enterprise appeared in some instances. Sven and his wife Asper had moved to another county, where he was working at a cotton gin. His employers were paying him $120 per year and planned to build a new house for him, his wife, and their future family. Laussen had broken soil, owned two horses and twenty-seven other animals. He was talking about sowing rice. Gunsteensen had gone to New Orleans to find work during the winter; "someone named Even" (pronounced "Ayvan") from Arendal or thereabouts had followed him.

Other stories were strictly personal. Birthe was staying with an American family. Lina had made a good match: she had married a German storekeeper who was very good to her and loved gardening. One item even hinted at bizarre misdoing. An old couple had moved in with Olsen at Christmas time. Both were now dead, "some say from fever, some say not—I don't know." When they died their only daughter stayed on with Olsen; rumor had it they would marry.

About Reiersen she wrote in considerable detail. As earlier noted, he was the former editor and publisher of the reform newspaper *Christianssandposten* and was known in Norway as a leading activist for emigration. His detailed report on America was titled *Veiviser for Norske emigranter til forenede nordamerikanske og Texas* (published in English in 1980 as *Pathfinder for Norwegian Emigrants to the United North American States and Texas*). Written after he made a thorough study of the northern plains states and Texas in 1843–44, was the most detailed and useful survey of its time. Anyone in Norway with the slightest interest in the New World had read it.

Inevitably he was a central figure in Elise's report about Brownsboro. In it she referred to him as Reinert, a name used by his friends, as if her readers knew him personally. He was doing well, she said. He had broken quite a lot of acreage, owned two horses, twenty-two cows with calves, and fourteen pigs, a throng amounting to considerable wealth by Norwegian standards. Most of the Reiersen family—Reinert's father Ole, six brothers, and two sisters—had come to Texas.

Old Ole had been *klokker* (sexton) at Elise's father's last church at Holt in Norway and, as we have seen, had helped to establish the cemetery at Brownsboro. Now deep in years, he was living three miles away with Reiersen's youngest brother and sister. The entire family had suffered hard bouts of fever, but all had recovered.

Johan Reiersen was keeping in close touch with events at the state legislature, where new counties thirty miles west of Brownsboro would soon be organized. He knew that once county government structures were in place, people would be able to secure land grants in the new areas. The land over there, bordering on the fertile Texas blacklands, would soon become Van Zandt and Kaufman counties.[17]

Besides chronicling information on the settlers, Elise once again put together a body of advice for the benefit of future emigrants. Her advisory list this time was shorter and less intense than the one she had sent from New Orleans. No longer anxious about bare survival, she was thinking about the requirements for settled domestic life and husbandry in the new land.

Grapes and plums were growing wild, she said. People were raising cultivated fruit—apple, cherry, gooseberry—in their gardens. The trees were reasonably productive, but sturdier stock would be even better: "Bring good apples, pears, plums, cherries, raspberries, black currants, and gooseberry bushes as well as all kinds of good yard seeds and root of hops and horseradish." While the hops would do well for brewing beer, anyone going through France or Germany should pick up fine quality grapevines for wine. The soil in Texas was so fertile any good rootstock and seed would thrive. She advised bringing whatever varieties came to hand.

Potatoes were a staple of the Norwegian diet. A German woman who lived near Reiersen had some of the same types as were found in Europe. They were growing right in her back yard and were very good. The more common native potatoes, though, were of poor quality. Elise recommended bringing an assortment of the best varieties to use as starter buds.

A man in Norway had been interested in sweet potatoes, an exotic food practically unknown to Europeans at the time. She addressed him as "Mr. B," perhaps avoiding use of his real name because he was an important public figure who might be embarrassed by showing an interest in emigrant news. Sweet potatoes, she told him, were delicious but took a long time to ripen and were hard to keep from rotting after harvest. She apologized to him for not fulfilling his request to send some over to Norway for his home garden. They would perish long before they arrived, and besides, even if planted in a hothouse, they would never grow to maturity in the short Norwegian summer.

In terms of planning for home comforts, she reported that beds in America were good no matter how poor other household furniture might be. Warmth at night, however, could be a problem. Winters were usually mild, but the north wind at times brought chill. When emigrants first arrived they nearly always had to live in hurriedly built log cabins, most of them out in the countryside where the construction might be crude.

They missed the solidly built houses and five-foot-high ceramic tile wood heaters found in Norway. The cabin fireplaces in Texas cast intense heat six feet out but spread little warmth through the room—"this is not comfortable," she reported. "You are cooking on one side and cold on the other." Heat might circulate better if the cabins were not so drafty, but "since one doesn't use windows to let in light and air, one either has to leave the door or the hole in the wall open."

Lacking casement-mounted windows that could be raised or lowered to control airflow, people depended on the small plank doors covering the openings in the cabin walls. The doors were removable or set on heavy hinges to swing outward. A tyrannical cold wind blew in when they were left open to circulate air. Elise gave solemn counsel to newcomers: "I would say that bringing windows, both the frame and the glass, as well as a cooking stove and good wood burner, would be very helpful."

Warm bedding and clothing were necessary, but both were high priced and in short supply in Texas. Prospective emigrants should bring good bedding, together with handkerchiefs, preferably linen, and wool stockings as well as other clothing made of wool. Feather down, commonly used in warm European-style comforters, was difficult to find and very expensive. Wool could be obtained but was costly. She suggested bringing down and wool in bulk.

Cotton, on the other hand, need not be brought—it was plentiful and available at prices below those in Europe. Clothing irons, which in those days were clunky blocks of cast iron that had to be heated atop stoves or on fireplace trivets, could be purchased only in a big city like New Orleans. She recommended bringing one along even though it weighed a lot.[18]

Once she joined Reiersen in Brownsboro Elise assumed that her advisory discourses would continue as regular features in the pages of *Norge og Amerika.* She may even have expected to put the magazine back under his control. If not, they would work in collaboration so that she could give up being its solo writer and editor. His role would be to contribute up-to-date information on land, business opportunities, and ranching, while she would write about people, garden plants, health matters, food, home furnishing, and the like.

Sharing the publication duties would make sense. *Norge og Amerika,* after all, had originally been his magazine. He had left it in her hands and she had done her duty by editing it for nearly three years and writing more than twelve thousand words for it since she had left Norway. She had no problem about sharing authority with him. They could write their articles independently and split the task of editing manuscripts submitted by other settlers.

Part of her eagerness to reach Brownsboro had been to fulfill a promise she had made to Kirkgaard, the printer back in Trondheim who had taken over *Norge og Amerika*. She had told him she would forward a manuscript from Reiersen as soon as she reached Texas. She never said, though, that Reiersen knew anything about this arrangement or that he had agreed to comply with it. Because he was such an avid emigration advocate, she took it for granted that he would be as eager as she to continue writing for the magazine.

When she reached Reiersen's residence in Brownsboro, no manuscript was forthcoming. Her expectation had lived only in her own mind. Her promise to Kirkgaard was a daydream. Reiersen was not about to write for the magazine again. What was more, he had decided the magazine must be shut down.

This decision seems to have come as a total surprise to Elise. At no time did she ever even hint at it or give any reason for it. Perhaps the magazine was simply too expensive to maintain. Reiersen may have signaled as much by not having a manuscript ready.

However painful the decision may have been for her, Elise said nothing more about it. She probably realized that closing the magazine made practical sense. It had subscribers, no question about that, but it probably required a subsidy to keep it going. Reiersen may have used his personal funds to get it started, and quite possibly Elise continued to support its printing and circulation costs herself when she became editor. They had no choice. Norway was far away, the magazine was bringing no profit, pioneering had its expenses, and there was other pressing work to do.

In its four-year life *Norge og Amerika* had been the main and perhaps the only regularly published source of emigration information in Norway. It had been a strong and useful voice that quickened the emigration fever beginning to engulf the country. For almost three of those years Elise had produced the magazine, first as its editor and then as its principal writer. It had lived constantly in her mind. Now she would write for it no more. Her career as a writer had come to an end.[19]

An incident following the end of *Norge og Amerika* suggests that angry words may have passed between Elise and Reiersen. Whatever they said to one another went unrecorded, but in early February, 1848, Reiersen suddenly reversed himself and produced a manuscript. Elise may have been badgering him, but he still refused to write for the magazine he had declared defunct. Instead he composed a strange letter for delivery to Andreas Gjestvang in Norway.

Gjestvang had been Elise's discovery. About him she said: "One fine day Gjestvang came to Christiania to interview the publisher [of *Norge og Amerika*] and was not a little surprised to find that E. Tvede was a woman. After that I often had letters from him."[20]

In Gjestvang's mind E. Tvede, editor of *Norge og Amerika*, had to be a man. A woman editor for a magazine—that was unheard of. Her signature avoided trouble. It freed her of female identity at a time when a woman magazine editor would be suspect; some people would consider such a person loose and shameless. Once Gjestvang got over his surprise at her guarded gender identity he entered into a spirited correspondence with her. He shared her ultramodern outlook. Writing to a woman editor caused him no problem. He even considered joining her emigration group.

Elise probably convinced Reiersen to write to Gjestvang when she realized the decision about *Norge og Amerika* was final. Reiersen in turn may have been willing to write to Gjestvang because he was a man of substance. Hamar, where Gjestvang was licensee for the government mail contract, was a sizable town at the mouth of Lake Mjoesa north of Christiania. A prominent man, he could arrange for publication of Reiersen's letter in *Hamars Budstikken* (Hamar Messenger), a newspaper with a wide circulation.

Knowing about Gjestvang's status may have prompted Reiersen to write his letter, but it also may have been what caused him to show that he cared not a hoot for the man's position. In Norway, Reiersen had been a belligerent critic of the established classes, and this attitude together with anger toward Elise may explain the tone of the letter he wrote. Whatever the reason, he began with a stinging attack on his former country, spewing words almost dripping with loathing. Norwegians, he flung out, quickly forgot their old world when they reached Texas: "I feel almost disgusted at the thought of writing to Norway, where I still see the truth, the naked, obvious, truth that I see with my own eyes every day, every hour, truth that is undeniable, being shaped into lies and fraud. These lies, though hidden in the most incredible stupidity, are presented and proclaimed in the language of pure oracles."

Having fired off this tirade he went on, presumably at Elise's insistence, to supply information on practical matters. He reported facts about Texas: the quantity of various crops produced; the price of land to the west of Brownsboro (50 cents to $1.50 per acre); the level of heat in the summer; the cold in the winter; his personal prosperity.

He threw in a few more fillips consistent with his opening diatribe. Poverty, he said, does not strike one in the face in Texas as it does in Norway. The ordinary citizen can influence policy—something quite impossible under royal rule back home. Hinting that Gjestvang's status in Norway amounted to little, he told him that in Texas he would achieve a rank far above his present position as postmaster. He closed with a peremptory tone. The gist of his words: "Come over and see for yourself!"

Reiersen's manner was hardly what Elise had in mind. Only the most avid emigrant-to-be would get to his factual report after reading his embittered opening remarks. She had always addressed Gjestvang in the most cordial terms. They shared a mutual respect and she meant to keep things that way.

As it turned out Reiersen gave her an opportunity to set things straight. He passed his letter to Gjestvang on to her for mailing. Possibly he wanted her to read it, but if so it was a mistake, because putting it in her hands gave her a chance to attach a postscript. She seized the opportunity without hesitation, coolly adding a passage meant to defuse Reiersen's hostility.

It was amazing that she took a stand against him so readily. She did not hesitate to tell people off in choice language when necessary, but Reiersen had been her mentor, the man who had first stirred her dreams of emigration. She had been so eager a disciple that he had put *Norge og Amerika* into her hands. When she took over his groundbreaking magazine she did it gratefully, but now she was opposing him.[21]

Her postscript seems like a mild demurrer, but actually it was another neatly executed, full-scale flank attack. She did not contradict Reiersen's assault on their Norwegian homeland; she merely questioned his factual accuracy on a couple of points. She took a low-key approach, deflating Reiersen's harangue with light stiletto jabs.

She observed that Reiersen's statements were not always quite accurate. This letter, for example, contained two flaws. The first concerned "the fever" in Texas—he had made it seem too mild. Medicine, he had claimed, easily cured it. This was not so. The disease was severe, "a great curse," as she had said about her own case. Medicine was rarely available for emigrants. Even then it only suppressed the disease and did not cure it. The fever struck again, bringing its victims more sweats and more chills.

Second, Reiersen had taken too strong a stand in urging Gjestvang to emigrate. She could have pointed out that in other writings Reiersen urged people of substance to stay home, but she made her case stronger by ignoring those statements. Instead, she asserted without qualification that only the poor would be better off in Texas. They could find plenty of work and would improve themselves by leaving Norway. Wealthier people had nothing to gain from emigration. Why would anyone who was comfortable challenge fate by starting out in the New World?

Nacogdoches to Brownsboro

Too, she countered Reiersen's innuendo regarding Gjestvang's position. Knowing Gjestvang was a man of polished tastes, she said she personally would be delighted if he decided to visit Texas with his family. Their society would be most welcome to her—the greatest deficit in Texas was that Norwegians with civilizing interests were too few and too scattered to form a community.

She closed her postscript in much the same way as Reiersen had but in a softer tone. She issued a polite invitation: come over and see what you think.[22]

With that she might have concluded her words, but she went on to make a startling disclosure: *"I have decided to stay in Texas."*

This was a crucial decision. It was the first time she ever said anything like it in public. Not only did it confirm her favorable attitude toward Texas; she knew her decision to stay would be well publicized in Norway. Gjestvang would arrange to publish Reiersen's letter in *Hamars Budstikken,* the main newspaper circulating in the area north of Christiania, and Elise's postscript would appear along with it. Moreover, *Morgenbladet* (Morning news) would spread the word far and wide. The country's leading newspaper published in Christiania, it commonly reprinted important letters from *Hamars Budstikken.*

Following her sensational disclosure she reported that she and Waerenskjold were thinking about buying land together with their friend James Staack. Brownsboro was a possibility, but they were also thinking about going farther west to the open prairie, the area where Van Zandt and Kaufman counties were about to be organized.[23]

Elise's postscript said nothing to indicate that her decision to stay rested in part on her ideals. This subject she reserved for the last issue of *Norge og Amerika,* where she made clear that there was more to Texas than making a good living. A spirit of openness and democracy prevailed in the country.

Reiersen had detected this spirit on his first visit to America. Elise in her final dispatch turned the clock back to that earlier day when his words had first sparked her imagination. He had written with pure enthusiasm then, making observations reminiscent of Alexis de Tocqueville's treatise *Democracy in America.* Like de Tocqueville, Reiersen saw an egalitarian spirit prevailing in America. Conditions in this land were open and fluid. There was opportunity. No one felt beneath his peers or that he could not rise up and become more than he had been.

Elise advanced examples from everyday usage in Norway to sum up her similar thoughts about Texas. In Norway, as in other European countries, people made social distinctions by using different forms of the word *you* when addressing superiors and inferiors—*De* was for a person of higher quality, and *du* was for a child, a servant, or a dog. Using this idea, Elise wrote: "Here all the white people eat the same food at the same table and stay in the same room, in other words all are treated in the same civil way. Everyone, even slaves, is addressed in the same polite way, not as at home where various degrees of esteem are expressed by addressing the upper classes with a respectful, impersonal *You*. The use of the superior and inferior expressions for *you* has always appeared insulting to me."[24]

She could not, however, allow her affirmative impression of Texas to stand without qualification: she pointedly omitted slaves when speaking about sharing common meals. She had in mind something like the "upstairs and downstairs" custom in Europe—masters were served upstairs in the formal dining room while inferiors ate at a bare table in the kitchen down in the cellar. Slaves in Texas might be spoken to politely, but it was only white people who shared an equality of status that permitted them to have meals together.

To make her point, she wrote: "One of the dark sides of Texas, in my opinion, is slavery . . . and I do hope that my fellow countrymen, even if they can afford it, will not forget their Christian teachings to the point that they will keep slaves."[25]

Her final dispatch to *Norge og Amerika* was sent from Nacogdoches, where she and Wacrenskjold had returned to pick up their baggage after their journey to Brownsboro. Somewhere along their way they searched out Andersen to say goodbye. At this point Elise was no longer referring to him as farmer Andersen. He was Torger Andersen, pure and simple.

In Norway when Elise was first in touch with Andersen he was identified by something even more modest than his occupational tag as a farmer. His surname was Noreodegaard, meaning North Abandoned Farm (farm abandoned during the Black Plague). This was not his own baptismal name; it was the name of the farm where he worked. His surname changed any time he moved from one farm residence or workplace to another.

The practice of assigning people a surname taken from where they lived dated from the medieval era. Andersen was a freeholder, a member of a defined class of small landowners whose link to the land was so strong that it became the source of their names. It was as if a man's identity was not his own. His being, the meaning of his life, came from the property or place where he lived and worked.

By dropping the surname Noreodegaard before he left Norway, Andersen had already made a first symbolic step toward dismissing his past social class identity. When he became just Torger Andersen to Elise it signaled the final break. And as plain Torger Andersen, he was finding Texas very much to his liking. He was going back to Norway to fetch his wife and children. Together he and his family would move and live in a land of opportunity, a place with a prevailing sense of equality, a place where a man's name could be his own.[26]

Elise said goodbye to her friend Thomine Grogard when she left Nacogdoches to return to Brownsboro. Presumably she was thinking they would exchange letters and perhaps see one another from time to time. This was not to be. Thomine was not as robust as Elise had thought her to be. She died in the winter of 1848.

Elise never mentioned Thomine's death until her own final days, when she wrote her last account of how the Norwegians in Texas had fared. In the winter of 1848, though, death was far from her mind. She was looking ahead to going farther west, ready to start a new life in pioneer country where the forest ended and the open spaces of the blackland prairie began.[27]

The future was promising. Death would not come into her life again for years, though when it did, the loss would be more overwhelming than anything she had ever known.

CHAPTER 5

FOUR MILE PRAIRIE

I T WAS ONE THING to admire the prairie west of Brownsboro
but quite another to get land there. Texas was in a period of massive
political development that was driving property acquisition into tor-
tuous channels. Elise pinpointed the problem in her last dispatch to *Norge
og Amerika:* "Before Texas joined the United States, the government gave
some of those prairies to a man whose name I have forgotten. Later, though,
this gift was annulled and the man brought a legal case against the government."

Getting secure titles to "some of those prairies" would take Elise and her
friends three years and tax all their ingenuity. Like other immigrant path-
finders, they would find initiative and flexibility essential to their success.
They were caught up in historic developments to which they must adapt, the
tumult of American expansion into new territory.

The man whose name she had forgotten was Charles Fenton Mercer.
Sam Houston had awarded him an *empresario* grant under a land distribution policy started by the Spanish in the 1700s, when Texas was part of that
country's empire in Mexico. Empresarios were given enormous tracts of
public land (one such grant made by the Spanish was for 600,000 acres)
in exchange for bringing in settlers and establishing law and order in their
territories. The empresarios, in effect, were immensely powerful real estate
agents. Mexico continued the policy after it gained independence from
Spain, even appointing some citizens from United States to the office.
Stephen F. Austin, for whom the Texas capital is named, was one of these.[1]

Empresario territories were called after the grantee, Austin's colony, Mercer's colony, and so on, but when Texas broke away from Mexico in 1836,
it abolished the system. Sam Houston, however, thought it was the best way

to promote settlement, and while serving as president of the Republic of Texas in 1841 he got it restored and then made the grant to Mercer in 1844. As things turned out, Mercer was the last empresario. Elise, Wilhelm, and Reiersen would have to be nimble to get claims on his terrain.

Mercer's colony ran roughly from Waco to Dallas and into East Texas, covering a territory so large that it was eventually split into eighteen counties, among them Kaufman and adjoining Van Zandt County, where Elise and her friends aimed to acquire land. The grant was perfectly legal, but land distribution was becoming a hot political issue swarming with angry adversaries.

Some opponents argued that Texas was giving away property and getting nothing in return. They were joined by veterans of the Texas war of independence who were aggrieved because they had been awarded land bounty certificates for their military service, but Mercer was challenging these when they made claims on his holding. Other individuals held headright certificates (land grants on condition of developing ranch or farm homesteads) that infringed Mercer's domain. A large contingent of squatters, politicians, and speculators hankering after soil favored direct government land sales to the public. Land certificates, sometimes representing hundreds of acres, were trading fast, adding to the confusion over who owned what.

Houston had made his award to Mercer on January 29, 1844. The next day the Texas Congress, goaded by the populist sentiment generated by the adversaries, passed a bill banning further empresario contracts. Houston vetoed the law, but the Congress overrode him. Charged up with victory, the Congress launched an investigation into the land certificates that Mercer had already sold to settlers.

Matters grew worse. Mercer's colonists found squatters as well as headright and bounty holders moving onto their lands. Surveyors from a county adjoining his grant came in, measured off parcels, and claimed them. Fighting broke out between the various parties, and Mercer's surveyors skirmished with civil and military forces when they joined in to settle things down. When Mercer sued in the courts to confirm the deals he had made, he was hamstrung by the furor and by having to litigate his rights. Buyers trying in good faith to acquire property on his grant were stymied.[2]

While this turmoil was going on, Republic of Texas authorities started negotiating an annexation treaty with the United States. If the treaty won approval, Texas would become part of the United States and its land, under ordinary circumstances, would become part of the U.S. public domain. At that point the land in Texas would be "Congress land," subject to distribution by the federal government. The state government would have nothing more to say about it, whether by empresario contract or any other system.

The circumstances, however, were not the least bit ordinary. Texas was under no obligation to join the United States. It was not an enemy but rather a friendly independent country with the power to negotiate the terms of annexation. Besides that, the United States was in an expansive mood. This was the age of Manifest Destiny, a time when nearly all Americans fervently believed the nation should take over the whole continent from the Atlantic to the Pacific. Although annexation of Texas could, as it ultimately did, provoke a war with Mexico, the action would bring a splendid prize.

Riding the wave of Manifest Destiny, the United States Senate and House of Representatives gave Texas special treatment. When the annexation treaty was done, the two houses adopted a joint resolution saying Texas could keep "all the vacant and unappropriated lands lying within its limits." Texas was the only state other than the original thirteen to retain ownership of its land.[3]

Annexation formally took place in December of 1845, nearly two years after Houston had made his grant to Mercer. At this point the state had to write a constitution, and opponents of the empresario system seized on the Constitutional Convention to end the hated scheme—they passed a resolution instructing the incoming government to void all land sales made under Mercer's empresario contract. The lieutenant governor was empowered to act, and when Albert Horton was elected to the office he summarily initiated suits to dissolve the deals Mercer had made with his hapless settlers.

A state district court then delivered what was supposed to be the final blow to Mercer: it moved in to dissolve Houston's empresario contract with him. Mercer's colony should have died on the spot. But the state supreme court came to the rescue. On appeal it overruled the district court, thus restoring life to the colony. Mercer and his settlers got their contracts back.[4]

All these legal wrangles drove settlement on the Mercer colony into an almost surreal world of chance. Elise could not know what the outcome of the turmoil over the Mercer case would be, and she wondered whether it was prudent to take property on his land before the confusion ended. She believed settlers who had made deals with Mercer before the litigation started would probably be allowed to keep their land, but what would happen to later buyers was anyone's guess. Although aware of the risk, she still found herself drawn to the winsome land west of Brownsboro.

Whatever else happened, the old empresario system had to be replaced. This task fell to the state legislature, and it adopted a "preemption" plan that would allow settlers to claim land directly from the State. Mercer colony contracts might somehow be folded into the new system.

Originally, Mercer had been allotting eighty acres to single men and 160 acres to families. The legislature's new preemption law, however, was more generous, and Elise's last dispatch to *Norge og Amerika* showed that he hastily changed his acreages to conform to it: "This land is now given away, I think, in slices of three hundred acres for a single person and somewhat over six hundred acres per family. After three years of working the soil you get a deed saying it's your property."[5]

The state law set up a series of stages and requirements for preemption grants. A settler would move onto unclaimed land. He would establish a home and bring at least ten acres under cultivation. After occupying the home and working the land for three years (the U.S. preemption law required five-year residence on Congress land), he would file for a certificate claiming his parcel—320 acres (a half-mile section) for a single man, and 640 acres (a square-mile section) for a married man. Near the end of his three-year residence he would pay for a survey that would show his boundaries and establish that he was neither infringing other claims nor exceeding his allowable acreage. When the surveyor's notes were confirmed, depending on the circumstances, the claimant would obtain the land free or by payment of from fifty cents to two dollars per acre. The title to the land was called a patent, and it was issued by the state for a small fee.[6]

Although the law was specific, it did not offer a solution to the Mercer colony problem. Nor had the state supreme court's decision supplied a way out. The ongoing tumult might still tempt the legislature to obstruct Mercer's sales. Individuals could also bring suits against the Mercer titles. In fact, some of those started during the ensuing years remained under litigation until 1936.

Despite the risk, Reiersen, Wilhelm, and Elise were eager to take claims in the Mercer colony. Reiersen naturally led the way. He had personally conferred with Sam Houston and other leaders during his exploratory visit to Texas in 1843, and he had been a resident of the state since 1845. A competent businessman, he had kept in close touch with land developments ever since his arrival from Norway. Judging from his actions in the spring of 1848, he knew what the state legislature would do to solve the Mercer colony problem.[7]

The legislature had to create new counties to get the preemption system going. It met every two years to adopt laws, and at its next session in 1848 it would be able to organize new counties in the pioneer areas including the

Mercer colony. The counties would then be able to set up the necessary government structure—clerks' offices, to be exact—to register land claims and transmit these to the state General Land Office, which would issue the official land patents. Once the counties were organized, the settlers could start preemption proceedings by moving onto land, building a house, and cultivating their ten acres.

The legislature could then take a second step at its 1850 session. It would reach back to 1848 and rule that there was a "window of time" in that year when settlers were authorized to take land in the Mercer colony. The 1850 ruling would be retroactive—anyone who had made a contract with Mercer during the 1848 window would be eligible to file a claim in accord with the state's new preemption system. In this way the Mercer colony would be folded into the state's preemption system. The problem would be solved.[8]

The time had come to act. In February, 1848, the legislature established Van Zandt and Kaufman counties. Very soon after, Elise said she was thinking about buying land either in Cherokee County or on the prairie—this in her postscript to Reiersen's letter to Gjestvang. She did not explain what she meant by "on the prairie," but she was clearly referring to the open grasslands west of Brownsboro where Kaufman and Van Zandt counties had just been established by the legislature. She was ready to leap into the future.

Reiersen set off first. In the spring of 1848 he left Brownsboro and put down in the southeast corner of Kaufman County on Mercer colony land. There he became the founding resident of Prairieville, the town that later grew into the local center. Waerenskjold followed in June and settled in the southwest corner of Van Zandt County. The area he chose was in Four Mile Prairie, just three miles east of Prairieville.

The two men's decision to take land in the Mercer colony shows that they must have known, or at least had a very strong inkling, about how the legislature would resolve the empresario problem. They had also selected desirable land because this part of the Mercer colony lay on the margin of the blackland prairie.[9]

During its 1850 biennial session the legislature did indeed rule that contracts made with Mercer during the 1848 window would be guaranteed. The window was open from February to October 25, roughly nine months, and because Reiersen and Waerenskjold settled on the Mercer colony within that period, their claims would be valid.

Elise never gave the exact date she moved to Four Mile Prairie; she said only that she settled there in 1848. All the same, in 1852 she wrote a friend saying, "a widow . . . lives in our old house." That statement implies a tem-

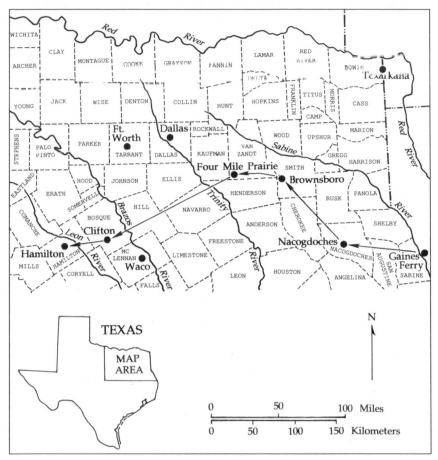

Map 3. Elise's Texas.
Map prepared by John Cotter, cartographer, courtesy of Charles H. Russell.

porary home built to set up a claim to land, and it also provides a clue, a flashback, to what Elise and Wilhelm did during the summer of 1848.[10]

The events went something like this. When Wilhelm moved to Van Zandt County in June he immediately built the house mentioned in Elise's letter. The house was probably a temporary residence, perhaps a log cabin, intended to serve as material proof to substantiate a land claim under the preemption law.

Wilhelm returned to Brownsboro after the house was built. There he presented himself to Elise and began a serious courtship. Previously he had been a single man with nothing more than youth, talent, and help to offer. Now he had sound material prospects—he would soon own a substantial property.

Undoubtedly he presented his case with appropriate graciousness, and Elise responded with interest. In talking about matrimony he may have pointed out, probably not for the first time, that married couples could claim a full 640-acre section, a square mile, double the number of acres available to a single person. He proposed. Elise accepted.

On August 14, 1848, they secured their license to marry. Elegantly inscribed, it was addressed "Greetings: To any regularly Ordained Minister of the Gospel or Judge of the District Court or Justice of the County Court or Justice of the Peace." They got the license in Buffalo in Henderson County, probably because it had the nearest office of local government. The license shows Elise's name as "Eliza Twede"—Eliza probably reflected the county clerk's Americanization of her name, and Tvede became Twede because Norwegians are inclined to pronounce a *v* as a *w* when speaking English, even today. Waerenskjold became "Warrenshield," probably during the clerk's struggle to cope with the Norwegian *ae* and *skj*.

They wed within a month after getting their license. The dates on their certificate show that there was a delay in recording it. When this was finally done, it read:

I do hereby certify that I did solemnize the rites of matrimony between William Warrenshield and Eliza Twede on the evening of the tenth of September at four of the Clock of sayd day. This given under my hand and private seal using a scrawl this 11th of Sept A.D. 1848.

A J HUNTER. J.P.
FILED FOR RECORD 9TH OCTOBER 1848
AND RECORDED 18TH OCTOBER 1848.
JAS BOGGS CLK CO CT HEN CO
BY JB HART DEPTY CLK

The certificate was recorded barely a week before the Mercer colony window was to close. Dangerously late, it still proved they had married in time. They were now eligible to claim a 640-acre section.[11]

Quite apart from its link to getting Mercer colony land, there was a peculiar connection between the date that Elise and Wilhelm married and her divorce from her former husband. She was a law-abiding woman, yet she married Wilhelm while still married to her first husband, the Norwegian sea captain Sven Foyn. Foyn and she had separated in 1842. For reasons unknown, their breakup dragged on for seven years. Their divorce did not go into effect until January of 1849.

Elise could not wait until 1849. She had to marry Wilhelm before October 25, 1848. Her marriage was unavoidably premature.

So what, one might ask? Well, being married to two men at the same time made her a bigamist. Is it fair to call Elise a bigamist? One could argue otherwise. Perhaps she did not know she had to wait until 1849 before she could remarry. Or perhaps she thought her waiting time was over and her divorce was in effect.[12]

These speculations are simply absurd. Elise was an intelligent, knowledgeable, and keen woman. How could she fail to know the final date of her divorce? How could she forget what the date was? Elise knew exactly what she was doing when she married Wilhelm in 1848.

One might reasonably ask other questions, though. Did she feel that Norwegian laws governing divorce no longer applied to her because she had decided to live in the United States? Did she become a bigamist without remorse, or was she just penetrating an ambiguous world where the old rules no longer applied and she simply did what she had to do?

The proximity of Elise's marriage to the October 25 deadline raises yet other questions. Did she and Wilhelm love each other, or was their marriage a calculated, mercenary step to get a large landholding? If not a loveless convenience, was theirs a simple companionate marriage? Or was their marriage perhaps the culmination of a long relationship that had started back in Christiania and ripened into maturity under numerous difficulties and ordeals during their journey?

The record shows that she and Wilhelm had been together at least since leaving Drobak. They had traveled across the sea in confined quarters but in the company of others. Their crossing had been hard, their wagon travel through the Nacogdoches Wold arduous. They were in Nacogdoches and Brownsboro together over several months. In the last days of February they considered purchasing land with their friend, James Staack, but by summer he was out of the picture. Wilhelm may have been seven years Elise's junior, but once he had proven himself a steady, reliable, and industrious young man, would she not accept his proposal of marriage?

One might ask, too, whether romance and physical attraction existed between the two. Later, in giving moral instruction to her sons, she showed that she understood physical desire. "Sexual desire is animalistic—I suppose," she wrote, the "I suppose" seeming to indicate a subtle admission of passion rather than any frigid Victorian inhibitions about it.

She elaborated on this point but never condemned feelings of desire. She warned her sons against sexual fulfillment "outside wedlock": "The person who . . . (sips) . . . the cup of sensuality will go further and further and seek to gratify his lusts among lewd women." Gratification of sexual desire outside wedlock grossly debased anyone who succumbed to it, but sexual desire expressed in marriage led to the "source of the purest human happiness in this life. I refer to the joys of fatherhood and motherhood."[13]

One might ask, too, about romance in Elise and Wilhelm's marriage. Did she ever experience a certain giddy feeling over him? Was a superlative love affair the foundation of their marriage? Although something of a visionary idealist, Elise was a practical woman who looked life square in the eye. Her letters show that she regarded Wilhelm fondly and respectfully, but she never wove romantic fantasies about him.

Intimate relations were certainly a part of their lives, but her marriage to Wilhelm was of the old-fashioned kind, rooted in mutual personal esteem and grounded in appreciation of the practical requirements of life—a home, a means to make a living, children, and faith in the other person's devotion. They may have shared an unspoken and refined romance, but speculation has to end with that.

Once Elise and Wilhelm established themselves at Four Mile Prairie, a period of peace and prosperity opened for them. Their enterprises were successful because they had settled on good soil. Although far away from the sea, their land was on the undulating Gulf Coastal Plain of Texas, a huge area that for millions of years was covered by a shallow ocean reaching far north into Oklahoma. When the sea retreated eons ago it left behind rich marine sediments where prairie grasses could grow in abundance. The grasslands, broken only by scattered trees and shrubs, spread for hundreds of miles past Dallas over to the Texas high plains. The great livestock trail drives on those western lands were just getting under way when Elise and Wilhelm came to Four Mile Prairie. [photo 8 about here]

Elise wrote that there was no need to manure fields when they first arrived. The soils were naturally fertile. For tens of thousands of years they had been carpeted by lush prairie flora—indiangrass, little bluestem, big bluestem, switchgrass, beaked panicum, herbs, forbs, and native edible legumes—that had died off and decayed into rich humus year after year.

The moderately acid topsoil, its dark brown color a sure sign of fertility, lay at least six inches deep above fifty-six inches of subsoil. The grasses had been fodder for buffalo. The territory had been a hunting ground for Native Americans and other trackers who stalked the great herds. Too, some of the animals died and left their bones on the earth during their annual migrations.

View of Four Mile Prairie land owned by Elise and Wilhelm.
Photo by Charles H. Russell.

The good range grasslands soon drew Elise and Wilhelm into livestock ranching, but in her first accounts of their life on the prairie she spoke mainly of crop raising. Compared to Norway, where the glaciers had scraped along for thousands of years leaving only boulders, rocks, and thin soil, this prairie land was easy to bring under cultivation. In most parts it did not need to be cleared, she said. All one had to do was fence fields to keep out the livestock, then plow and sow. Even the careless planter could grow wheat and corn; food was so plentiful that rye, barley, and oats—crops made into bread in Norway—were used as browsing fodder for animals.[14]

There were cash crops of cotton and flax, but her greatest interest was in garden produce. She spoke of melons, pumpkins, peas, sweet potatoes, and a regular cornucopia of garden plants—beans, peas, carrots, parsley, radishes, cress, lettuce, fall turnips.

All of these produced their own seed for next year's planting, an advantage, she said, because seed could not be bought anywhere in this pioneer country. Cool-weather fall plants—May turnips, cabbage, cauliflower, kohlrabi, and Swedish and French turnips—could not be grown. No seed for them could be had, and even if immigrants brought some with them, the plants would rot in the hot summer before they reached seed-producing maturity.

Of fruit trees only the peach was cultivated, she reported. It did not bear until the third year—not a bad rate of growth but a long wait for new settlers hungering for an edible crop. Elise had seen small groves of apple and cherry in Nacogdoches, but the real-life Johnny Appleseed, a famous wanderer who had planted and cultivated orchards on the frontiers, had not come to her southwest pioneer territory. Although grapes, plums, and cherries grew wild, they did not match the quantity and size of cultivated strains. Bees, the pollinators, did well and produced wild honey for the gathering.[15]

She observed that the breed of cows, probably the common black cow brought by settlers from the South, was not very good. Besides, the animals received minimal care. They stayed out of doors year round. During winter there was so little forage that the milking cows produced small amounts. Butter was scarce. Little milk was left for human consumption because calves were allowed to suckle until the mothers weaned them. To increase milk production, Elise advised future Norwegian immigrants to build shelters for their cattle and to cut the natural prairie hay to store in outdoor ricks for winter feed.

She reported that the Norwegian settlers engaged in subsistence farming after they arrived. Money was rare; barter was the common way to obtain products. Settlers exchanged produce with one another and their American neighbors. They traded garden yield, eggs, corn, loaves of home-baked bread, and milk.[16]

Although Reiersen opened a country store in Prairieville, it would be a few years before thriving communities grew up in that small settlement and over in nearby Four Mile Prairie. Existing markets were far away. Dallas, then barely more than a trading post, was more than fifty miles away and Nacogdoches more than 120 miles distant. Later on, Shreveport in Louisiana would become a major way station on a livestock trail that led from Dallas through northeast Texas over to the Mississippi and down the Red River to New Orleans. For now, though, Shreveport was far off and mainly a landing point for settlers heading into Texas.

Elise wrote that both Americans and Norwegians were coming in, and that everyone lived by an annual round of hard work: plow in late January and early February, plant in March, start harvesting field crops in June, slaughter animals and smoke meat in late summer and fall, and pick cotton in October. To attain subsistence in the early days required self-reliance and frugality. Hardy simplicity was the rule of life.[17]

Elise and Wilhelm built their second and permanent home as soon as they achieved a measure of settlement, probably in 1850. A photograph of the place made before it was torn down in the 1930s seems to show it was

Elise and Wilhelm's home in Four Mile Prairie, late 1890s, showing its fieldstone chimney. Photo courtesy of Derwood Johnson, Waco.

a dog-run house built in two sections, with a chimney in each. One of the chimneys, visible in the photo, is built of rough fieldstone cut to different sized blocks and neatly fitted together. The other, showing only the flue top in the photo, Elise said was brick.

In addition to mentioning the chimneys, she spoke of having a kitchen range and stove for wood fires. Both had iron pipes that she said went through the roof; together they provided warmth as well as ample space for cooking and baking. She recommended that emigrants who could not afford a kitchen range or stove should bring cookery implements for their chimney fireplaces. These included a large metal drawer to hold ashes, fire tongs, and a pair of *braendejern,* probably andirons on which to set frying pans, kettles, or pots.

Alongside the house, about twenty feet away, the photograph shows a split-rail fence forming a rustic barrier. It separates the house from an adjoining field or perhaps a dirt road that ran from ranch to ranch. Elise spoke, too, of having an oak-log stable, big enough to provide shelter for their horses and for those of overnight guests. For her sheep she had a roofed shed open to the south and east for warmth against the blue northers that swept down from Canada in the winter. This and her chicken coop, she said, "are an extravagance in Texas."

She described the wood fences to keep livestock and hogs out of home yards and off cropland. The rails were cut from oak tree trunks into eight- to ten-foot lengths and then split with an iron wedge driven by blows from a wooden sledgehammer. Posts, in pairs, were pounded into the ground, and ladderlike slats were nailed between them to serve as rests for the rails. Fences around homes had rails set four or five levels high. Out in the fields, though, they were stacked up eight or nine levels—as the saying went, the fences had to be "pig tight, horse high, and bull strong." A good rail splitter, she reported, could make two hundred rails a day and be paid seventy-five cents to a dollar per hundred, plus his board. Barbed wire did not replace split-rail fencing until the 1870s.[18]

As to the clothes Elise wore, photographs made at intervals over the years show her in formal wear. Her dresses—made of dark, shiny material, most likely crinoline—are appropriate for church or other decorous occasions. Most of the time, though, she worked tirelessly around the ranch: she raised garden produce, herded and sheared the sheep, milked the cows, and may occasionally have helped round up the beef animals and worked in the fields. For this daily ranch work she probably wore the same sort of garb as her contemporaries.

Even in hot southern climates numerous petticoats and bustles underlay formal dresses, but for work, women put on simple, light clothing. "Monday wash dresses" were the rule for laundering when things had to be soaked in boiling water, scrubbed by hand with homemade soap, wrung out, and hung in the open air to dry.

Work around the ranch required the "short dress." This was a loose garment worn over cut-down petticoats. The material was gingham, calico, or a cheap cloth such as sheeting. It had to be dark to avoid showing the dirt smudged on by leaning against animals, handling tubs, filling mangers, and tracking around in corral and stable muck. Short dresses reached only to the ankle so that hems would not drag in the yard mud and road dust.

Over the shortened skirt women wore at the waist an apron made of coarse linen cloth. Pinafores, full-length smock-type garments that covered dresses from shoulders to hem and tied or buttoned at the back, were used for housework. Bonnets made of better quality linen were worn indoors to keep the hair in place and outside for protection against the sun. Lighter shoes and slippers were kept for house wear, but outdoors the ranch women wore thick boots. Some of these were finished with wooden soles.

Makeup at the time was worn only by "painted ladies"—prostitutes and showgirls. Jewelry was almost unknown in pioneer areas and was generally limited to wedding rings or other modest adornments like cameos. Even considering this, Elise probably wore only a small brooch to close her collar, like one that shows in one of her photos. She once professed that a simple and frugal life suited her well.[19]

As Elise and Wilhelm settled in, holiday observances followed as a matter of course. Pioneer life, at first, was too lean to allow anything like parties. In Norway, though, she had been accustomed to religious observances at Christmas and on other holy days. In one of her early letters she noted that even these were absent in her new country. Later on she mentioned sharing in a cheerful Christmas celebration with neighbors. Until then, she wrote, it had been impossible to get "a simple thing like ale because of the lack of yeast; but as the last immigrants brought yeast with them, almost all of us brewed ale for Christmas. It has never tasted so good to me as now." She emphasized the point: "I haven't tasted a glass of wine in . . . years."

Before long she and Wilhelm would celebrate Independence Day with their American neighbors. On one such occasion each person contributed food or money for a community party, and Elise reported that her husband gave half an ox and fifty cents. The celebration started in the morning and lasted more than twenty-four hours. "They ate and drank lustily. A few danced a little," she said. Her own participation in the party was limited, but about Wilhelm she reported: "Waerenskjold made a speech . . . such things are just to his liking, especially when he can be the head of the whole affair."[20]

Whatever Elise thought of Wilhelm's style, he was making headway in assuring the two of them stability. Their community was growing. In 1850 fourteen families had arrived from Norway, and that same year Wilhelm filed the first of their two land claims under the legislature's preemption plan. The Archives and Records Division of the Texas General Land Office in Austin shows that Colony Certificate 359 was issued to "Wilhelm Warenhold" on May 1, 1850. Apparently this claim reflected his original status as a single man. The survey, done on July 27, 1850, showed that his parcel was for 313 acres. After he paid the necessary costs for the survey and certificate, the property was registered to him under land patent number 992.

The second claim evidently was for the additional land he and Elise were entitled to as a married couple. That survey, made on April 21, 1851, showed 297½ acres, with the parcel registered as patent number 993. The two properties together comprised 610 acres. Although their holdings were 30 acres short of the full 640 acres allowed to married couples, Elise and Wilhelm were now solidly established Texas property owners.[21]

The reputation of the Four Mile Prairie Norwegians spread rapidly. Elise's dispatches to *Norge og Amerika,* together with Reiersen's earlier *Pathfinder for Norwegian Emigrants,* were having their effect. As early as 1849 Cleng Peerson had heard of the Texas settlement. Father of Norwegian emigration to America, he had convinced the first expatriate group to cross aboard the sloop *Restauration* in 1825. Now, as he always had, he was roving in search of new land for his countrymen.

His career illustrates the way Norwegians settled in the northern plains as well as Texas. He began as a pathfinder by leading most of the *Restauration* group to Orleans, New York. After that he moved on to Fox River, Illinois, and then took a colony to Shelbyville, Missouri. The Shelbyville colony failed, but it was fifty miles west of Mark Twain's home in Hannibal, Missouri. Peerson would have fitted well in that Mark Twain venue. He was a character right out of a novel, the kind of a wanderer one might meet on any real or fictional riverboat or in any dusty borderland.

When he turned his attention to Texas he quickly earned a reputation in the Norwegian colony. He was reported to go striding over the countryside dressed in a black top hat and long black tailcoat. It seems he wore this garb to display respectability when negotiating land deals with clerks and public officials.

On arriving in Four Mile Prairie he visited with the Reiersens as well as Elise and Wilhelm, but he soon left to look for more and better unclaimed land elsewhere. For weeks he tramped over a two-hundred-mile territory west of the Trinity River below Dallas. Forty-five miles beyond Waco he found what he was looking for—unclaimed open prairie, rich with the dark soil of the Texas blacklands, watered by the Bosque River. The area spread for miles and was ideal for raising field crops, cotton, and beef cattle.

Peerson returned to Fox River, Illinois, where he told his Norwegian countrymen about the superb rolling prairie he had found in Texas. Ole Canuteson was the first to move to the area from Fox River. A generous man who constantly helped other Norwegians with land purchases and general business dealings, he was a natural leader for a new settlement. He and his family, together with Peerson and others, became the nucleus of the Norwegian colony that settled at Clifton.

The Clifton colony overtook the Four Mile Prairie and Brownsboro settlements, and by the Civil War it had become the main Norwegian center in Texas. Peerson himself owned a 320-acre tract of Bosque County land there. According to a local legend, the parcel was given to him free of charge as a reward for bringing so many Norwegian pioneers into the state. The legislature supposedly voted it to him without his knowledge, but more likely he acquired his property by preemption, 320 acres being the standard allotment for a single man.

Peerson got his land in 1856. Soon afterward he placed a personal notice in a newspaper back in Fox River offering half his acreage to anyone who would give him a home—room, board, and care—for the rest of his life. Ovee Colwick took up the offer and moved to Bosque. He prospered there and built a splendid prairie home that stood until the 1960s when it burned down.

Peerson lived with the Colwicks until he died at age eighty-three at the end of the Civil War. Elise knew him well, calling him "old Peerson" when telling about his first arrival in Four Mile Prairie. "Often," she said, "he made long visits to the Reiersens and Waerenskjolds. He was always a welcome guest."[22]

Johannes Nordboe was another visitor who turned up early at Four Mile Prairie. According to Elise he had lived in Texas just south of Dallas for years. In fact, he had been there ten years when Elise arrived in Four Mile Prairie in 1848, but his route to the state was remarkable. In Norway he came from Gudbrandsdalen, a charming valley north of Christiania where the Norwegian playwright Henrik Ibsen placed his lying hero, Peer Gynt, who claimed to ride a giant buck reindeer over the mountains and to dally with the Woman in Green, daughter of the menacing troll king. Nordboe left this valley and sailed away from his homeland aboard the ship *Delta* from Lisbon, Portugal, with other Norwegian immigrants in 1832. He followed Cleng Peerson's lead first to Orleans, New York, and then to Fox River, Illinois.

How or why he moved on to the Dallas area is unrecorded, but he had traveled over one thousand miles on his way there from Fox River. He reached Texas soon after it gained independence, a time when the unsettled Indian frontier lay along the line from Dallas to Waco. According to Elise, when Nordboe came to Four Mile Prairie he had not seen any Norwegians since he reached Texas. "He held his countrymen in such warm regard," she said, that "nothing could hold him back when he heard about the Reiersens and Waerenskjolds. He insisted on visiting us."

Almost eighty years old, Nordboe was not strong enough to make the journey on horseback. His sons, having no interest in Norwegians, refused to take him to Four Mile Prairie in the family buggy. Determined to meet his countrymen, he traveled the more than fifty miles from Dallas to Four Mile

Prairie on foot. Walking that distance must have taken him three to four days, and at night he would have had to sleep by the wayside or stop at strangers' cabins along the dusty wagon trail. It was a remarkable journey for a man his age.

He arrived in Four Mile Prairie just before Christmas of 1851 and stayed for weeks. About him Elise observed: "He was an interesting old man who had seen, read, and thought much." She said he seemed to be very kind and "took a great interest in the study of history and the wonders of nature." When the time came for him to return to Dallas, Peerson came over to walk him home. "I do not think Nordboe was very happy about it," Elise remarked, "as it was too strenuous for him to keep up with Cleng."[23]

Life had become peaceful for Elise and Wilhelm. They got their second land patent in early 1851. Three months later, on May 5, Elise gave birth to her first child. They gave him a full complement of names according to the custom of Norwegian families with upper-class roots: Otto Christian Wilhelm Waerenskjold.[24]

Elise was thirty-six years old at the time, and in those days thirty-six was a late age to be starting a family. She never gave any details concerning Otto's birth, nor the births of her other children, for that matter. One can infer, though, from diaries written by other women that a "lying-in woman" or friends would have attended her births. There were no physicians close by, and birth with attending women was they way things had to be done.

Elise's complete delight in her son showed through in her correspondence. When Otto was a year and a half old she wrote to her friend Thomine Dannevig back in Norway about an early gift she and Wilhelm made to him: "A few days after Otto was born, he got a little colt, which will thus be two years old in the spring and will then be broken in. It is already so gentle that Wilhelm can sit on it whenever he wishes, so I think it will be a good riding horse by the time Otto gets big enough to ride. It is named after my father's brown horse, Perris, which perhaps you remember; we have another beautiful colt named Alida."

In another instance she showed her affection mixed with protective indulgence when describing Otto's forays against their barnyard animals: "I think your boys would enjoy seeing all of our many domestic animals. Otto already has a lot of fun with them, especially with the poultry, of which I have various kinds: hens, turkeys, guinea hens, geese, and two kinds of ducks. When I give them grain and they all gather around me, it is Otto's greatest pleasure to run among them with a little stick, and he is terribly pleased when they scamper. He also wanted to chase after the pigs when they were small, but I didn't dare leave him alone with them for fear the sows would bite him."

Later, in telling about her hopes for him, she called up her vision of equality in America: "My wishes for my little Otto's future are very modest. All I ask is that he may become an upright and able farmer, possessed of such knowledge as every cultured man should have. I have always had a liking for farm and country life, and if one is otherwise happy in his position, I cannot imagine a more pleasant or more independent state, for in this country a tiller of the soil is respected as much as anyone else, be he official or merchant. This is not as in Norway, where the farmers constitute a lower class."[25]

Life was good. Elise had established herself in a new world. Now she had entered upon motherhood, not because it was expected of her as it was of women in Norway but because of her own natural desires and her exercise of free choice.

CHAPTER 6

IN DEFENSE OF TEXAS

J UST DAYS after Otto's birth, Elise was abruptly recast in her role as a writer. Her friend Andreas Gjestvang in Hamar had forwarded scurrilous newspaper articles attacking Texas. Although he expected a reply, Gjestvang hardly guessed that the articles would revive Elise's taste for robust journalism. When the slanderous items reached her, she burst back into the world of writing and never left it again.

A "Captain J. Tolmer" was the purported author of the offending articles. According to Tolmer's story, he was a French military officer who was writing a newspaper series about his travels through the United States. On the western leg of his journey he claimed he had detoured into Texas and gone on from there to St. Louis. He pulled off this trip of more than six hundred miles in only one day, obviously an impossible feat at the time.[1]

He said he had written his Texas account in St. Louis and sent it from there to France. It was published in *Le Journal des Debats* (Journal of debates) in Paris, then translated into Norwegian and forwarded to *Hamars Budstikken*, the newspaper in Gjestvang's county. In 1850 Avenarius and Mendelssohn of Leipzig, Germany, published the letters in French with the title *Scènes de l'Amerique du Nord* (Scenes of North America).

Elise immediately doubted the authenticity of Tolmer's account: "It is hard for me to think . . . that people would accept this product . . . at face value; it strikes me as nothing but a poorly written adventure story. I wonder if the people in Norway were not simply confused if they took Tolmer's account as anything but a piece of fiction. It is impossible for me to believe that Tolmer would have the audacity to offer as truth such a mass of gross . . . lies to so highly cultured a nation as the French."

She was right. The *Scènes de l'Amerique du Nord* description of Texas comes across as pure fiction, the granddaddy of Wild West frontier adventures written long before ten-cent cowboy pulp novels began to flood the market. The author even felt he had to deny that he was violating the French maxim *A beau mentir, qui vient de loin*—"He tells fine lies, who comes from afar."[2]

The modern historian Philip Jordan, writing in the *Southwestern Historical Quarterly*, has shown that the letters were a fraud, a total fabrication. There was no Captain J. Tolmer in the French army or navy, and the real writer may never have been in the United States, much less Texas. According to Jordan, the make-believe account was cobbled together from bits of Americana narratives written by famous English and French travelers. My own speculation on the basis of Jordan's analysis is that the writer was probably a professional novelist, perhaps even Alexander Dumas, author of *The Three Musketeers,* who was linked to the *Journal des Debats.* Dumas, or an imitator of his florid style, had put together a potboiler tale contrived to sell to an unsuspecting public.[3]

Translated from the original French, Tolmer's story starts this way: "I crossed Texas and, wonder of wonders, I'm still alive. But not because of the inhabitants." He then describes them. "The word *inhabitants* hardly fits so bizarre a population, mixed, nomadic, heterogeneous, fantastic, composed of fugitives, savages, Americans, Spaniards, Portuguese, *metiz* (mestizos), French, Germans, and even of Indians and Negroes who often have had petty run-ins with the law."

From here the story goes on to present Texans as braggart villains who address one another as "judge" and "general," however lowly their occupation. A gang of these sleazy people in Galveston—presumably heirs to the pirate Jean Lafitte, who once ran the town—tries to seize Tolmer. "Judge" Peters, a famous bandit, leads the desperadoes on a chase to capture him, but Tolmer escapes to Nacogdoches with the help of aristocratic Spanish hacienda owners. His getaway is made by an incredible overnight journey— Galveston is an island on the Gulf of Mexico shore more than two hundred miles south of Nacogdoches.

To this the bogus Captain Tolmer added other insulting and mendacious observations: "The United States flings out to its frontiers a refuse boiling with crime." About Nacogdoches specifically, he said: "The annexation of Texas to the United States had not brought the slightest happiness to its former (Mexican) population, once so spirited, so gracious, and so flourishing."[4]

When Gjestvang sent the reprints from *Hamars Budstikken* to Elise, he asked to know if this portrait of Texas was accurate. Elise's nearly five-thousand-word reply was crushing as well as detailed. She began it by giving Gjestvang a ringing verbal slap: "You . . . ask me and other Norwegians here to let you know whether Mr. Tolmer's account is true or false. Even though it seems to me that the contents of the letters should answer this question clearly enough for you and any other sensible Norwegian who is not totally ignorant of other countries and especially the United States (to which Texas has now belonged for several years), I shall comply with your wish."[5]

Elise denied the author's competence as a writer and then disagreed with him point by point. He had described the inferior quality of southwestern life relative to Europe, then said: "The struggle between man and nature is even more intense (in Texas) than in the Mississippi Valley." Not at all, Elise replied, "People have far less difficulty in Texas than in Norway—or in any other part of Europe, no doubt." With that, she went into an extended discourse on the generous soil and copious produce of Texan land, adding for good measure that "labor is of greater value here than in Norway, and many kinds of work can be done by children as well as adults."

Tolmer presented Texas as a primeval world where predatory alligators, jaguars, snakes, and bears roamed about menacing people. Elise admitted there were "quite a few beasts of prey." Among these, she said, were panthers (she described them as "a kind of tiger, the size of a dog but shaped like a cat"), bears, wolves, foxes, opossums, skunks, several types of snakes, and alligators in lakes and rivers.

She said she had never heard of a single person being attacked or harmed by wild animals. To show that the animals were inoffensive, she reported that people slept in their wagons or on the ground while out on the trail, and she described one of her own dramatic encounters: "Snakes can be a nuisance and may crawl clear up to the second story, especially a type called the chicken snake because it eats chickens and eggs, which it swallows whole. The reason for its intrusion into houses is that the hens usually have their nests under the beds and up in lofts. These snakes are harmless, however; but of course, such an uninvited guest can put a scare into newcomers, as happened to the Grogards and me in Nacogdoches, where such a snake had made its way to the loft."

Tolmer claimed he had traveled on horseback from New Orleans to Galveston. Never, said Elise. Modern historians confirm her assertion— there was no land route from New Orleans to Galveston at the time. The basin of the Atchafalaya River alone creates a twenty-five-mile swamp barrier, and even today the most seasoned horseman would not try to find a path alone through the sloughs and bayous along the Louisiana coast. In Elise's time, the only direct way from one port city to the other was by sail across the Gulf.

Tolmer wrote that he escaped with the help of an armed escort. Watchdogs brought along by his bodyguard scared up a *mastingo* (mustang) from the woods. One of his metiz escorts jumped onto the horse and rode it with ease. He let it go when they came to the next hacienda stronghold, a place fortified with iron doors and steel window shutters.

Elise acknowledged there were wild horses around but countered with: "I do not suppose anyone is simple enough to believe that a person can, without further ado, jump astride a wild horse and ride it." Besides, no one needed the company of an escort, armed or otherwise—"only the most miserable coward would travel with one." Furthermore, there were no fortified haciendas anywhere near Nacogdoches or across the Sabine in western Louisiana.

As to Tolmer's portrait of Texas populated by thieves and brigands, Elise replied that there was no need even to lock your doors—people in Texas did not need to steal. And Comanche with poisoned lances! Nonsense! She had never so much as seen an Indian.

The Tolmer account had him holding off the bandit chief Judge Peters with a *cravache,* a horsewhip. Elise laid the cravache back on Tolmer himself. With fine invective she asserted: "Neither will any American allow himself to be threatened with a whip; the good Mr. Tolmer would soon have had a bullet through his body if he had dared such a thing."[6]

When she came to Tolmer's remarks about Nacogdoches she simply dismissed everything he had to say, including the specific details. Because of her own stay in the town, she well knew that the people there were mainly Americans and Europeans rather than Mexicans. Besides, there was no palisade around the town, no Red Eagle Hotel, no Spanish hotelkeeper, no broad river crossed by a bridge, no prairies in the neighborhood, "and still less crocodiles and jaguars." She finished off with: "Nor are the Americans afraid of beasts of prey—no more than they would be afraid of giving the good Captain Tolmer a sound thrashing for all his lies if he were here."

If Tolmer deserved a thrashing for all his lies, what were Texans really like? The main part of Elise's response was devoted to observations about customs and manners she had seen at work among real Texans. As in her earlier dispatches to *Norge og Amerika,* she spoke with the impartiality of an anthropologist describing the ways of newly discovered civilization in a far-off land.

Tolmer had said you could not count on receiving justice in Texan courts. "No doubt this is in part true," she said, "but to no greater a degree than in old Norway." She knew about justice in both countries, especially in Texas, where she and Wilhelm had recently acquired their land after legal resolution of the Mercer colony imbroglio. The problem, she said, was that the laws in both countries had flaws, and besides, they were written in ambiguous language. They were also subject to misinterpretation, sometimes getting twisted to accord with personal opinions and the biases of juries.

Mindful of the treatment of women and children in both countries, she listed specific Texan laws that were ahead of those in Norway. In Texas $250 of a married man's property was tax-exempt ($250 was equivalent to about $7,500 today), while unmarried men paid taxes on all their property. If a husband ran up debts, his creditors faced restrictions on their claims: they could not seize property owned by his wife; they must leave sufficient land, home and kitchen furnishings, and livestock to maintain his family; they could not take the tools or books of craftsmen and professional men. Historians of Norwegian immigration to the United States support Elise's view from another angle: taxes and debt burdens in Norway were so onerous that they helped drive the exodus to America.

She came back once again to the democratic spirit she encountered in her new home. "It is not here as in Norway," she wrote, "where equality and liberty are found on paper but not in real life." She supported her case with examples. In Texas civic duties and privileges were the same for all citizens. All free adult males had the right to vote regardless of financial status. Defense of the country was an obligation on all persons.

Back in Norway civic rights and duties depended on people's social class membership, with the heaviest burdens and fewest privileges going to the lower classes. In Texas all but slaves were equals. Settlers coming from Norway could forget their former lives, where social barriers and family backgrounds gave some people preference over others. In Texas it was what you were, not who you were, that mattered.

Slavery, of course, was to be condemned. The practice was less prevalent in Van Zandt County than in other places in Texas, but Elise could not excuse it for any reason: "There are very few free Negroes here, but unfortunately, there are many slaves because most rich Americans are slave owners.

Much as I despise slavery, I cannot deny that the slaves are treated rather well and that numbers of them are better off in many respects than free laborers in Europe. But the loss of liberty cannot be replaced by anything."

She felt obliged to report one other flaw in the Texan character. Although Texans are not brigands, she noted, "they are much too prone to avenge every real or fancied insult with a bullet or a stab." Dueling had been illegal in the state since the days of Sam Houston's republic, but men still displayed the inflated sense of honor that demanded retribution for whatever they considered a personal affront. In years to come, this hard spirit of revenge for presumed insults would cost her husband his life.

In spite of these failings, Texans had great public virtues. They were "friendly and helpful" toward foreigners as well as their own kind. There was no need for poor relief—she had personally witnessed the case of a widow with a large family (presumably her friend Thomine Grogard in Nacog-doches) who had "not only received substantial gifts in the form of food and clothing, but besides, the tuition fees for her children—which are quite high here—were paid for her," in part by people who had never seen her.

Then, too, Texas was a hunters' paradise. The countryside offered unique opportunity to satisfy the most ordinary as well as the most refined European tastes for game. There were a great many deer, rabbits, and squirrels ("very tasty," she said), turkeys, geese, various types of ducks, and prairie-chickens. Dove shooting went on in the fall, the hunters firing off their muzzle-loading rifles packed with buckshot: "The doves come in by the millions; they look like a dark cloud and there is a sound in the sky as if a great storm is ap-proaching. My husband killed about thirty with one shot, and where they roost at night wagonloads can be killed."

She summed up her attitude toward Tolmer's articles with this: "His whole silly story did indeed give me, and several others who happened to be here, a hearty laugh when I received the letter and read it to them."

Her reply to Tolmer's false portrait of Texas was sent to Gjestvang. In 1852 it appeared in *Hamars Budstikken* and afterward in *Morgenbladet* (Morning News) in Christiania, the leading newspaper in Norway. Avidly read by the emigration-hungry Norwegian public, it helped to build an image of Amer-ica as a land of opportunity where people could expand their minds as well as improve their material conditions.[7]

It may have been seen by Ole Bull, the popular Norwegian concert vio-linist, widely appreciated in Europe and the Americas for rivaling the great Italian Paganini with his showy virtuoso performances. In 1852 Bull decided to create a utopian colony for Norwegians in the United States.

CHAPTER 6

A prodigious violinist but no pioneer, Bull established his colony in the mountainous woodlands of western Pennsylvania. Alas, the area was isolated and cursed with thin, acidic soil unsuited to farming, and the enterprise failed. Elise knew two of the individuals who joined the colony. At one time she inquired about them, but she learned only that they had abandoned the place. Years later Bull would reenter Elise's story in a roundabout way; but, for the present, he should have chosen Texas, where things were going well.[8]

As for Gjestvang, a flurry of letters went to him following Elise's reply to the offensive Tolmer articles. Some of the letters were sent by Elise herself and others by her friends, all of them aiming to persuade him to visit. If Gjestvang would come to Texas it would make a good impression on potential immigrants in Norway, and if he chose to settle, scores would follow.

Elise and her friends seemed to assume that Gjestvang would find Texas irresistible. The Texan Norwegians were becoming established in two years, much faster than the immigrants going to states like Illinois, Iowa, and Wisconsin, where many reported long periods of hardship before getting started. In 1852 Elise confidently wrote to Gjestvang advising him on how to obtain land and what to bring to become a successful rancher.

Come he did, but he chose not to stay. In one of her letters written after the Civil War, Elise related that Gjestvang had arrived in 1853 to "inspect the country." He took in Bosque County as well as Four Mile Prairie, then, without comment, turned around and went back to Norway. Some of his neighbors from the Hedmark district where Hamar was located, north of Christiania, came with him on his inspection tour.

A few of them stayed, but Elise had to report: "No one ever found out what account Mr. Gjestvang gave of Texas upon his return; but this much is known—emigration from Hedmark to Texas stopped until two years ago." In spite of her suspicions about Gjestvang's accounts back home, the two maintained a correspondence for a few years. The zest was gone, though, and their exchanges eventually dwindled away.[9]

CHURCH, GOD, AND INTELLECT

A S THE TOLMER INCIDENT and Gjestvang's visit faded into the background, the issue of religious observance captured the Norwegians' attention. Reiersen, for all his radical criticism of conditions in Norway, was sufficiently aware of his homeland's religious traditions that he considered the provision of sacred observances essential to the building of a successful colony. Likewise, Elise's dispatches to *Norge og Amerika* had shown that the Brownsboro settlers viewed ordained religious leadership as vital to their community. It was time to provide a sound system of Lutheran worship to satisfy people's spiritual yearnings.

At first the Norwegians of Four Mile Prairie and Prairieville held baptisms, weddings, and funerals in their homes. Lay members of the community led these, but the lack of a church as well as ordained pastoral leadership was taking its toll. Some of Elise's friends slipped away from the Lutheran faith—Andreas Orbeck and Mads Vinzent joined the Campbellites (now the Disciples of Christ); Marie Grogard, daughter of Thomine, went to the Episcopalians; "Mother" Staack became a Methodist and her brother a Baptist.[1]

Elise herself, though firm in her commitment to the Lutheran Church, tested the waters of local religious practice. She attended a religious camp meeting that she described in two separate letters.

The first was to Gjestvang. Camp meetings, she told him, took place in the fall and were held in the woods. The sponsors of the one she attended erected a large roofed shed with the sides open to the surrounding forest trees. Five preachers, sometimes more, conducted the proceedings, preaching day and night for eight days. People brought great quantities of food that they shared with one another.

On arriving to join in the events, Elise and Wilhelm were immediately invited for a meal with American families. After the meal they attended daytime services that seemed perfectly ordinary. In the evening, though, the men and women split up for what Elise described as "so-called secret prayers." Things now took a new turn. The groups went to different parts of the wood where they sang psalms in raucous voices. One by one people began reciting long prayers, and then the worshipers "become so inspired . . . that one after another they begin to sing and clap their hands, crying out 'Glory! Glory!' as loudly as they can. They begin pounding on the ones nearest to them, throwing themselves on their knees or on their backs, laughing and crying—in short, conducting themselves like perfectly insane people."

Ecstatic expressions of religious feeling were not part of Elise's tradition. She was accustomed to formal proceedings led by a pastor, with minimum personal exhibitions of uninhibited spirit. The hymns she sang were solemn, and the ancient prayers that she heard read by the pastor were set in pre-scribed religious language. Quiet, sonorous sermons, dignified rituals, and well-modulated hymns, these were the traditions she knew.

She called the camp meeting event a comic performance, "the oddest form of Christian worship any person can imagine." The preachers, she said, "exerted themselves to the utmost to rouse the people to the highest state of ecstasy. At these camp meetings people are baptized, married, and tendered the Lord's Supper. The emotions that the whole thing aroused were hardly devotional."

Her second letter was to Thomine Dannevig, her closest childhood friend in Lillesand. Thomine Dannevig had always been her confidante, but when Elise's exchanges with Gjestvang began to decline, Thomine became her main correspondent. Elise wrote to her about practical details—ranch-ing, stock, land, and prices—but that was not all. Her most inward thoughts and deepest feelings, together with news about family and friends, were her subjects. When Otto was born it was to Thomine Dannevig that she ex-pressed her joy. She named her third son, her favorite, Thorvald August, af-ter Thomine's eldest boy.

In telling Thomine Dannevig about the camp meeting, she was less flip-pant and tongue-in-cheek than she had been with Gjestvang. Forceful and blunt, she declared the naked truth as she felt it. The people at the camp meetings acted as if "possessed by the devil." When they threw themselves on the ground, she said, "the others press around (them) and continue singing and praying. The same mad scene takes place in the evening after the sermon and the minister's most zealous incitement. Apparently they believe that they cannot get into Heaven unless they take it by storm. There is no edification for me in this."[2]

In 1853 the Four Mile Prairie Norwegians decided to establish their own place of worship, and Elise and Wilhelm joined their neighbors in putting up a small log cabin to serve as a Lutheran church. A parishioner who made a pencil sketch of the building for a church anniversary celebration in the 1970s imagined it with a pair of oxen yoked to a peasant cart standing outside the front door. This form of transportation, common at the time, gives the place a proper rustic appearance, while the cabin itself, utterly crude by comparison with present-day churches, looks more like a woodsman's hut than a religious building. Its single wooden door seems to be made of wide, heavy planks suited to a stronghold. The wall openings—there are no windows—are covered by hatches made of boards held together by black metal bands that would have been forged by a local blacksmith if the drawing truly resembled the building as it was in Elise's time.

Like many log cabins, the church would have had a dirt floor, hard packed and swept clean. The drawing shows no chimney, which means the parishioners would have sat through winter services without heat. The hatches and door would have been kept open to admit light, and candle-bearing lanterns were perhaps hung from the ceiling beams to illuminate the dark interior.

Although wood logs would seem to be a primitive construction material for a religious building, the Norwegians had for centuries known log churches in their home country. Called *stavekirker,* these sanctuaries were built in Viking times, the timbers finished like ship masts, so smooth that they seem almost polished. In some cases the "stave" churches were decorated with superb carved designs not unlike those created by the pagan artists of Norway's pre-Christian era. Although the Four Mile Prairie log cabin church was plain to the utmost degree, it served for years as the colony's house of worship, the place for baptisms, weddings, funerals, and the prayers that carried the people's lives along.[3]

Elise's second son, Niels, born on December 12, 1853, may have been baptized in this cabin church before it was consecrated as a religious building. The blessing of a building to make it a holy sanctuary had to be performed by a trained pastor, and in 1854 the first educated man came to Four Mile Prairie from Norway. He was Anders Emil Fridrichsen, zealous enough to take a post in hard pioneer country.[4]

Fridrichsen had not yet received final ordination from a bishop, but the

Log cabin Lutheran church at Four Mile Prairie. Drawing by A. M. McFarland, courtesy of Betty Ann Trednick, Four Mile Prairie.

Four Mile Prairie community welcomed him because he had completed theological studies and knew how to perform the major pastoral functions. One of his first acts was to dedicate the log cabin as a true place of worship; along with that he probably blessed the ground behind the church, making it a hallowed site for a cemetery.

Elise reported that the families in the congregation contributed anywhere from three to eight dollars per year toward his salary, and unmarried women and widows gave one or two dollars each. These sums, along with offerings on special feast days and fees for weddings, baptisms, and funerals made up his entire income. To make a quick calculation of his earnings, one might estimate thirty families contributing an average of five dollars each. Adding fees, and special offerings, and the donations by single women, he might have had an income in the vicinity of two hundred dollars a year. Equivalent to about six thousand dollars in present-day currency, this amount would barely have been enough to scrape by. For this salary Fridrichsen was serving Four Mile Prairie and riding circuit to the settlements in Bosque and Brownsboro, a territory covering 150 miles.

His pastorate lasted to 1857, only three years. It was not only that his salary was wretchedly low. People with a zealous spirit do not always have an agreeable personality, and Fridrichsen apparently offended some members of his flock. Elise reported that four adults in Four Mile Prairie refused to be confirmed by him. She noted that one of these dissenters was a married woman, presumably someone of reliable judgment who needed confirmation because it was expected of married people. The four may have been alienated by a superior attitude on Fridrichsen's part. Elise said he considered himself better than others—an offense against Norwegian attitudes as well as against the spirit of pioneer Texas.

When Fridrichsen left, Elise wrote a letter to *Morgenbladet* saying "it would be fine if we could get a Christian-minded minister." But, she added, "he must not come expecting any temporal gain," for he could not "count on more than three hundred dollars annually and a simple house." Such a low salary would require someone with an exceptionally keen religious spirit. Perhaps for that reason the Four Mile Prairie parish never attracted another minister from Norway.[5]

Instead Elling Eielsen, an itinerant missionary, came from Wisconsin in the winter of 1860. Eielsen had arrived in America in 1839 and had been ordained in Chicago, the first Norwegian Lutheran pastor to be ordained there. He was known to be a "Haugean," a follower of the lay preacher Hans Nielsen Hauge, initiator of a pious evangelical revival movement that had spread throughout Norway. Considered an upstart by authorities of the Lutheran state church, Hauge had been jailed for violating the nation's law forbidding preaching by anyone but an ordained pastor.

In spite of Eielsen's Haugean orientation, Elise had enormous respect for him. She wrote to Thomine Dannevig in March, 1860, about his arrival from Wisconsin. He came without any guarantee that he would be repaid for his journey or would even receive a salary. Once in Texas the fifty-four-year-old Eielsen served the three Norwegian settlements spread over 150 miles, yet he refused to accept any money from church offerings. Elise doubted that people contributed more than a hundred dollars (the equivalent of about three thousand today) to his work. "He is a Haugean, to be sure," she said, "but a particularly capable person who is an untiring worker even though he is an old man. He visited all the Norwegians and preached every day—nearly all day." Such earnest piety earned her admiration.

During his months in Texas, Eielsen convinced the settlers that they should set up Sunday schools, then a new religious initiative, though these later became an essential feature of church life. Even more important for Elise was his work in organizing a temperance society in Brownsboro. She reported that Eielsen spent most of his time at that settlement, "where the Norwegians are great lovers of intoxicating drinks." In telling Thomine Dannevig about this she had to explain what whiskey was—people in Norway were familiar with brandy but not with American sour mash bourbon or rye. Whiskey, she said, was a stronger brew than beer and wine, one that readily induced drunkenness.

Her husband Wilhelm had previously tried to start a temperance society in 1855, but it had failed over a misunderstanding about whether drinking whiskey should be allowed. Present-day temperance advocates favor total abstinence; by that standard Elise and Wilhelm were too moderate—they both drank wine and beer. In their approach to temperance, only distilled alcohol was to be banned.

The 1855 temperance society broke down over how much inebriation was acceptable. Some of the society's members insisted that drinking distilled alcohol was acceptable as long as the imbiber did not get drunk. When Wilhelm helped Eielsen get the new society going, Elise observed: "This time we hope that with God's help it may fare better, since they [the Brownsboro group] seemed to be deeply moved by the pastor's presentation and admonitions."

Eielsen did not remain in Texas for long. While he was there, however, whatever objections there may have been to his Haugean background simply disappeared. Elise reported that the congregations hoped to have him move down from Wisconsin to be their pastor. She added her own conviction: "I do not think we could find anyone better fitted for the work here."

When Eielsen left he had told them he could not return, but he promised to send a replacement. So eager were they for spiritual leadership that he may have felt a twinge of pastoral regret over leaving the Norwegian Texans alone to care for the religious well-being of their linked but widely separated communities.[6]

It is no surprise that Elise should have respected Eielsen in spite of his Haugean leanings. Her religious views were hardly orthodox. She held fast

Embroidery of Jesus made by Elise at age thirteen
using black silk thread on ivory-colored satin.
Photo by Charles H. Russell, courtesy of owner William Van Shaw, Dallas.

to a firm moral outlook and a stout, unsentimental Lutheran faith, but her reasons for doing so were entirely her own. It was as if she had written her own script based on her examination of religious subjects and study of the Bible.

Elise's independent religious thinking started early. At the age of thirteen she created an embroidery portrait of Jesus. It was executed in black silk thread on luminous ivory-colored satin, the stitches so tiny that they seemed to flow together and give the appearance of an etching. The picture was a masterpiece for a girl her age.

CHAPTER 7

It was daring, too. Portraits of Jesus had been the province of great artists who aimed to induce a spirit of awe and reverence in viewers, but Elise's image reflected her personal vision. She pictured Jesus as a known person, someone who had actually lived, someone who need not be approached with shrinking humility and worshiped as an overarching God.

This insight can be seen in the way she treated Jesus' general appearance. Although she showed Him with long hair and a full beard as in traditional portraits, she based her image on the secular fashions of her own time, the Romantic Era. Poets and artists were represented as debonair, wearing flowing wind-blown curls and, if not clean-shaven, displaying elegantly groomed whiskers. Although Elise's Jesus bore a serious expression, He was handsome and wore hair that hung in elegant whorls down to His shoulders. His beard was fine, discreet, gently curled, like that of a Romantic figure, someone with whom a young girl could fall in love.

Furthermore, one can see that Jesus' right eye is a colorless blur, as if the iris is damaged. His left eye, however, is clear and sharply delineated. It has a penetrating quality as if He is looking right into His viewer's soul.

Elise herself had a blank spot in her right eye; it shows in her daguerreotype portrait made in Texas when she was in her mid-forties. This colorless spot was the result of an injury she received at birth. The appearance of a similarly damaged right eye in her portrait of Jesus was no accident. Artists often have used themselves as models when creating images of people. Elise must have looked in a mirror and used her own reflection when making her picture. At age thirteen she had the confidence in her religious convictions to create a representation of Jesus seemingly with elements of her own likeness.[7]

At the time she made this portrait she may have been generating the doubts about the Trinity doctrine that she later recorded in her "Confession of Faith." Her pastor father Nicolai Tvede had been influenced by the Rationalist philosophy that dominated Europe in the eighteenth- and early nineteenth-century Enlightenment period. Elise in turn absorbed elements of Rationalist thought, including the idea that religious believers should express their faith through good works.[8]

In its extreme forms Enlightenment Rationalism led to religious skepticism and atheism, but for many serious Christians it meant replacing rigid doctrines and unquestioned obedience to church fathers with reason and common sense. Consistent with this dissenting attitude toward traditional dogma, Elise came to the conclusion that the doctrine of the Trinity (Father, Son, and Holy Spirit) was an obstacle to her faith. From her practical point of view, it was impossible to imagine that God could be one person and at the same time three people.

Disclosure of her thoughts concerning this major tenet of Christian faith would have been utterly shocking to most other believers. She revealed it in private, and then only on the eve of the Civil War, when—sensing that shattering experiences were coming on—she set down her religious ideas, her "Confession of Faith," for her sons. Her title, probably derived from the "Augsburg Confession" written by the Protestant theologian Melancthon in 1530 and used since as a guide by Lutherans, indicates the vital importance the document had for her. She had to pass her personal creed on to her boys; they needed a defense against "scoffers and doubters, seducers and offenders, of whom there are altogether too many."

After first declaring her disbelief in the Trinity Doctrine, she put forward her own understanding of God. God was a single person, the originator of being, who sends His holy spirit out to accompany humans at all times. Jesus was not the same as God. He was the teacher and the redeemer, a real, living person on earth who had saved humanity from its evil ways. She did not trouble herself that her idea of Jesus might make Him divine. She just went on, confident in the faith she was passing on to her sons.

Her vision of God was deep and direct: "He is possessed of the most noble and majestic attributes, and . . . in His sublimity embodies everything that we can imagine," she wrote. "I believe that His essence is infinite love which embraces all His creatures, the greatest and the least." Because of His attributes, God would accept believers no matter what they thought about the Trinity Doctrine. Besides, "we should be all the more inspired with love for everybody," and therefore faith should "reveal its power in good deeds, in love toward our neighbor."

She held that the salvation offered by Christ reached people in any faith if they genuinely practiced what they believed. In her words, Christ was their redeemer "insofar as they have sincerely sought to obey the will of God as realized by them." This led her to an appreciation of Judaism. Rather than speaking of the Old Testament, she repeatedly wrote "Moses tells us," when quoting from the first books of the Christian Bible.[9]

Her convictions about God gave her an inward ethical guidance system for judging current issues, and in the Confession of Faith document she directed her judgment first of all against the improper treatment of women. Had she lived in a later age she would surely have become a strong advocate of women's political rights, but the movement in the mid–nineteenth century was too young to reach her. At that moment, though, "scoffers and doubters, seducers and offenders" were saying that "Christ was an illegitimate child"—in effect attacking the merit of his mother Mary, the most representative of all women.

That the mother of Jesus could be an immoral woman—"I actually shudder at the thought of it," Elise wrote. Not many years before she penned these words, the doctrine of the Immaculate Conception had been published by the Roman Catholic Church: the Virgin Mary was worthy to be the mother of Christ because she was free of original sin from the time of her own conception. Apparently interpreting this idea in her own way, Elise asked, would God choose a man like Jesus for his holy work—a man "whose mother had behaved so loosely as to have a child with one man while engaged to another? No! this I absolutely cannot believe; on the contrary, I take it for granted that the mother of Christ was a noble woman—and immaculate, as the Bible tells us.[10]

From her defense of Mary she moved on to actual perpetrators of violations against women: men whose religious doctrines allowed them to take several wives. "Bigamy," she called it; today we call it polygamy or polygyny—having multiple wives. *Mormons were practicing Bigamy!*

The Mormons may have been far away, but they seem to have been firmly present in Elise's mind. In Illinois more than 150 Norwegian men had joined the Mormons. Some came from Fox River, Illinois, the settlement started by her friend Cleng Peerson; a number had even become leaders of the denomination. In 1846, as the Mormons were trekking from their original capital in Nauvoo, Illinois, to the future Salt Lake City, the news about their Norwegian members traveled back to Norway. The Lutheran Church authorities there expressed disapproval of the polygynous denomination and denounced the defection of their members to it.[11]

Elise did not say in her Confession of Faith that she knew Norwegians had joined the Mormon Church, but she was keenly attuned to what was going on in the world beyond her prairie home. She must have known that some of her countrymen had become Mormons, for surely her furious outburst against "bigamy" was provoked by such knowledge.

Muslims as well as Mormons must be condemned. Both were spreading a doctrine that "degraded half the human race, namely, the women"; her reference to half the human race foreshadows the resonant modern feminist rallying cry. Warring against the foul agents of polygyny, she wrote: "It should be obvious that it is a degradation for a woman to share her husband's love with several other women (I cannot permit myself to call them 'wives')."

Church, God, and Intellect

How would it be possible for a man to cherish a deep and warm love for several women at the same time?

This is contrary to human nature, and the feeling a man has for his several wives must therefore be identical with the passion that drives him into the arms of a harlot, she told her sons. Children will suffer in multiple-wife marriages because their fathers' "many women" will live in conflict with one another. They will be rivals for the man's love and will compete for "supremacy in the house." A man, she declared, cannot love and treat his children equally if they are born of many women. Not only does bigamy degrade women to a position "little better than that of slaves," she suggested; it also "demoralizes . . . the men and children."

Propagandists and missionaries for a doctrine that said bigamy was God's bidding were "liars and cheats of the worst sort . . . they confuse and mislead their fellow men." She must have been pleased when many years later, in 1890, the Mormon Church outlawed multiple marriages, just as she would be pleased, were she alive today, to know that American Muslims are monogamous. The issues are different today, but the ardent sentiments she expressed about polygyny prefigured the women's rights crusade.[12]

She left denouncing bigamy for a happier topic: advising her sons on how to treat their wives. Being a strong believer in the work ethic, she told them to lead industrious lives before contemplating marriage. Then, when they were "really mature," and lucky enough to find a girl with whom they could hope to lead a happy life, they should wed. A capable and thrifty wife, she said, would help them acquire wealth more rapidly than if they remained bachelors. Besides, when committed to a wife they would "be free from more temptations than the unmarried man—or at least much less exposed to them."

Aware that laws of her time gave husbands mastery over their wives, she admonished her sons to follow a basic rule: "make as little use of the right as possible." If the family income were sufficient, "then let them always have money of their own to dispose of as freely as you do yourself." And do not insist that they ask your permission to buy every item they want, she said, or make them give you an accounting of how they spend every penny.

Some of her counsel to her sons regarding common practices of her day sounds ludicrous in our present time: "Do not expect your wives to ask your consent to visit the neighbors" or to go where they want, because this reduces them "to the status of children."

Other advice she gave them was less time-bound. Never keep secrets from one another. Be reasonable in what you expect of your wives. Be courteous, and trustful—your wives will be more polite and trusting if you are. Above all, "deal lovingly with your wives; do not make them feel that you are their masters." She closed by commending equality in spousal relations: "If one is to rule over another, then love and marital happiness will soon vanish."[13]

With her interest in what was going on beyond Four Mile Prairie, Elise was quick to take up subjects stirring the public mind. One of these was the theory of evolution, a fact that dates the composition of her Confession of Faith to the summer of 1860 or to the fall harvest months about the time of Lincoln's election.

Darwin had published the theory at the end of November, 1859, but it was not until June of 1860 that it spread outside scientific circles. It became known to the public when Samuel Wilberforce, the Church of England bishop at the university town of Oxford, decided to launch an attack against it at a meeting of the British Association for the Advancement of Science. Unfortunately for him, he chose to ridicule the theory by making a derisive reference to the "simian ancestry" of one of the other speakers. The man he made fun of was the brilliant scientist T. H. Huxley. In reply Huxley destroyed the bishop by saying he would rather have an ape for a grandfather than a man who used his wit to bring ridicule into a meeting where a serious scientific subject was under discussion.

Huxley's sharp rejoinder not only blew Wilberforce away; it catapulted the new theory from the halls of science into the public arena. Out there, in general public discussion, questions of religion and theology reigned supreme. Elise picked up the resulting furor and, like other religious people, condemned the theory of evolution for its conflict with the biblical account of Creation.

But she did not stop with a simple condemnation. She avoided Wilberforce's error and went on to criticize the theory's scientific underpinnings. In doing so, she used her customary approach, the best she knew—rational thinking. She found the theory neither reasonable nor logical. Had her views been presented at the British Scientific Association meeting, they might well have been respected and have earned a reply.

She considered the theory and the idea of evolution itself absurd. How could plants have evolved from minerals? How could animals have evolved from plants? How could humans have evolved from "one of the most perfect animals, namely, the ape which is very like the human in form"? How could this "slow and peculiar process" have taken place?

What was more, the theory was lacking in hard evidence. "History goes

Church, God, and Intellect

back thousands of years in time and it tells us nothing to substantiate this kind of view of the creative process." If evolution had been ongoing, why had the process stopped? If true, the theory implied that things had reached perfection—and she did not believe "that the human being is so perfect that he cannot reach further perfection." This teaching, she concluded, "I find wholly and completely unacceptable and just as contrary to sound common sense as it is against the Bible."

Elise had not seen the enormous body of evidence Darwin drew upon to adduce his theory. Nothing in any of her correspondence shows that she ever did consult it. Nor do any of her writings indicate that she ever considered the theory again or that she changed her mind about it. Her interests lay in morality and faith for daily living, and that was quite enough.[14]

She next turned her attention to various aspects of inner being, the soul, the mind, and veiled inward personal experience. Spiritualism had captured her notice, so she addressed it. This esoteric belief came into vogue during the mid–nineteenth century, apparently following the religious revival that had spread across the United States in the early 1800s. Its devotees held that one could communicate with, and even recall, the dead.

Spiritualists with clairvoyant powers were needed to make these contacts. Their method was to put themselves into a trance during séances and to communicate in their dreamlike state with members of the spirit world. On these occasions various phenomena occurred—ghostly voices, rapping, emanations of ectoplasm, and so on—all supposedly produced from the spiritualist's contact with the occult realm.

Elise viewed spiritualism from her religious perspective. She believed deeply that humans have a living inner being, a soul, an actual inward body just as real as the physical body. When the soul leaves the human body at the time of death, she said, it continues in a glorified state, free of human imperfections.

She did not, however, think that souls ever returned to earth. Parents did not come back as spirits to visit and advise their children, as some people thought. In fact, she wrote, "I cannot believe either that the many stories of revelations by the departed are anything other than frauds or the creations of an excited imagination."[15]

She looked also at phrenology, which was an early attempt to develop a theory of human psychology. Although an ill-founded psuedoscience, phrenology had achieved notoriety for its efforts to tie psychological theorizing to actual observations of people. Phrenologists thought there were twenty-six faculties in the mind—wonder, hope, amativeness, firmness, combativeness, destructiveness, and so forth. These faculties were innate, built into the individual from birth.

According to the theory, bumps on people's skulls lay over each of these faculties, and maps of shaved heads were drawn delineating protuberances that disclosed the faculty underneath. By study of people's skull bump zones, phrenologists claimed they could read a person's character.

Scientific research eventually disproved the claims of phrenology, but Elise immediately and flatly rejected it. Humans have free will, she believed. They are not born with faculties already defined. They have the power to choose what they do. God, she asserted, could not "have created one individual from birth to be a thief, another a murderer, a third to become a libertine, and so on." Experience and common sense told "sensible people" phrenology was wrong, "no matter how many of those whom the world calls enlightened and wise accept it as truth."[16]

Ethical treatment of animals was yet another subject that Elise linked to inward being. By the late 1850s she and her husband were owners of a large stock of cattle, sheep, hogs, and chickens. All the processes relating to ranch animals—breeding, birthing, milking, feeding, cleaning, shearing, roundup, branding, and slaughtering—were part of their daily or annual routine.

Elise held that animals have souls. They have a will. They feel sorrow, joy, love, and hate. They remember their experiences, and "draw conclusions as to what will happen." For her, all these capabilities were evidence that animals had a lively inward being.

She was not sure that animal souls were immortal. It seemed reasonable, though, that they might be. Souls cannot die, she observed, and besides, "it would increase my joy if the many animals who have made me happy here also would live and enjoy themselves forever."

Whatever one may think about Elise's views on animal souls, she felt strongly that humans had obligations toward all living creatures. It might be necessary, she said, to kill animals in self-defense or for food, but this should be done as quickly and humanely as possible to minimize their suffering. Animals should never be allowed to starve to death through "carelessness or laziness or stupid stinginess."[17]

For all her attention to these engrossing topics, Elise's deepest reflections concerned the institution of slavery. She addressed more words to it than to any other subject in her Confession of Faith. The essence of her thought, eloquent in language and powerful in feeling, was cast entirely in religious terms:

We are all of us, the children of God, created for the same high destiny, and whereas all of us have our origin in God, all of us are redeemed by the blood of Jesus; all have the same hope of salvation.

I believe to the fullest degree that human beings are born with equal rights. Consequently it is repulsive to me to hear people read their Declaration of Independence and deliver their bloated Fourth of July orations in honor of liberty while there are millions of slaves among them.

. . . I believe that slavery is absolutely contrary to the law of God, because the law commands us to love God and our neighbors as ourselves, and further, that whatsoever we want others to do unto us, that we should do toward them. These rules are as simple and easily understood as they are true, and if we would only accept them as the guiding lines in accordance with which we regulated our behavior toward our fellow men then we would not easily go astray.

. . . Let us now ask ourselves if we would be satisfied with being slaves, with being sold like animals, with being separated from our mates and our children whenever it might suit our masters, with seeing our children brought up in thralldom and ignorance without the slightest possibility of rising above the miserable state into which we were born, despite the fact that we might have the highest abilities and the greatest eagerness to learn.

To all this we must without qualification answer "No!"—answer that it would make us immeasurably unhappy. Consequently slavery must be contrary to the will of God, must be an abomination.

When she expressed her abhorrence for slavery in public a snide racist question had been flung in her face: "People have asked me if I would tolerate having a Negro woman as a daughter-in-law." She made no pretense of bridging the great divide between the races of her time, but brusquely replied: "I must admit it would not please me very much, but I would rather have it thus than to have grandchildren who are slaves."

Such a mindless racist challenge forced her to think again, to go beyond principle. She put the issue in personal terms, telling how the grandchildren of a white person could actually become slaves: "Let us now assume that . . . a lecherous person seeks to satisfy his passions among Negro women and as a consequence becomes the father of slaves, either his own or those of others. What will become the fate of these children? Yes, they will be brought up as thralls, as something halfway between men and brutes. They will be sold as beasts and denied opportunities for spiritual or intellectual advancement; and this dire degradation is passed on as an inheritance to all their descendants."

She closed her condemnation of men who satisfy their passions among powerless slave women with this: "How can then such a father who so absolutely has neglected to further the spiritual and temporal welfare of his children—how can he survive the wrath of God's Judgment Seat? Will not his child or children and the descendants appear as the most severe plaintiffs against him?" One would have to read far to find any more forceful statements against slavery than Elise made in her Confession of Faith.[18]

Interest in subjects beyond the world of Four Mile Prairie required finding practical ways to stay in touch with popular tastes. Many Norwegians—people like herself, Reiersen, Gjestvang, and Ole Bull—drawn to America by ideals expected the favorable air of democratic equality to enrich their minds as well as their material circumstances. In spite of this, Elise occasionally felt cut off from the stimulating life she had known in Europe.

By the late 1850s there were enough residents in her area to attract spectator shows. She told Thomine Dannevig about circus riders performing in her area. A freak show had come too. It exhibited a man who was nothing but skin and bones—"a frightful sight to behold," Elise wrote. This grotesquerie drew her interest—"I would very much have liked to see him because probably nowhere on this earth could his like be found"; but sights and circus amusements were not enough.

She looked for something more. She complained that except for Gjestvang's occasional letters, she received no mail. When the newcomers arrive, she said, "we usually get a lot of newspapers, too, and a few books," but that was only once a year. The items they brought briefly satisfied her tastes, but the feast was too meager. The hunger remained. "We read (these) over and over until the next year, when immigrants come again."

One way she tried to gratify her appetite for wider culture was by joining with neighbors in starting a reading club. They were a group of Scandinavians—Swedes and Danes as well as Norwegians—sixteen families in all. Money for things of the mind was scarce, but by pooling their resources they hoped to buy books they could exchange with one another and discuss at meetings. They managed to put together twenty-two dollars, but Elise considered this a meager sum even though it would buy fifteen to twenty satisfyingly ample books, all hardcover. On her initiative the club members appealed to publishers, friends, and relatives in their homelands for book donations.

Church, God, and Intellect

She mentioned having read Harriet Beecher Stowe's anti-slavery book *Uncle Tom's Cabin,* evidently together with the members of the reading club, but she never recorded what became of the club or how long it survived. The mere fact that it existed, though, showed there was time for something other than work.[19]

Toward the end of the 1850s life was flourishing. A post office had opened in Prairieville as early as 1854. She and Wilhelm had expensive daguerreotypes made of themselves and their two boys, Otto and Nicls; their youngest son was not yet born. Most likely they made an overnight trip beyond Brownsboro to Tyler, the nearest sizable town, for their sittings.

Texas was booming. According to the ten-year United States census, the population grew from 212,592 in 1850 to 604,215 in 1860, including freemen and slaves. Van Zandt County went from 1,348 residents to 3,777 during those years.[20]

In the fall of 1858 Elise gave birth to her third son, Thorvald. Forty-four years old at the time, she wrote to Thomine Dannevig: "God be praised, that the little baby arrived happy and well on the fourth of this month. I cannot tell you how glad I was that everything went well because, after all, I am no longer young, and I was worried for fear that I might have to leave my be-loved children. Neither Wilhelm nor I have a single relative in this country, so it isn't easy to say what he would have done with the children if I had died."

Two years later when Elise wrote to her mother-in-law and sisters-in-law about weaning Thorvald, she told about the help she had from maids: "Recently I have tried to wean Thorvald from his mother's milk. It has not been easy for either of us to do this, but it had to be done sometime, and I thought that it would be the best thing for both of us. The maid I had last winter is about to leave me now, and the new one arrived two weeks ago. This was the main reason why I wanted to wean Thorvald just now, for during this time, Berthe, whom he loves so much, has plenty of time to look after him."

About this time, too, Elise related that she and Wilhelm owned seven horses. Wilhelm had to trade away their old mare, and Niels was unhappy about it. The boy, now almost eight, considered the mare his own. He cried all day when animal was taken away, but Elise would not comfort him; he would be getting a younger and better mare and a gold dollar. The exchange did not console him.

Business was prospering. Wilhelm and Reiersen joined with Ole Gunderson to buy a lumber and flour steam mill in Brownsboro for $6,000 (about $180,000 today). Wilhelm also obtained a contract to build a courthouse

Waerenskjold family portraits composite, about 1855.
Otto, bottom left, Niels right. Thorvald, born in 1858, may never have been
photographed. Photo courtesy of owner Ophelia Sparks, Denton;
copy at the University of Texas Institute of Texan Cultures at San Antonio.

for $6,000. The 1860 tax rolls for Van Zandt County show that Elise and
Wilhelm were among the wealthiest people in their area. They owned over
940 acres, 150 cattle, and 185 sheep. The total value of their personal property—excluding the land, their home, and Wilhelm's share of the sawmill—
was $4,040 (about $120,000). The $320 (about $10,000) Wilhelm had felt

sufficiently affluent to put out on loan had been repaid, and Elise was think-ing about making a visit back to Norway.[21]

And yet, while all this success seemed to confirm their wisdom in choos-ing to emigrate, there were disquieting signs in Texas. The legislature in 1858 had passed a law saying that no free Negroes could reside in the state. Freemen must either leave or voluntarily choose a master under whom they would return to slave status. The big planters who controlled the politics of the state were hardening in their attitudes. Word of secession was spreading throughout the south, and in Texas it was being pushed in spite of opposi-tion by Governor Sam Houston.

In March, 1860, Elise wrote Thomine Dannevig her last letter before the Civil War. She reported that the winter had been "a most unfortunate one for Texas." November was so warm that the trees and grass were "in luxuri-ant growth," but then the worst snow and cold "anyone could remember" broke over them.

It began with a sudden nighttime freeze. By morning the turnips, cab-bages, and other winter produce were ice hard. Entire trees—pears, figs, mul-berries—and grapevines all were dying. Never expecting such cold, people had scythed their grain and hay and left it out in the fields, where it froze and rotted on the ground. Cattle, sheep, and pigs had stood about covered with ice. Many had starved and died. "Spring is very late this year," Elise wrote, "and the old saying 'While the grass grows, the cows die' has been literally fulfilled, for most of the cattle died after the grass began to grow."[22]

A great abyss was about to split the nation. Like other Americans in the South, the Norwegians in Texas were about to go to war against their coun-trymen in the North.

CIVIL WAR

OR ELISE THERE WAS only one cause of the Civil War: slavery. "I am convinced," she wrote in her Confession of Faith, "that slavery will be abolished by gentle means or force, because I believe that institutions founded on injustice are doomed to fall."

Her statement about abolition was prophetic. Conflict was boiling between the North and the South, with the planter aristocrats who controlled the politics of the South claiming that slavery was essential to their region's agricultural economy. They drew on constitutional theory to maintain the institution. The Union was a "compact" between the states, and the southern states had a right to secede if abolitionist sentiment in the North were to threaten their economic survival.

Elise cared nothing for these legalities and economics. She shared the growing sentiment against the system that southern apologists were calling "our peculiar institution." Most European nations had ended slavery in their colonies and were attempting to stamp out the slave trade in the Americas. In the United States the North was insisting Congress must do likewise. A climax came with the 1860 election when the Republican Lincoln won over the Democratic Party (split into northern and southern factions, each with their own candidate) and the Constitutional Union Party.[1]

The inaugural arrangements of the time gave the defeated southern Democrat secessionists opportunity for drastic action. Lincoln could not take the office until March 4, 1861. As the outgoing President James Buchanan dawdled to the end of his term, South Carolina, longtime leader of the movement to break up the Union, seized the initiative. In early December it declared the Union dissolved. Alabama, Mississippi, Georgia, Florida, and Louisiana followed suit.

Elise was writing her Confession of Faith as the fever spread to Texas. In late December the state's secessionists set up a convention to withdraw from the Union. Sam Houston, governor of the state, opposed secession. He tried to forestall the proceedings by summoning the legislature to deny recognition to the unauthorized gathering. Instead, the legislature rejected his position and endorsed the convention. With this legal power, the convention adopted a secession ordinance by a lopsided vote of 166 to 8. In spite of the feeble showing of dissent—fewer than 5 percent of the delegates said "nay"—several leading citizens shared Sam Houston's sentiments.

At Houston's insistence the issue was put out to public referendum. Late in February, 1861, the people of the state did choose secession, 46,153 to 14,747—but 22 percent were opposed. The convention next required state officials to take an oath of loyalty to the Confederacy. Houston refused. The delegates deposed him by declaring the office of the governor vacant and appointed Lieutenant Governor Edward Clark in his place.

In Van Zandt County, where the foreign-born population and northerners nearly equaled the number of residents from the lower south, the 1861 vote was 181 to 127—41 percent opposed secession. The majority of voters in seventeen of the other 122 Texas counties also opposed secession, in one by 96 percent and another by 97 percent. In eleven more counties over 40 percent were opposed.

As a woman Elise was ineligible to vote, but according to her testimony most Norwegians were Unionists and against secession. They were but a small part of the dissenting group; the bulk of the opposition came in counties with large German, Mexican, or northern populations.

During February, 1861, the states of the Deep South met in Alabama and formed the Confederacy. Texas joined in March. On April 12, a South Carolina shore battery opened fire on Fort Sumter, the federal fortress in Charleston harbor. Lincoln proclaimed the southern states in insurrection and summoned a volunteer army to suppress the rebellion. Slavery would be struck down by force.[2]

During the early war years an extraordinary inconsistency appears in the record of Elise's opposition to slavery. Although she remained intensely hostile to the institution, the property tax records for Van Zandt County for 1861 and 1862 show that Wilhelm and she owned a slave.[3]

The documents bearing witness to this startling fact were created almost 150 years ago. They can be viewed today in a voluminous set of microfilm rolls housed at the Texas A&M University library at Commerce. The pages recorded on these films are photographs of the Van Zandt County tax register volumes kept from 1848 to 1886. The documents thus preserved are products of routine government business. Turned out on orderly printed pages, they are neatly inscribed with the elegant handwritten script of the time. Their very elegance and bloodless appearance drives home the monstrous outrage of slavery. It was a practice almost beyond imagining.

Column headings at the top of each record show that human beings were classified with animals. The first two categories on each page are for NAME and REAL PROPERTY (land and homes). Next comes PERSONAL PROPERTY, under which NEGROES is the first subheading, followed by HORSES, CATTLE, SHEEP, and MIS. PROPY (miscellaneous property). People were material assets, chattels to be used like animals, bred, bought and sold. They were objects to be routinely taxed by a government deeply entrenched in a system that was being declared rotten in the rest of the world.

Elise and Wilhelm's ownership of a slave has to be reconciled with her repeated condemnation of the institution year after year. Nowhere in her writings did she ever acknowledge that they owned a slave. Was she ignorant of it? Was her silence a cover for guilt? Was her hatred of slavery a pretense? Or did an effort to get around the legal standards of the time underlie this glaring contradiction in her attitudes?

One possibility is that Wilhelm recorded an employee as a slave without her knowledge. Men at the time were responsible for family business affairs, and Wilhelm undoubtedly took care of reporting their property to tax authorities. He might have reported a slave surreptitiously to demonstrate loyalty to the Confederacy during the dangerously rising tensions at the beginning of the Civil War. He might also have felt obliged to show ownership of a slave in order to gain some advantage in case he had to enter the Texas Confederate army—by the end of 1861 twenty-five-thousand men had volunteered to join, among them some of his fellow Norwegians.

But Wilhelm and Elise generally shared opinions on matters of principle, and he surely agreed with her anti-slavery outlook. True, he deeded ownership of the slave—apparently a female house worker—to Elise when he was going to join the Confederate Army, and he might even have done so without telling her. As a soldier going off to war, he was making sure to put the woman in his wife's hands. Elise would undoubtedly treat her well and give her freedom as soon as possible. This would be a way for him to express the values he shared with his wife.

Yet the suggestion that Elise knew nothing about their ownership of a slave seems utterly farfetched. Much more likely, Elise knew about it because Wilhelm and she acquired possession of a person as a result of the 1858 Texas law banning freemen. The law required emancipated Negroes either to leave the state or to become slaves. If they decided to become slaves, they had the right to choose their masters. The United States Census of 1860 reported that there were six black freemen in Texas who owned real estate with an average value of $5,133. They and others who enjoyed liberty must have escaped the ban against freemen for a few years. The pressure of the Civil War probably turned the situation around and forced them into compliance.[4]

Elise's silence most likely came about because the person listed as their property had voluntarily chosen to enroll as their slave. In that case, she and Wilhelm would simply have accepted the arrangement; they would not have had to "buy" the individual. In Elise's mind that person would not have been their property—an employee, perhaps, but not a slave. Under such circumstances, she would have had no need to mention the fact in any of her letters.

There are reasons to believe that such an explanation is more than mere speculation. The tax records for the Waerenskjolds' property start in 1851, the year they acquired their second land patent. In no year from 1851 through 1860 is a slave listed as one of their material possessions. During that entire period the persons they employed were free people. Some of them were probably indentured servants—persons who contracted to work for an employer in exchange for payment of their travel to America—brought from Norway, but no slaves.

Elise and Wilhelm could easily have owned slaves during those years. Although Van Zandt County had fewer slaves than nearby counties, several persons listed on the same tax record pages as the Waerenskjolds owned five or more, and Harrison County due east of Van Zandt had one of the largest slave populations in the state. Some of the Waerenskjolds' Norwegian friends, including relatives of Johan Reinert Reiersen, were slave owners.

Furthermore, the taxable value of the person owned by the Waerenskjolds—entered as $150 for 1861 and $100 for 1862—bears no relationship to the real price of slaves. Values varied according to the individual's age, gender, health, and strength, but the average price of slaves in Texas in 1860 was $800. The values of other slaves appearing on the tax register pages with the Waerenskjolds' property are much higher: one at $1,000; two at $1,800 ($900 each); two at $1,500 ($750 each); three at $2,000 ($666 each); seven at $4,000 ($571 each); three at $1,500 ($500 each); three at $1,200 ($400 each); and ten at $3,500 ($350 each). Apparently the nominal value declared by the Waerenskjolds was artificial, put down for simple documentation.[5]

The records show that Elise and Wilhelm owned a slave only in the first two years of the Civil War, in 1861 and 1862. In 1863, 1864, and 1865, while the war was still going on, slavery remained in effect in Texas. Texas was one of the last states to abandon the institution, giving it up only when federal troops entered Galveston on June 19, 1865 (now celebrated as Juneteenth by descendants), two and a half years after Lincoln's Emancipation Proclamation and two months after the Confederate surrender at Appomattox.

The person listed as Elise and Wilhelm's property disappears from the record in 1863. Why? Although Texas had passed a law that no slave owner could voluntarily manumit slaves, when Lincoln issued the Emancipation Proclamation in September of 1862, Elise and Wilhelm may have freed the individual. Even Sam Houston—who had by now gone with the will of the people of his state and was supporting the Confederate war effort—told his slaves they were free soon after Lincoln's proclamation.[6]

Wilhelm's service in Confederate military forces during the war, another seeming anomaly, is easier to explain than the matter of slave ownership: Confederate actions gave the Norwegian Texans little choice but to join the state's armed services. Part of the reason was that early in the war it seemed the South would succeed in breaking up the Union. In the first two years of the war the Confederates won a stunning series of victories, some of them on battlefields close to Washington, D.C., that might have forced the North to accept secession.

Developments in Texas were equally threatening to the Union. After the state joined the Confederacy, the secession convention appointed a Committee of Public Safety to run the war effort. Its first task was to deal with federal troops posted in the state. Major General Edward Twiggs, commander of the U.S. Army forces in Texas, met with the committee's representatives in San Antonio and agreed to evacuate his approximately three thousand troopers from frontier forts. With that Twiggs followed the lead of Robert E. Lee and many other southern military officers. He resigned from the U.S. Army and took a commission in the Confederate forces.

Other successes followed. A Confederate Texan brigade defeated a federal unit at El Paso and went on to invade New Mexico and capture Albuquerque. Federal troops that had occupied Galveston in 1862 were attacked on New Year's Day in 1863 and forced to surrender.

Later in 1863 General Banks, the Union commander in New Orleans, tried to land a four-thousand-man army at Sabine Pass on the Louisiana-Texas border, where the Sabine River flows into the Gulf of Mexico. He was aiming to take Galveston and Houston, and he came in strength with his troop transports escorted by four gunboats. As the flotilla sailed through the narrow gap of Sabine Pass, it came under fire from Confederate field artillery manned by forty-seven men under the command of Lieutenant Dick Dowling, an Irish saloonkeeper and liquor importer from Houston. Without suffering a single loss Dowling's men sank two of the gunboats, captured 315 of the invaders, and drove the flotilla off.

Elise reported that Wilhelm was in the Texas military forces three times during the conflict, a fact confirmed by Confederate military records housed at the Henry B. Simpson History Center at Hill College in Hillsboro, Texas. His first term of service was in the regular army and began on February 8, 1862, more than a month before the Texas legislature passed its general conscription law. Like many other Texas residents, he evidently chose to volunteer in anticipation of the draft.

His decision to enlist may also have been influenced by a widespread public detestation of foreign residents whose loyalty to the Confederacy was in doubt. Early in the war sixty German settlers from the San Antonio area tried to escape to Mexico. Pursued and trapped by a one-hundred-man Confederate detachment, they tried to fight their way out. In the mêlée they killed two of the Confederates and wounded eighteen, but thirty of them were slain. The rest were captured and massacred.[7]

Whatever Wilhelm's reasons for becoming a soldier, his enrollment before the conscription law passed allowed him to join the regular Confederate Army. He signed on for a one-year term in Company E, 11th Regiment, Texas Volunteer Infantry, a unit that followed the democratic practice of electing its officers.

He entered the service at the town of Canton, then as now the government center for Van Zandt County. His company elected him as a second lieutenant, perhaps because his family in Norway was known for its long military tradition. His father, a lieutenant at the coastal fortress at Fredrikshald (now Halden) bordering Sweden, came from a line of aristocratic military officers. He was descended from Jens Wernersen, a successful businessman who started the military tradition in the family (like the Junkers in Prussia) to guarantee his sons' future after the king of Denmark-Norway raised him to the nobility in the early 1700s and renamed him Waerenskjold. (The name meant "shield," according to Elise.)

Wilhelm's activities as a Confederate second lieutenant seem to have been confined to quartermaster functions, as far as the surviving military records show. On April 21 he was reimbursed for buying six pounds of coffee for his company at a cost of $2.90. On May 14 he purchased ten pounds of bacon at $2.10. His pay was $80 a month.

When the conscription law was passed in April of 1862, it applied only to men aged eighteen to thirty-five. Being thirty-nine years old, Wilhelm was overage and under no obligation to finish his enlistment term. He was not reelected to the second lieutenant rank, an event that may have occurred because he resigned or perhaps because his pro-Union and anti-slavery inclinations were becoming known; one suspects the latter, because he was relieved from duty and dropped from the regimental roster on June 23, 1862, by order of Brigadier General McCulloch. In September that year he received a closing disbursement of $132.66, back pay to the time from May 1 to June 20 when he was still in officer's uniform.

After he was discharged his regiment participated in a series of engagements in Arkansas and Louisiana. One of these was at Bayou Teche near St. Martinsville in the Mississippi Delta, a town noted for its statue to Longfellow's poetic heroine Evangeline, standing in the garden of St. Martinsville de Tours Catholic Church. Evangeline was a French Acadian refugee. After being driven out of Nova Scotia by the British in 1755, she made a lifelong search for her beloved fiancé Gabriele. She found him at last lying by Bayou Teche, old and dying. Wilhelm was fortunate to avoid the military engagement at that dreamy place. The war was no romantic adventure.[8]

Later the Texas legislature broadened the age range for conscription to include men aged seventeen to fifty. In November, 1863, Wilhelm was called up for a second term as "W. Van Shaw," an identity he used in place of the unpronounceable Norwegian Waerenskjold (the Van Shaw name has also been adopted by some of his present-day descendants).

During this tour of duty he was a private in Company F, 1st Regiment Cavalry of the Texas State Troops, a local militia. In that unit he was reported as being thrown from his horse. Injured and unable to ride, he was dropped from the company roster. He was enrolled a third time as a private in 1864, but there is no record of his unit or length of service—perhaps by then Confederate record keeping had fallen victim to a wartime clerical manpower shortage.

Wilhelm's intermittent service in the Confederate military forces tells little about the Norwegian participation in the Civil War. Most of his countrymen fought for the Union, their numbers in the northern armies being estimated at more than four thousand soldiers. Many were in the 15th Wisconsin Regiment, which displayed exceptional bravery in a battle with the Confederates at Chickamauga, Tennessee, in September, 1863. Their army commander, General William Rosencrans, was a poor soldier, and the regiment lost half its men. The regimental leader, Brigadier General Hans C.

Heg, was killed soon after being promoted. When Ulysses Grant took command of the Union army in Tennessee, Norwegian soldiers from the North contributed to his victories as he campaigned eastward. Later they joined Sherman's march through Georgia, and at the end of the war some were fighting in Virginia.

As for the Confederate Norwegian Texans, their names are recorded in a book written by Martin Jensen, pastor of the Four Mile Prairie Lutheran Church in the late 1980s. This book lists eighty men, most of whom served west of the Mississippi, generally in Texas. Jensen's great uncle, Ole Foss, was one of those who fought outside the state. Captured at Vicksburg, Mississippi, when Grant won his long siege of the city in July, 1863, he enlisted in the Union Army. After the war Foss went back to Texas, and in his late years he received a United States pension for his service as a Union soldier. The payments were made to him until he died.

Jensen's other great uncles in the Confederate Army came from Clifton in Bosque County rather than from Four Mile Prairie. Two of them fought at the Battle of Gettysburg but deserted after the battle. They managed to slip back home and spent the rest of the war dodging Confederate officers who came searching for them—when the officers left their district, the men's wives hung out the wash as a signal for them to come back from the hills. One of these Gettysburg veterans buried his guns deep in the earth after he returned, caring for nothing else than to forget the brutality of the war.

Norwegians in the Union army knew about their countrymen in the Texas Confederate forces. In February of 1862, the Union major Charles Riis wrote home that he had seen thirty of the Norwegian Texans in Chicago, where they had apparently been taken after being captured in the Mississippi-Tennessee military region. Riis said they all wanted to join the 15th Wisconsin but were unable to do so owing to War Department red tape.

His count of thirty captives seems high. Norwegians in Confederate forces numbered about one hundred men at most, and few of them ever served outside Texas or nearby states. If Major Riis's report were true, nearly a third of them would have been taken prisoner on the Mississippi-Tennessee front very early in the war. All the same, Jensen's account names eight men who were killed or died in the Confederate service, a considerable loss.[9]

At the end of the Civil War Elise reported on how she and her family had fared during the conflict. Her main account was printed in *Kristianssands stiftavis* (Kristiansand County news), published in the city closest to her former hometown of Lillesand. Her story opens with a final blast against slavery—

"I would rather have left Texas a beggar than have had my children fight to preserve slavery." From that declaration she went on to tell how they had "got along far better than one might have expected, though not always as we may have wished."

She said places in the South where the war had been fought had "suffered terribly from our own armies and from the armies of the enemy," adding: "But, God be praised, our part of the country escaped this double visitation, and consequently endured far less." She reported that during the war there was no lack of money, except that it was all in Confederate paper dollars. With inflation, the exchange rate was twenty dollars to a single gold dollar. Everyone had to barter for goods. Her best trade item was wool, the fleece sheared from her 278 sheep.

While Wilhelm was in the army she and her sons ran the ranch. On one occasion he stayed in Bosque County between military enrollments, and she felt compelled to complain that he was over there relaxing with their Norwegian friends, enjoying himself while his family worked.

In Texas, cut off from the northern states, manufactured consumer goods could almost not be had during the war. The prices were ridiculous: a pound of sugar cost ten Confederate dollars, and a yard of cloth ran from fifteen to twenty dollars. She could only get prewar value for her wool, twenty cents a pound, while wheat went for one gold dollar per bushel. Near the end of the war a few products came in from Mexico, but scarcity remained.

The government and the press had lied during the war, she said. It claimed victories that were actually defeats and reported battles that were never fought. No newspaper editor dared print the truth for fear he would be killed. Anyone who tried to escape from conscription was likely to be tortured if caught.

Elise told about a "substitute" law that had been put into effect along with conscription. This allowed a man who had been drafted to pay a fee to have someone not yet conscripted take his place. She reported that the government repealed the law after a time. The substitutes were forced to stay in the army, and the people who had paid fees for them were summarily conscripted.

"There was shameless profiteering on the part of officials from the highest to the lowest," she reported. She and her fellow ranchers had to turn over to the government one-tenth of everything they produced. All kinds of goods were commandeered at one-quarter their value, supposedly for use by the army. If the goods had actually gone to the soldiers it would not have been so bad. One of her friends, a "Mr. B" who had immigrated from Lillesand, had loaned the Confederate government ten thousand dollars. (This may have been the same Mr. B she had addressed long before about sweet potatoes; see chapter 4.) He expected to get practically nothing in return. In considerable understatement she observed: "Many families lost considerably during the war, which is only to be expected."

Elise was concerned, too, with the tragedy that afflicted former slaves in the aftermath of freedom. Some of them were viciously abused, their owners terrorizing them into staying at work and in some cases even murdering them. Others were simply released or just abandoned the plantations where they had worked. Thousands were left with nothing to make a new start, not even clothing for their bodies. Although she feared many would lead worse lives as freemen than they had as slaves, she was happy to report that "practically all the Norwegians have hired Negroes, and among us they are well treated."[10]

Her unemotional tone in describing their experiences suggests that she did not know how narrowly she had escaped two events that would have wrought wartime havoc in Four Mile Prairie. In the spring of 1864 the Union forces from New Orleans came up the Red River on a major campaign to gain control of Shreveport and northeast Texas. Lincoln called for this invasion because the French had used American preoccupation with the Civil War to install the Emperor Maximilian as head of their puppet regime in Mexico. French imperialistic ambitions might lead them into an attack on Texas and introduce a new enemy into the war to preserve the United States.

The federal invasion force was defeated at the Battle of Mansfield downstream of Shreveport. Had Union soldiers won the battle, they would have headed for Dallas, passing through Canton in northern Van Zandt County on the way. The soldiers would likely have foraged southward to the Four Mile Prairie area, looking for cattle, horses, and produce. Because northeast Texas was well known for supplying the Confederates with arms, men, and food rations, the Union force would have burned down the ranches as it had destroyed the plantations around Alexandria on the Red River in Louisiana. Although the Union effort ended in defeat, it succeeded in discouraging the French from further exploits.[11]

The second threat came near the very end of the war, when breakdown of public authority allowed lawless elements to infest northeast Texas. Taking refuge in the state were violent men like Jesse James and the Younger brothers, members of William Quantrill's Confederate raiders at the massacre of the male population of Lawrence, Kansas. One of their hideouts was the family home of Belle Starr, later known as the Bandit Queen.

CHAPTER 8

Quantrill himself rode into Texas with his raider cavalry. He was accepted as a loyal Confederate by the Texan military authorities and assigned to round up cattle rustlers, deserters, and conscription dodgers in northeast Texas, where Four Mile Prairie lay. His operations were murderous and proved so worthless that Confederate troops were called to drive him out of the state. Fortunately the troops succeeded before he could spread his terrorism into Van Zandt County.[12]

Elise may not have known about the danger from invasion or from Quantrill's raiders, but she did record one instance of the violent hatred that had accompanied the war. While writing her report for *Kristianssands stiftavis* she suddenly interrupted herself to say that a group of men were marching three prisoners past her home. The prisoners had been members of the Confederate Home Guard, local enforcers charged with finding deserters and runaway slaves. In May, 1864, they had led a lynch mob against pro-Union men, taking twelve of them captive and hanging three on Whitsunday.

Wilhelm and other Norwegians believed to have pro-Union sentiments had been among the twelve seized by the mob. Reprieved from hanging at the last moment, they were taken to Shreveport and then down to Alexandria in Louisiana, where Wilhelm was drafted for his third term of service in Confederate military forces.

After the war, Union civil authorities arrested the three lynch mob leaders. Although branded the "Whitsunday Gang" and tried as murderers for the hangings, none of them was ever punished. Two were acquitted and the third fled while on bail. Elise remarked with bitter irony: "One of the men was a pastor. What do you think of that? Is it not a noble thing for a minister to be an executioner!"[13]

"An ocean of tears and blood," the distinguished English historian Paul Johnson called the Civil War in his masterful *History of the American People*. This was not to make a judgment. He was describing the war and its hatreds with absolute accuracy.[14]

CHAPTER 9

DEATH

LISE'S MATTER-OF-FACT LETTER reporting their wartime experiences was written on November 18, 1865. Two months later she wrote to her sisters-in-law in Norway: "The news I have for you is very sad. It has pleased the Lord to take from us the dearest thing we possessed on this earth, our most beloved child Thorvald."

The death of her youngest son opened a year of tragedy for Elise, her own time of unremitting blood and tears. Within months of her young son's death her husband Wilhelm was vilely murdered. Her letters reporting these devastating experiences display a surface calm, but underneath her emotions rise—stark, intense, searing her heart.

Thorvald was seven years old when he died. During the summer he and his brother Niels had been ill—cholera and typhus were common sicknesses at the time—but by fall both were fully recovered. With their return to health, the family went about its usual work on the ranch and celebrated a quiet Christmas.

In mid-January 1866 neighbors asked Elise and Wilhelm if they could hold their daughter's wedding at the Waerenskjold home. The neighbors' house was small, and they wanted to invite two hundred wedding guests. The Waerenskjolds willingly agreed, and the nuptials took place on Friday, January 19. The festivities went on for a week with great quantities of rich foods being served.

On the Sunday after the wedding, Elise and her family dined with several of the wedding guests who were staying at their house. After dinner they decided to spend the evening with Danish neighbors who lived a mile and a half away, a short walk for people accustomed to ranch life. On the way over Thorvald ran along beside Elise, "happy and gay as usual."

They visited with the neighbors for a while, and then Elise told the gathering she needed to go home to bring in her sheep. She asked if anyone cared to come along. It was too early, the others said; "only my sweet little Thorvald wanted to go home with Mama." A nightmare followed:

He chatted with me as was his wont, and there was not the slightest indication that anything was wrong with him.

We had taken hardly more than ten steps, however, after his last words, when suddenly, without uttering a sound, he collapsed beside me. When I looked at him I could see that he had the cramps.

I picked him up in my arms and carried him home as fast as I could and sent for Wilhelm and the doctor.

Thorvald was ill three days, and I am afraid he suffered a great deal. On the third day he spoke a little, but it was very difficult for him to pronounce the words distinctly.

I was so unspeakably happy when he began to talk on Wednesday morning, for I began then to hope that God might still let me keep my dear child.

But no, it was not to be. About noon he began to breathe more heavily, and around four o'clock he died. He was buried on Friday of that week.

A few months later when writing to Thomine Dannevig she laid bare her deepest feelings: "Yes, little did I think the Friday before when the house was filled with gay wedding guests, that the next Friday I should lose the dearest treasure I had on earth. My little Thorvald was such a sweet, lovable boy, and all who knew him loved him. I cannot really enjoy anything, and my only desire is to be with my Thorvald once more."

As if Thorvald sensed his oncoming death, on the night before he collapsed he asked Elise if he "didn't think it would be too bad if he died now." Not imagining that such a dreadful thing could possibly happen, she asked him why. "Oh," he replied. "If I died I would always keep this bad breath which I have just now."

He asked many other things, she said—"about resurrection and the next life . . . much more than I was able to explain to him." "Now my little angel knows all that he wished to know—and all that is still a mystery to us."

It is not easy to turn from Elise's account to a medical explanation of Thorvald's death, but doing so helps us understand his pain and her agony. In her first letter she had looked back to Thorvald's July illness for an explanation: "I believe that from that time on the disease which finally caused his death was in his body, although he apparently had recovered." In the second she added, "Perhaps the abundance of cakes and fresh meat that were provided for . . . (the wedding) . . . was harmful to Thorvald."[1]

To appraise his death in terms of present-day medical knowledge, Dr. Bernard Patten examined these statements and Elise's other accounts of Thorvald's collapse and subsequent decline. Patten had recently retired as vice chairman of the Department of Neurology and chief of the Neuromuscular Disease Division at Baylor College of Medicine in Houston. In his judgment Elise was wrong in her first surmise: Thorvald's summer sickness did not linger on to cause his death. Heavy meals during the wedding celebrations, however, may have been a contributing factor. The problem, said Patten,

> was the bad teeth and poor oral hygiene. From the periodontal infection the bacteria seeded the blood and probably ended up on his aortic valve causing an infection known as subacute bacterial endocarditis (SBE). The bacteria grow there a while and break off into the main arterial stream seeding the rest of the body with infective foci of bacteria.
>
> When a part breaks off and impacts on the artery to the speech center in the left hemisphere (Broca's area) the child would experience a stroke with loss of ability to speak. When the embolism moves downstream, as usually happens, a partial recovery occurs because blood flow is now restored to the brain's speech center. That is why . . . [Thorvald] . . . appeared to get better. The time course of the event and the time course of his recovery are classical for a cerebral embolism from an infected aortic valve.
>
> After that an infected embolism probably ended up in the artery to the gut causing an infarction and the belly pain, perforation of the gut, peritonitis and death.
>
> The more I think about it the more I am sure that SBE was the cause of the problem. Unfortunately, SBE was a fatal disease in those days and nothing they could have done would have saved the [boy]. Now we would treat with high doses of intravenous antibiotics, and if the aortic value was significantly damaged, we would have replaced it.

CHAPTER 9

Sadly, during the summer Thorvald may have been given mercury-based calomel. Calomel was a common treatment for illness at the time. It is now known to loosen teeth.[2]

On Wednesday morning when Elise's hopes rose for Thorvald's recovery, he gave "Mama a last kiss." He died, as she said, in the afternoon.

"I miss him so terribly. Yet I am calm and composed in my grief." Being fifty-one years old, she believed she would not have long to wait to join him. When she was very young she had felt she would be happy to die anytime God called her, but since the birth of her children she had "wanted to live for them." "Now that one of the strongest ties that bound me to life here on earth has been severed, I feel so much more drawn to heaven."

This was not resignation, nor was it stoic endurance. Elise was no fatalist. Her vision of God was affirmative. In her Confession of Faith she had seen God as the author of all creation and being. He did not enact senseless events. Her thoughts linked to Job's faith in the Bible—humans may not be able to fathom why things happen as they do, but events that cause inexplicable and crushing pain are part of a larger eternity that God is leading toward good.

Elise revealed this faith in the letter she wrote her sisters-in-law: "Thorvald was a blessing to me as long as he was alive, and now I hope that in the loving wisdom of God his going, too, may prove a blessing for me and mine." His death was a call from God, she said, "a forceful reminder to us to be prepared for death and judgment, and I hope we shall never forget it. The life we live here is not a very spiritual one. We think far too much of earthly things and lack all concrete reminders of the existence of God's heavenly kingdom."

She was reminded once more how sad it was to be without a pastor, a man who had been ordained to perform funeral services and other divine rites according to proper formal procedure. Her two surviving boys, Otto and Niels, were nearly old enough to be confirmed. There was no ordained man present to carry out the service, nor was one likely to come soon.[3]

Little Thorvald was laid to rest in the patch of land that had been hallowed as a cemetery behind the Four Mile Prairie log cabin church. His grave is still there to be seen today, located near the middle of the cemetery where a great oak once stood. If you walk to view his headstone in summer, the dry prairie hay crackles underfoot and grasshoppers burst up for short flights, their rasping wings beating in the hot, sun-drenched air.

With the passage of the years since 1866, Thorvald's headstone might have become gray and worn, but it has been kept blanched clean and bears only a few spotted growths of lichen. The lettering reads:

THORVALD AUGUST WARENSKJOLD
SON OF WILHELM AND ELISE WARENSKJOLD
BORN OCT 4 1858
DIED JAN 24 1866

The footstone marking the end of his short resting place bears his initials, T. A. W.[4]

Elise was subjected to her second incredible loss under circumstances that almost defy belief. During the painful weeks that followed Thorvald's death, she and Wilhelm were called upon to perform an act of outstanding charity. It was a deed of compassion willingly done, but it led to ruination—Wilhelm's murder.

His death occurred on November 17, 1866. Elise's account of it appeared in Norway on February 14, 1867, in the newspaper *Aftenbladet* (Afternoon post), a political and literary journal published in Christiania. Being unfamiliar with her handwriting, the newspaper editor transcribed the name of the murderer, Dickerson, as "Dickson," and rendered "Shreveport" as "Shrewsport."

The tragedy opened when neighbors—people Elise called "a very respectable Norwegian family who took in travelers"—came to her for help. They had taken a young woman, Mary Reagan, into their home at the request of her aunt. Mary came from a good family, the aunt had told them, but her parents had died when she was a child. She had been living at the aunt's home out on a country ranch, but now she was planning to move on to other relatives in Tennessee. She needed temporary housing in town until she could find and join someone who would be making a wagon journey east.

The Norwegian family agreed to the aunt's request, but when Mary arrived at their home she came with a baby. Mary was white. The child was of mixed race; the father was black. The aunt had told the Norwegian family nothing about this.

According to Elise, Mary's brothers and sisters had "disowned her entirely when they discovered her condition." Although the aunt had accepted her and the baby without reservation, trouble cropped up in her home. This was with Dickerson, the aunt's husband, the "Dickson" referred to in the *Aftenbladet* article. Elise described Dickerson as a sometime Methodist preacher.

Dickerson had fixed his attentions on Mary. She was vulnerable, staying in his home helpless and dependent, with a mixed race child, without a future. Dickerson used her weaknesses to propose an indecent alliance. If she would flee with him to another state and live with him as his wife, he promised to desert her aunt and their daughter. The aunt discovered this "'fine' plan"—Elise's words—and decided she must get Mary out of her house.

Unwilling to risk refusal from the Norwegian family whom she asked to take Mary in, she told them neither about the baby nor about Dickerson's shameless proposal to Mary. Instead, she fabricated the story about Mary's imminent departure to go and live with relatives in Tennessee. When Mary came to the Norwegian family's house with the child, they realized at once that she had too little money to pay for travel. Besides that, her clothing for both herself and her baby was inadequate.

The Norwegian family told Elise they were turning to her because their house was small and they could no longer accommodate Mary and her baby. Elise accepted their statement, thinking they were too humane to "put her out on the street." She and Wilhelm were known for their kindness, and the Norwegian family assumed the Waerenskjolds would dismiss any scruples they might have about the child's paternity and birth outside wedlock. They would be willing to help.

Elise explained how Wilhelm joined in deciding to take Mary and the baby into their home: "I consented, providing my husband would allow it. He was usually always willing to be of assistance, when and where he was able. But this time he was reluctant to do so since he knew that Americans considered such a lapse by a female a greater offense than any other, while they didn't regard it a sin or a shame when white men had children with black women, which was very common. However, when the old and respected (Norwegian) man in whose home she was staying came over and described the unhappy situation to Waerenskjold, he permitted her to come here."

Soon after Mary and the baby arrived at her home Elise discovered Dickerson lurking outside. She asked him to come in—the only time she ever spoke to him—believing that as Mary's uncle, he wished her well. Dickerson expressed gratitude that they were allowing Mary to stay with them, and he asked if they would not mind keeping her until spring when her departure could be arranged.

Elise agreed, but from then on Dickerson came skulking around the house "like a thief." At first Elise thought little about it, but then Mary disclosed what had happened at her aunt's home. Dickerson had tried to injure her, she said. He had tried to seduce her. She had shunned his heated advances. Elise commented, "She would rather die than commit this sin."

To support her assertion about Dickerson's unwanted advances, Mary showed Elise letters he had written to her. They "clearly disclosed his impure purposes," Elise wrote in *Aftenbladet*. He had even taken the precaution of forging a signature, but it was still obvious that the letters came from him. Not only was he harassing young Mary, but in one letter he made an outright threat to bend her to his lustful will. He told her that if she did not run off with him, "May the deepest Hell become my highest Heaven if I do not take revenge."

After seeing the letters Elise apparently told Dickerson to stay away from her house. In return he tried to "infuriate" their American neighbors against her and Wilhelm, claiming they had accepted Mary into their home so that they could induce Negroes to work for them. He made other accusations that Elise did not report. They may have been too unseemly to record.

Wilhelm and Elise disagreed about how to respond to Dickerson's calumnies. She was not greatly concerned about them herself because she knew she and Wilhelm were well respected in the community. Wilhelm was an elected justice of the peace—people would listen to him and ignore Dickerson.

Wilhelm thought otherwise. He wanted Dickerson to retract his accusations openly. "Being informed," she said in the account published in *Aftenbladet*, "he could not tacitly endure such undeserved insults, and he had one of his friends go with him to Dickson, (whereupon) he requested that Dickson withdraw what he had said about us. At which Dickson swore that he would rather see Waerenskjold in Hell before doing that. My husband told him that he knew the motive behind his course of action and that he was in possession of his letters."

Looking back on the events that followed, Elise realized that after this confrontation Dickerson decided to kill Wilhelm. From that time on, she wrote, Dickerson "always went armed with a six-barreled pistol and a large butcher knife. I did not know (it) until afterwards."

In a few months Mary Reagan went on her way and Elise and Wilhelm assumed that the trouble had passed. Not so. Dickerson, apparently incensed that Mary had gotten away, began following Wilhelm around, trying to find a moment where he could "carry out his bloody intention." Elise gave an account of Wilhelm's murder:

They . . . met at Reiersen's country store, but since there were many people around Dickson kept quiet there. But when my husband went to the post office he followed, and when he found only the postmaster and a young man there, both unarmed, he found that his opportune moment had arrived.

He began with insults, to which my husband answered calmly: that he could not prove what he had said about him. It appears my husband believed Dickson was not evil enough to use a weapon against an unarmed man, but unfortunately he was mistaken.

Just as Waerenskjold turned toward Dickson, Dickson took the opportunity to, from behind, thrust his knife under the left arm straight to the heart, so that he fell dead without uttering a word. The murderer ran to his horse and had disappeared before anyone could chase him, and so far there has been no success in finding his tracks.[5]

James Bowlden, the postmaster, witnessed the horrible event at his store in Prairicville. He said Wilhelm had declared he was not afraid of Dickerson. A grave mistake. Wilhelm was unarmed and should have remembered the advice given to Lord Fafnir, a figure in ancient Viking religious mythology: "Listen, Lord Fafnir, and listen carefully! Three angry words are three too many if spoken to a bad man; and the better man often comes off worse when the bad man's sword starts talking."

Bowlden reported that Wilhelm had staggered out through the front door and fallen down the post office steps. He pitched forward and lay on his face, his dark blood pooling in the dirt. The physician who examined his corpse reported that the knife had sliced through the muscle of his left arm. It had struck Wilhelm between the fifth and sixth ribs. The knife blade had been driven right to his heart.[6]

Elise said no one chased Dickerson, but men did mount up and ride after him. Nevertheless he made good his escape out of Prairieville and fled to Arkansas, where he was eventually found and returned to Texas for trial (see chapter 11).

Otto, now fifteen, was working at the sawmill in Brownsboro at the time of Wilhelm's murder. Elise immediately sent for him. When he reached Four Mile Prairie they held the funeral. Wilhelm's body would lie in the earth next to Thorvald's.

It was barely a year since the end of the Civil War, and now Elise had lost

Portrait of Wilhelm.
Photo by Charles H. Russell, courtesy of William Van Shaw, Dallas.

her husband as well as her beloved youngest son. One might suppose her personal tragedy following the grim years of war would crush her religious faith, but it did not. Her words in *Aftenbladet* show that her faith never faltered. She was sustained by it: "On Monday Nov. 19 we placed my husband's earthly remains to rest beside those of our little Thorvald, and there, when it is God's will, I also wish to rest when the Lord calls me. I had woven a wreath of the flowers from Thorvald's grave to place on the coffin, and many women among the numerous in the funeral procession brought wreaths and bouquets."

She wrote of hymns being sung and a talk being given by an old school teacher. Then she continued: "This event is so sorrowful for me and my poor children that it is a great consolation to know that he died innocent, grieved by many, respected and admired by all who knew him, not only our countrymen but also Americans."[7]

Wilhelm lies alongside his son. His grave marker has been blanched clean like Thorvald's. The inscription on his headstone reads:

WILHELM WARENSKJOLD
BORN FREDERIKSHOLD NORWAY
AUGUST 24 1823
NOVEMBER 17 1866

Two months after Wilhelm's funeral Elise wrote a letter to Commodore Thorvald Dannevig, Thomine Dannevig's son, for whom she and Wilhelm had named their youngest boy. In that letter she reported that her close friend and mentor Johan Reinert Reiersen had died of a fever in 1864. Cleng Peerson had died the following year.

Elise was the last of the three early Norwegian publicists for Texas. The state had become her world, but now she was about to enter a void. To Thomine Dannevig she had written, "I cannot really enjoy anything." Could she ever again speak warm words about her adopted home?[8]

Chapter 10

Escape from Sorrow

I N TIME THE DEEP SHADES of mourning would disappear from Elise's world, but now they surrounded her constantly. It was as if she were back in the Nacogdoches Wold struggling through the dark forest without her companions and capable guide. No new endeavor beckoned, no pioneer country lay ahead waiting to be conquered.

Nothing could lighten her way. Her matter-of-fact attitude, so plain in her report on the Civil War, was gone. In its place came depressing memories of hard times. She reported that thirty of the cattle she and Wilhelm had raised so diligently died in the first year of the War. Forty-seven starved the following year, and then in the most recent winter twenty cows about to deliver calves were lost before birthing. There was a dearth of forage and half her sheep perished.

People had no cash to pay their debts. She and Wilhelm had sold eighty-two wethers (castrated rams) for three dollars each during the summer before his death, but months later she still had not been able to collect a cent. For fifteen oxen she got a partial payment of twenty-five dollars. The going price was twenty dollars per head, so she was $335 short.[1]

Property was worth one-third to half of what it had been worth before the war. For example, old Erick Bache, a neighbor, had died and left his widow "well provided for," but low prices were keeping her from selling her land and returning to Norway. Elise's situation was equally bad. She thought about moving away to some other place, but that was impossible. Old friends were moving to Bosque County, and no one could afford to buy her property in the chaos of Reconstruction. As with the old saying, she was land poor.

Only God knows, she thought, what other deaths might come to her family; she worried about her own. When pregnant with Thorvald at age forty-four she had wondered how Wilhelm would fare if she died in childbirth. Back then she worried because it was "absolutely against the custom of this country for a white girl to keep house for a widower—and as for a stepmother, well, they are seldom good."

Her sons Otto and Niels, now aged sixteen and fourteen, were not old enough for legal or personal independence. In Norway she knew there would have been close friends and relatives who would gladly have taken care of her boys. In Texas she felt she was alone in a foreign land, without "assurance that anyone would assume the responsibility for providing a Christian training for my children or of safeguarding their inheritance."[2]

Thomine Dannevig's son Thorvald had sent her some photographs from Norway. He was just a boy when she left in 1847. When he reached adulthood he obtained an officer's post in the navy. Now he was prominent, a commodore, and she turned to him for solace. Writing to thank him for the photographs, she asked if he would send pictures of Lillesand harbor and of the Dybvaag parsonage where she was born. She said she had been only eight years old when her father moved away from Dybvaag, but she remembered "every detail" of the place better than their fine homes in Lillesand and Holt. Her request was hesitant: "Is it not possible . . . to get pictures of landscapes, or is the price prohibitive?"

She closed her letter to him with dreadful news. An Indian band had raided the Bosque Colony and carried off a Norwegian boy. She did not mention the boy's name, but he was Ole Nystel, a fourteen-year-old youngster who was helping his neighbor, Carl Quaestad, cut cedar poles at a copse several miles from home when the Indians attacked. Nystel was shot through the right thigh with an arrow and taken, but Quaestad, knowing full well that an Indian raiding party would immediately kill any full-grown male, made a run for it and got away.

Elise's own lost son was in her mind as she wrote to the commodore about Nystel's capture: "It was hard to bury little Thorvald, but it would be much harder to know that he was among wild, heathen people who would torture him every day and bring him up as a pagan."[3]

Unexpected natural hardships added to her grief. In the fall of 1868 she wrote to her friend Kaja (Kaya) Poppe in Lillesand about an invasion of locusts in Four Mile Prairie: "I had never realized grasshoppers could fly so high. The air was filled with them as far as one could see." Remembering the story of the biblical invasion of locusts before Moses led the Israelites out of Egypt, she called the misfortune an "Egyptian plague." She lost a planting of sprouted wheat, fifteen bushels of seed that had cost fifty dollars—gone. The locusts destroyed the entire crop and consumed everything else that was green.[4]

Drought prevented her from planting more wheat for two months, but just before Christmas she was able to sow again. After the wheat sprouted in the spring the locusts returned and devoured her crop a second time. The crackling dry grass, the only thing left by the monstrous swarm, brought prairie wildfires, "causing great trouble."

During these years Elise had her photograph taken wearing a Victorian mourning dress. The dignified portrait, probably made in Tyler, shows her wearing a delicate bonnet partially covering her hair. Cloth "widow's weeds" stitched to the veil frame her face. They hang in clusters down to her shoulders. She is wearing the second stage bereavement costume. According to Victorian custom, during the first stage she would have worn a lace veil pinned to her hair and long enough to hang to the small of her back. When out in public, she would have drawn the veil over her face.

Some ten years before this photograph was taken, she and Wilhelm had the daguerreotypes made of themselves and Otto and Niels (see chapter 7). Those were days of contentment not long before Thorvald was born. In that picture she wore a millinery headpiece, festively decorated with white bows and a white ribbon that tied under her chin. In the new portrait, the entire coif is black—veil, weeds, and ribbon.

The mourning dress she wears is stiff and formal. The bodice closes with small rounded buttons running down the front. The black cloth, presumably a plain weave silk taffeta, has a tight, shiny finish. The sleeves, full and puffed out from shoulder to wrist, end in taut cuffs. The narrow black belt that cinches her waist shapes the top of her skirt into crisp pleats. The skirt, bouffant style, spreads over her petticoats. Her hands are held in her lap with the fingers lightly closed. They look surprisingly strong, rugged reminders of the hard work she did on her ranch.

Handkerchiefs trimmed with a black border were carried with Victorian mourning dresses. Elise holds a handkerchief in her right hand, and though white it conforms to the proper fashion. In the earlier portrait she was wearing a collar of hand-tatted lace. In this one her collar is plain white, undecorated. Previously her face gave the hint of a smile. In this second portrait nothing relieves her somber expression. Although her eyes are not downcast, her look is serious to the point of being severe. It suggests austere and controlled sadness.[5]

In spite of these desolate years of mourning, moments of lightness did

Elise in widow's weeds, ca. 1870.
Courtesy of Wisconsin Historical Society.

Escape from Sorrow

occasionally penetrate her prevailing gloom. Elise and her community had been trying to attract a permanent pastor for fifteen years, and in her 1866 letter to Thomine Dannevig reporting young Thorvald's death, she was able to mention some success in efforts to raise a subscription of three hundred dollars to bring a man from the northern plains states. Then in 1868 she wrote to her friend Madam Staack in Clifton about their continuing effort, telling how she gave a dinner at her home where the guests came expecting to make pledges for a pastor's salary. In spite of her success in attracting guests, Elise complained that all the married women came but "without a single cake or pie."

In that same letter she wrote about attending a lively party in Prairieville. The guests all wore different costumes, and to her surprise her son Otto turned up in knee breeches, a cotton blouse, and an Indian cap, looking so strange that she almost did not recognize him. There was dancing, she said—"I have not seen so many people together in many years." She went on to mention three other parties, adding, "You will see from this that we can have some merriment in Four Mile."

She reported, too, that a particularly encouraging moment had come when she was able to borrow money from a friend in Norway. The loan was to pay off debts she had run up while restoring her herds and crops. Her letter to Kaja Poppe had told how she was saving money by getting along without a maid, and how two Negro women had helped her with milking her cows during the summer when "milking was heaviest." Because of this she was able to put aside fifty dollars' worth of butter for sale.

She told Kaja that she was leading a leisurely life because she was renting part of her cropland to Negro sharecroppers who conducted themselves "much better . . . than the white Americans." The arrangement may not have worked out well in the long run; she later commented that "many of the freed Negroes are lazy and do not care to exert themselves more than necessary to provide 'plenty to eat,' and that is easily done in Texas." However, as she was generally sympathetic toward former slaves, this remark may merely have been a fleeting judgment reflecting difficulties during the first years of emancipation. Before long she was writing that her fruit trees were bearing well, and that "many people, black and white, acquaintances and strangers, come for plums."

Finally, in June of 1869, she confessed to the sadness she had experienced during the past three years. In a letter to Wilhelm's sister Emilie Syvertsen in Denmark, she mentioned poems Wilhelm had written after the death of their Thorvald. Then she added: "I have never felt quite happy since

CHAPTER 10

—132—

the deaths of Thorvald and Wilhelm and have worn mourning ever since they died."

This frank admission seems to have marked a turning point for Elise. She went on to relate far more pleasant news than usual, beginning by telling Emilie that at last a Norwegian pastor was due to arrive. He was Ole Estrem, coming from Illinois to settle in Bosque County. He would ride circuit to Four Mile Prairie, and Otto and Niels could be confirmed—"my wish for a long time."

There was good news on her ranch. "Plums and blackberries have been ripe for several weeks—early, is it not?" Emilie could appreciate this because nearly a whole month would pass before fruit would ripen at her home in Denmark. Elise's field crops were doing well, too. She had taken in seven acres of wheat and six of rye, and she had twenty-two more acres of cotton and fourteen of corn growing nicely. Otto, just turned eighteen, had begun his first independent project. He had sown eight acres of cotton to harvest and market on his own.

"Hogs pay the mortgage," so it used to be said. Elise could only guess how many she owned—somewhere "between two and three hundred." The previous winter she had earned three hundred dollars by selling slabs of bacon along with some of her hog herd. There had been buyers, too, for her oxen and wethers, and her turkeys had brought in twenty-five dollars. Collecting the money was "an annoying affair," but now that "I have paid off my debt, we manage fairly well." Things were looking up.[6]

Then quite unexpectedly, just days after she had written to Emilie, she received an extraordinary request. *Billed-magazin* (Picture magazine), the Norwegian-language weekly published in Madison, Wisconsin, asked her to write the story of Norwegian settlement in Texas.

It was an exhilarating call. Responding to it would interrupt her ranch activities, and writing would be difficult—the sweltering July heat of Texas would make letter paper stick to her perspiring wrists. Besides, *Billed-magazin* probably expected her to do the job free, gratis, or for a mere token payment. All the same, the opportunity to break into print again was overwhelming. She took it up at once.

She immediately contacted her old friend Carl Quaestad, the man who had escaped capture when the Indians took Ole Nystel in Bosque County. Quaestad was a former neighbor, a member of one of the thirty-four Norwegian families that had lived in Four Mile Prairie at one time. In the early 1850s he had moved away to establish a new homestead on the rich blackland of Clifton. As Elise had remained in Four Mile Prairie—hers was one of seventeen Norwegian families still there—she needed someone to give her detailed information about the Bosque settlement. Quaestad was known for his obliging spirit; she could look to him to fill in the gap.

Her letter to him was polite to the point of fawning: "Excuse me for taking the liberty of sending you these lines. . . . I . . permit myself to ask you, dear Mr. Quaestad, to be kind enough to send me all available data about Bosque: when it was first settled and by whom; who arrived later and from where; its present population; the physical nature of the area and its products; how much can be raised per acre; in short, anything that may be of interest."

All available data! Eight subjects by count of her list, plus "anything that may be of interest." Quaestad would need strong motivation to comply with her request. She pressed him: "I assume you agree with me that it would be to our own interest as well as to that of our country and our many poor countrymen if a part of the migration from the Scandinavian countries could be directed toward Texas. I therefore hope you will be good enough to contribute whatever you can toward this end."[7]

This combination of self-interest and altruism was certainly a strong appeal, but it seems that Quaestad did not respond to Elise's request. Instead, he must have told her he intended to write his own account, because Elise said in her article that one of the oldest settlers at Clifton in Bosque County had "promised to write a separate account of it." She was doomed to disappointment; more than twenty years later she was still urging Quaestad to get the job done. Out of deference to him, however, she gave Bosque and Clifton no more than a couple of sentences in her 1869 report.[8]

Elise may have regretted bypassing the Bosque County settlement, but the omission was actually a blessing. It left her free to concentrate on the vision of democracy and a new life that had brought her to Texas. She could tell about those deep impulses as well as what had become of the settlers who came in those first years.

Elise's easy reference to "our own interest" and "those of our country and our many poor countrymen" was far more subtle than it seems at first glance. These were essentially philosophic ideas, and she put them into her letter to Quaestad as if they were simple, easily understood assumptions, commonly held with full awareness by most of her countrymen. In fact, Quaestad and most of Elise's fellow emigrants may scarcely have acknowledged such reasons for their leaving Norway. Their motives were highly practical and down to earth: they hoped to escape poverty, get land, and make a living for themselves and their families. All the same, the causes Elise considered important were vital impulses that gave life to the emigration movement.

The story of these causes becomes clear when Elise's *Billed-magazin* articles are put together with an essay on Reiersen written by the American historian Frank Nelson. Together these two accounts show how the settlement in Texas rested on aspirations to improve the human condition. Nelson related the facts of Reiersen's life and emigration, showing how he discovered and developed his ideas and how his commitment to ideals eventually failed. Elise showed how Reiersen's ideas became part of her own motivation, how she moved because of them, and how, in contrast to his loss of idealism, she remained committed to the good of her fellow beings.

Her *Billed-magazin* article ran to more than five thousand words, long enough to appear in three consecutive issues from February 19 to March 5, 1870. She opened by reporting that in the early 1840s Reiersen had attracted the attention of several persons in the district of Kristiansand who "had been giving special attention to the emigration problem." Elise had been one of them, but in her usual style for formal writing she did not mention herself.[9]

Frank Nelson's story of Reiersen's life begins with his own personal experiences at the beginning of World War II when he was a student in Norway. A descendant of Norwegian immigrants himself, Nelson was studying in Norway when the German army overran the country in 1940. He was trapped and jailed by the Gestapo but was exchanged when the United States entered the war.

During his months of confinement he learned of the deep courage and idealism of the Norwegian partisans fighting the invaders. Impressed by this show of national resolve, he returned to Norway after the war, newly married to his wife Jeanette, and with her assistance started a research project. Considering the patriotism he had witnessed, what could have motivated three-quarters of a million Norwegians to emigrate to America?

He never got a solid answer to his question, but because Reiersen seemed to offer a promising lead, Nelson studied him in depth. He discovered the Reiersen document collection in the University of Oslo archives. Along with the guidebook *Pathfinder for Norwegian Emigrants to the United North American States and Texas,* the collection contained copies of Reiersen's newspaper *Christianssandsposten* and a curiously venomous set of statements about him that appeared in the then unpublished memoirs of his one-time friend Knud Knudsen. Reiersen had written in the *Pathfinder* guidebook that he could not "hope to escape the merciless criticism of opponents." Knudsen's memoirs in all their asperity certainly fulfill that prophesy, but they provided Nelson with a rich mine of information.[10]

The trouble with Reiersen was that he was a misfit, a man filled with a contentious spirit from an early age. Bright and studious, he passed the rigorous *artium* exams for admission to the University of Christiania (today the University of Oslo). Typical of European institutions of higher learning at the time, the university was home to blue-blooded scions of the upper classes. Reiersen's father Ole belonged to a low-status occupation; he was a mere *klokker*—a church sexton and local schoolmaster. Young Reiersen lacked the cachet of wealth and aristocratic family ties needed to fit into the typical university student's world.

According to Nelson he got into a scrape soon after he arrived at the university. A fellow student had a money order waiting for him at the post office. Reiersen heard about it, made a rash joke of it, rushed ahead to claim it, and signed for it with the student's name. The exploit was a youthful jape, but it caused a furor. Reiersen had to flee to mainland Europe to escape the legal consequences.

He spent several years in Europe variously employed as a tutor, absorbing the growing revolutionary sentiments of the time, and learning the elements of the newspaper business by writing for short-lived political sheets. He returned to Norway and because of his obvious experience in publishing quickly raised the capital to begin *Christianssandsposten*. From its first issue in 1839 he devoted its columns to progressive causes, advocating freedom of the press and religion, reform of poor laws, rights for women, public education, and free enterprise for business and industry. Some of his more inflammatory articles got him fined by government authorities, but the newspaper rapidly became recognized as the voice of reform in Norway. Even the editor of the leading conservative newspaper grudgingly acknowledged that he was one of the best writers in the country.

The newspaper brought him wealth and comfort, but his outrage remained. The oppression and injustice he saw in his homeland still rankled. No matter how much success he or anyone attained, no man could rise above his original social standing. A designated class of royal officials surrounded by impenetrably rigid barriers ruled the country. Wealth and achievement were not enough to break into it. You had to be born into this upper stratum.

While Reiersen was living chilled by his personal discontent, his fellow countrymen were suffering acute material privation. Potato rot had for several years caused major destruction of the common people's food supply staple. Primogeniture, the practice of granting inheritance of land and property only to firstborn sons, relegated younger family members to poverty. Farm owners were burdened by debt, interest, and taxes while the elite governing class got preferential treatment in taxation and even in military service.

Poverty was everywhere and people were becoming desperate. By the 1840s they were beginning to leave the country in droves, and Reiersen filled the columns of *Christianssandsposten* with debate about emigration and letters sent home from America. Departure from Norway was becoming a movement with a momentum of its own.[11]

During Reiersen's years abroad and emergence as a newspaperman championing progressive causes, Elise was building her personal sense of independence. She may have been the person who brought him to the attention of her group of social thinkers in the Lillesand district, but in any case she related in her *Billed-magazin* article that the members learned of Reiersen's planned exploratory visit to the United States. Recognizing that his journey might produce findings useful to the poor in Norway, the group subscribed three hundred Norwegian *speciedaler* (gold coin currency probably worth some nine thousand dollars today) toward his travel expenses. In return Reiersen agreed to write a detailed report on what he found; the *Pathfinder* was the result.

Elise described Reiersen's trip to America in her *Billed-magazin* article. He went first to the northern plains states to tour the existing Norwegian colonies. While there he met and interviewed leaders of the emigrant communities, among them Gustaf Unonius, a Lutheran pastor from Sweden (Norway was part of the Swedish kingdom at the time), and Hans Gasmann, a prominent man and former member of the Norwegian parliament who had emigrated because he feared his children would not be able to earn a living in their homeland.[12]

Nelson's essay supports Elise's account and adds that Reiersen observed much failure, sickness, and death among the settlers in the northern plains. These troubles, he believed, were caused by inadequate planning and the settlers' unwillingness to accept the leadership of persons who knew most about pioneer conditions in America. He left the northern states firmly convinced of the importance of "self-interest," namely that Norwegians should establish orderly colonies and seek to promote themselves as a group rather than as separate individuals.

He went south through Illinois, Missouri, and Louisiana, intending to sail back to Norway from New Orleans. In New Orleans he met the consul for the still independent Republic of Texas (presumably William Bryan, the republic's representative in New Orleans at the time), who suggested that he look things over in Texas. Reiersen accepted this proposal, and instead of returning immediately to Norway he traveled up the Mississippi and Red River, over to San Augustine and Nacogdoches, and on to Austin.

In Washington-on-the-Brazos he had a personal interview with President Sam Houston. Eager to bring in settlers to build up the republic, Houston encouraged him to immigrate and form a Norwegian colony. From there Reiersen made a long swing southeast through established towns—Bastrop, Rutersville, and the like—down to Houston and Galveston. By the time he reached the port at Galveston he had seen most of the settled countryside.[13]

He returned to Norway in 1844 captivated by the spreading Texas prairies, the agreeable people, and the rich land. When he duly wrote his *Pathfinder* guidebook, he included a special chapter praising Texas, hoping to induce a large number of emigrants to follow him and establish a colony in the soon-to-be state.

For a time Reiersen's guidebook was the most valuable emigration manual in Norway, but it failed to turn the flood of Norwegians to Texas. It was not reprinted after the first run sold out, and Reiersen himself departed, leaving *Norge og Amerika* under Elise's control to advocate emigration to Texas as a solution to poor people's problems.[14]

Elise's *Billed-magazin* articles took up the story from June of 1845, the month and year Reiersen arrived in Texas; the young republic was formally annexed by the United States in December of that year. Using letters he sent home to friends soon after his arrival, she related that he found people free of the overpowering exclusiveness characteristic of upper social circles in his homeland. In Nacogdoches, she said, he attended a ball at the town courthouse. Prominent figures were there, among them General Thomas Jefferson Rusk, a hero of the Battle of San Jacinto, secretary of war during the Texas war of independence, and about to be appointed a United States senator. Also present was Nicholas Adolphus Sterne, an early Nacogdoches resident, friend of Sam Houston's, and a financier of the Texas war of independence.

Elise quoted Reiersen's words about his introductions: "'General Rusk, Mr. Reiersen from Norway; Colonel Tom, Mr. Reiersen; Judge Sterne, Mr. Reiersen; Dr. Louis, Mr. Reiersen; Captain Walding, Mr. Reiersen'—and thus the presentation of generals, colonels, judges, and doctors proceeded until the whole party had made the acquaintance of 'Mr. Reiersen from Norway.'"

Reiersen knew these were some of the most prominent men in Texas. Elise's quoting of his comment on the occasion clearly reveals how meeting them spurred the bitterness he felt over the haughty disdain with which he had been treated back home: "I looked around in amazement at this company of high ranking persons dressed in light, varied summer attire, but could not discover the least trace of that superciliousness that usually characterizes our upper classes and betrays itself even in their poorly disguised condescension. Here everything was straightforward, free, and easy," Reiersen had written.[15]

From telling about Reiersen's initial impressions Elise turned to his failure to establish a large colony in Texas. Some of the first settlers who came with him to New Orleans went to Missouri and the northern plains states rather than to Texas. When some who followed him to Brownsboro took sick and died, he was blamed even though he had warned them against settling in pestilential bottomland. From these experiences he learned that his countrymen were too obdurate and independent to fit in with his grand colonization theory. His scheme for planned settlement was obviously not going to work.

Elise hinted that Reiersen was disappointed at this development, but Nelson's account is explicit—Reiersen was disillusioned by the failure of his theories. He gave up "his active crusade for organized immigration" even though he continued "to welcome those Norwegians who found their way to Texas in a small but steady stream." Not only that, but his "zeal for public causes . . . ebbed away," so much so that he turned a blind eye to the injustice of slavery in Texas. Nelson cited Elise to confirm his judgment about Reiersen's apostasy from ideals of human rights—"the silence of Mrs. Waerenskjold, who loathed slavery, is eloquent on this point."[16]

Nelson, writing late in the 1970s when liberal causes still very much occupied the American public mind, seems not to have understood that Reiersen's dedication to humanitarian ideals had probably never been as strong as Elise's. Reiersen was always a restless and contentious entrepreneur. During his stay in Europe he lived in a turbulent world agitated by the energetic philosophy of free enterprise capitalism shaping the industrial revolution, the era English historian Paul Johnson described in *The Birth of the Modern*. Elise in one of her letters called Reiersen a "Rationalist," meaning that he accepted the anti-religious features of Rationalist philosophy. Evidently he absorbed more of the spirit of individualism and industrial-commercial enterprise than of the humanitarian and progressive reform hopes of the time. In contrast, though Elise appreciated the importance of enterprise, she remained committed to ideals, perhaps because of her religious outlook.

It seems that Reiersen found the exclusiveness of the ruling elite in Norway galling more because it restrained independent enterprise and prevented people from rising than because it trampled people's abstract rights. In the new settlement called Normandy he abruptly dismissed his successful past as a progressive reform journalist, becoming reluctant even to relay what he was learning back to his native country; his desire to attain material success was that avid. Although his projects were on a modest local scale—a general store, a boarding house, a sawmill at Brownsboro, investment in land, and founding the Prairieville settlement—he could pursue them untrammeled by legal restrictions, in liberty, and with respect. He now turned to material concerns and no longer held to the same desire for broad human improvement as did Elise.[17]

One might surmise that Reiersen did not actually leave his idealism behind at the dock in Norway. His ideals probably rose out of another branch of philosophy seen later in Nietzsche, Ayn Rand, and other thinkers, who endorsed individualism and rational self-interest as the best way to advance human life. That philosophy subsumed material achievement, and in that respect it has never left the modern world. Elise herself put it into words when she wrote after Thorvald's death: "The life we live here is not a very spiritual one. We think far too much of earthly things and lack all concrete reminders of the existence of God's heavenly kingdom."[18]

For her part, Elise never forgot her commitment to the general well-being of her countrymen. She remained dedicated to people, and it showed in her essay for *Billed-magazin*. After telling about Reiersen and the early years in Texas, she populated her account completely with individuals— there were fifty in her article, with names like Halvorsen, Hansen, Olsen, Lindberg, Staack, Terjesen (Teryesen), Gjestvang, the Reiersens, Grogards, Baches, and many others.

There was also Knudsen, one of the founding members of the Bosque colony, who changed the spelling of his name to "Canuteson." Elise's own husband had adopted the name Van Shaw during his last term in the Confederate Army, but she advised against this practice, "so that people can understand how stupid it is for Norwegian newcomers to change their names." To illustrate her point she told the unfortunate story of a man whose name was Nielsen when he arrived in Texas. He worked for a time in Marshall near the Louisiana border, and then changed his name and joined the army to get ahead. None of the Norwegians, not even Elise, learned his new identity, but he worked as a military blacksmith for fifty dollars a month and, as Elise put it, "earned a bit on the side by playing the violin"—fiddles were part of the folk music tradition in Norway's country provinces. During these years he saved fifteen hundred dollars, a very large sum indeed, which he meant to use beneficially by returning to Norway and bringing his parents and brothers and sisters back to Texas. Unfortunately, he died while making a trip to El Paso (presumably while he was in the army, though Elise did not say so).

The funds he had earned were on deposit with the American government under his assumed name. There was no official record whatever for a soldier named Nielsen. When word of his death reached his parents in Norway they tried to claim their legitimate inheritance. They commissioned the Norwegian consul in New York to act on their behalf, but he could do nothing. The whole matter ended in total futility. The money simply vanished into the obscurity of military coffers.[19]

In the closing section of her *Billed-magazin* report Elise turned once again to showing how her countrymen could improve their lives by coming to Texas. Because she knew religion was important to them, she first described the Norwegians' success in setting up Lutheran church services and then went on to say: "I will add a few remarks concerning the country." With that she launched into a six-hundred-word discourse on the merits of the state.

She began with the weather. It was generally mild, she said, and though the summer temperature did occasionally reach 104 degrees, "one never hears of sunstroke here." In the winter the north wind could be "sharp and penetrating, but the cold lasts only a few days at a time—and even on Christmas eve I have seen butterflies flitting about."

The soil was "very fertile," the usual crops being cotton, corn, and sweet potatoes, with peach the most common fruit. It was not necessary to feed domestic animals. They roamed around at will, and "a man may own several hundred head of horses, cattle, sheep, or swine—yes, farther west, even several thousand." As for the native prairie grass, it had once given away to weeds, but the affliction of locusts that had destroyed her wheat crop brought it back—the horde had consumed the tender spring weeds along with everything else.

Because the state was short of workers, it was "a paradise for poor people." There were good jobs in every season, and children could earn "good money picking cotton," bringing in two hundred pounds a day at seventy-five cents per hundred pounds plus board. Land prices were on the rise, but renting a field was easy for "half or two thirds of the yield, depending on whether the owner or renter supplies the horses, equipment, and seed." She added that foods were inexpensive and gave sample prices—"fresh salt pork $.05 per pound, corn and sweet potatoes $.50 a bushel, and wheat $1."

She closed with a warm endorsement for Texas: "I have no doubt that immigrants would do much better in going to Texas rather than Minnesota. I am strengthened in this view because a Norwegian and a Dane, both of whom lived here awhile but now live in Minnesota, have written that they want to return to Texas this winter."[20]

A few months after her articles appeared in *Billed-magazin* she received another call for information on Texas. This time it came from *Faedreland og emigranten,* published in La Crosse, Wisconsin. It was obvious that she had become the preeminent authority on the state.

Her greatest satisfaction came later the same year. She was able to tell her sister-in-law Emilie that Pastor Estrem had been in Four Mile Prairie for an entire month. "Thus," she wrote, "my wish was granted: to see my children confirmed before I die."

Meanwhile Otto had become engaged to Ophelia Florence Spikes, "a very beautiful American girl of his own age." They were married early in 1871, with the wedding held at Ophelia's parents' house followed by a party in the evening. Elise described her own contribution to the event, a dinner at her house with a dance for 130 guests: "We butchered two hogs, three turkeys, and twelve chickens. It does not cost as much to give a party in this country as in Norway, since people here do not use any other beverages than coffee, milk, and water. We do not have as many different courses either. At this dinner we had only roast, stew, several kinds of cake and pie. What was left over from dinner we served cold in the evening with coffee, and later that night we had coffee and cake for the third time. Everybody seemed to be having a good time."[21]

With the wedding her years of mourning came to an end. The years of sorrow were behind her, but she was due to face quite another kind of test that could thrust her back into gloom again.

DICKERSON'S TRIAL

S EVEN YEARS PASSED before Dickerson was found and brought to justice for the murder of Elise's husband. In early 1874 someone in Van Zandt County read a religious newspaper that said Dickerson had attended a conference in northwest Arkansas, where he was preaching the gospel. Johan Reiersen's son Christian got this news and passed it on to Elise.

A grand jury in Kaufman County had indicted Dickerson (see appendix) and issued a warrant for his arrest in February, 1867. The warrant had been reissued in 1868 and 1870, but any attempt to bring him back from Arkansas had to be authorized by the Texas governor, Richard Coke. He had only recently taken office and was heavily burdened, but Elise was determined to have Dickerson brought to trial as soon as possible. On February 7, 1874, she sent Coke a certified copy of the indictment and information on Dickerson's whereabouts, asking Coke please to "use such force" as necessary to bring Dickerson "to justice."[1]

Christian Reierson moved things along by writing to J. M. Harrison, a member of the state legislature who resided in Four Mile Prairie and knew about the Dickerson case, asking him to support Elise's petition. Within days Coke issued a proclamation for the "arrest and delivery of said N. T. Dickerson," accompanying it with a five-hundred-dollar reward for bringing him to the Kaufman County sheriff and depositing him "inside the jail door." Armed with this authority, Christian Reiersen traveled to northwest Arkansas (he had been in military campaigns there with the 3rd Texas Cavalry during the Civil War) and located Dickerson. Possibly Christian convinced him that the passage of time since the murder had reduced the likelihood of a severe sentence, but in any case he took Dickerson into custody and brought him back to the sheriff, who imprisoned him on May 25, 1874.

News of Dickerson's return to Kaufman County was first published in Galveston, the main Texas port 240 miles south of Four Mile Prairie. Galveston was the largest and most cosmopolitan city in the state, and its highly regarded newspaper, the *Galveston Daily News,* was known for its statewide coverage of important events. The *Tyler Democrat,* published in the main town of northeastern Texas, fifty miles east of Four Mile Prairie, featured the news on the day Dickerson was jailed.

Both papers reported that Dickerson had killed Wilhelm Waerenskjold (the *Tyler Democrat* erroneously called Dickerson "Dixon"); both noted that he had escaped to Arkansas; both identified him as a gospel preacher; and both said it was Christian Reiersen who fetched him back. The *Galveston Daily News* added that Wilhelm was "a very influential Norwegian."[2]

Preparation for Dickerson's trial took months. Residents of Prairieville and Four Mile Prairie were for the most part scattered rural folk unaccustomed to traveling miles from their homes to appear for thorny legal cases. Summer harvests were beginning, and cotton culture and ranch stock operations would last through late fall.

Although most witnesses were subpoenaed without incident, some had to be "attached"—taken into custody—to assure their appearance. Mack Norman, a key witness because he was present at the murder scene, was particularly dilatory. In June Otto Waerenskjold was appointed as special deputy sheriff to arrest Norman and take his bond for $250 to make sure he would appear at the trial. Even at that, in October when the final groundwork for the trial was being done, an attachment had to be issued to bring his "boddy" (the actual spelling in the document) before the court.

An account book recording Dickerson's purchase of weapons was considered vital evidence. The prosecutor had the court issue a special Subpoena *Duces tecum* commanding M. L. Elliott, son of the man who employed the blacksmith who had made Dickerson's weapons, to produce the book and also to appear at the trial.[3]

Finding a suitable date for the trial took some time. The defense attorney was George Washington Chilton, a prominent man who lived and practiced in Tyler. The trial was to be held in Kaufman, the county seat of Kaufman County, nineteen miles beyond Four Mile Prairie for someone coming from Tyler. As Chilton had to ride seventy miles, which was two days' travel each way, he would be absent from his home office for a week during the proceedings. The trial date had to conform to his schedule.

Elise's journey to Kaufman took more than half a day, so she too had trouble getting there. After the trial she wrote to Mrs. James H. Staack, a friend in Clifton whom she always addressed respectfully as "Madam Staack," telling her about the difficulties with the trip. She complained that she had had to go to Kaufman seven times and on the last occasion had had to stay an entire week.[4]

As there is no evidence that Dickerson posted a bond, he probably remained in the county jail during the months leading up to his trial. He was served with the indictment on October 14, 1874, six months after the Kaufman County sheriff took him in. The wheels of justice continued to grind slowly for another four months and then whirled at turbine speed. The trial started on February 13, 1875, and ended the same day.

Elise's letter to Madam Staack shows that she clearly understood the charge and the proceedings, and this together with her one-week stay in Kaufman suggests she was present at the trial. Besides Dickerson and his defense attorney Chilton, the other main figures were William H. Martin, district attorney for Kaufman County and the prosecutor in this case, and M. H. Bonner, the presiding judge.

The indictment and charge were issued "in the name and by the authority of the State of Texas," upon oath of "the grand Jurors for the State of Texas, duly elected impanneled, sworn and charged to inquire in and for the body of the County of Kaufman in said State." The wording of the charge, with all its strange and archaic legal phrasing, variously spelled Wilhelm's last name "Warenskgold," "Warenskold," and "Warrenskjold."

The key portion read: "N. T. Dickerson late of the County and State aforesaid, on the 17th Day of November, 1866, with force and arms, in the County aforesaid, in and upon one William Warenskgold, in the peace of God and of the State, then and there being, feloniously, willfully, and of his Malice aforethought, did make an assault . . . giving . . . Wilhelm Warenskgold . . . one mortal wound . . . of which said mortal wound, the said William Warenskgold did then and there instantly die."[5]

Dickerson was being charged with more than simple murder. His act had been performed with "malice aforethought." If the prosecution could prove he had planned what he did with premeditated design—malice aforethought—justice would be harsh. The verdict would be murder in the first degree. The sentence would be death.

The defense, for its part, had to counter the charge of malicious intent. It was widely known that Dickerson had committed the murder, and the proof was likely to be incontrovertible. The defense, however, could contend that he had acted under provocation, almost in self-defense, rather than killing Wilhelm by malevolent plan. If the defense could make this case, Dickerson would be convicted of murder in the second degree. The sentence would be a few years in jail. He would escape death.

A "Statement of Facts" was made as the trial proceeded. It was a narrative recital of the witnesses' testimony rather than a verbatim rendering of every word said. Because the questions put by the prosecution and defense attorneys were not recorded, they can only be inferred. Written in longhand probably by a male court secretary, the transcript effectively catches the vivid phrases and language used by the witnesses.

After the trial this handwritten statement of facts was formally filed by Henry Erwin, district clerk of Kaufman County, and stored in the county courthouse cellar. It gathered dust there until the early 1960s when it was brought to light by Derwood Johnson, a young attorney of Norwegian descent who later became judge for the 74th State District Court at Waco in McLennan County. Johnson had searched long and diligently for this document with Lorena Gould, Elise's great-granddaughter. Gould actually discovered it and took it out of the file box; Johnson was so excited that he snatched it from her and had to apologize. Finding it was like unearthing an archeological treasure, and Johnson immediately set about making a typed copy.

This typed document, which records the longhand original with complete accuracy, shows Dickerson identified as the "defendant," variously abbreviated to "Deft," "Deft.," "Def't," "deft," and "def't." Likewise, Wilhelm is identified as the "deceased," variously abbreviated to "Dece'd," "Dec'd," "dece'd," "decd," and "dec'd." For all its terse language and abbreviations, Johnson's typed transcript fairly shrieks out the horrible reality of the murder itself. The shock of the event pervades the entire trial proceedings.[6]

The prosecution's first witness was James Bowlden, postmaster and owner of the grocery store where Wilhelm was murdered. Bowlden was an eyewitness to Dickerson's crime. His testimony is consistent with what Elise wrote in her letter published by *Aftenbladet* in Norway in 1866.

Wilhelm was an elected justice of the peace, and the transcript shows Bowlden saying that Wilhelm was reading something, presumably an official document, to him when Dickerson came into the store. Bowlden described the encounter between the two like this: "Some words passed between them. do not know what it was about. Deft. did not appear satisfied. Dece'd said he had proof of what he said . . . there seemed to an altercation about some private business."

CHAPTER 11

Dickerson put his hand to the hilt of a knife he was wearing at his belt. "Dece'd told him he was not afraid, put his hand down. Dece'd went to door and pulled off his coat, when deft struck him with a knife, went partly through his arm, into his left side." Wilhelm was turning toward Dickerson when Dickerson struck.

Bowlden continued: "I don't suppose deceased lived half a minute, he fell out side door." The weapon was "about 5 or 6 inches long, home made hunting knife. Deft ran off, I called out for help & neighbors came immediately. Deft got on his horse & rode off first at a walk afterwards at a canter.

"I did not examine the wound. I saw it but did not examine it. It bled right-smart, dec'd fell on his face, I do not know whether Dec'd had weapons, he died almost instantly after he was stabbed."

Upon cross-examination by the defense, Bowlden added an item that at first seems trivial and irrelevant. The transcript shows him saying, "Am an Englishman." But he did not stop at that. He went on to say, "dec'd was a foreigner."

Foreigner? Why add this? And why did the prosecution not object to this irrelevant question and other statements concerning anyone's nationality or ancestry? Bowlden had just declared he was an Englishman. Apparently the defense was seeking to have the jury infer that English nationality was acceptable while Norwegian nationality was suspect. Even if Bowlden meant only that he was of English descent, nothing in the transcript suggests any reason to add that Wilhelm was a "foreigner."

Bowlden brought up Wilhelm's "foreign" nationality again when later the defense was seeking to test his credibility. He testified that when Dickerson came into his store, Wilhelm "rose politely said good day," and that he thought he remembered doing the same himself.

"Deft said he wished to have an explanation about some letters . . . both seemed tolerable angry, and both spoke quickly. . . . Dec'd walked with his back to deft toward the door and took his coat off (Deft made no attempt, no attempt to strike him until he had got his coat off & had turned around) (Dec'd had put his coat on the counter with his left side to Deft and was in the act of turning towards North door when deft stabbed him with a knife.)"

Bowlden now returned to the matter of nationality. He said, "Oscar Rierson, John Rierson, & Christian Rierson, and others went after him, dont remember who the others were." Then he added gratuitously, "The Riersons and dec'd were foreigners, Norwegians. Rierson and Dec'd were very friendly."

Bowlden's testimony on the matter of the pursuers put a sinister cast on the Norwegians. Furthermore, later testimony by J. Barnett, the first person to ride after Dickerson, contradicted him. Barnett himself was a native Texan and he identified two other pursuers. One was Obe Erwin, a fellow Texan, and the second was Oscar Reiersen, a Norwegian. Bowlden's testimony regarding the pursuers gave the impression that Wilhelm and his friends were not only foreigners but were practically in conspiracy. This was false and grossly prejudicial.[7]

The prosecution failed to counter this image of the Norwegians as a gang of foreigners. For example, it was never brought up that two of the Norwegians Bowlden named had served loyally in the Confederate Army throughout the Civil War—John Reiersen, whether he actually rode after Dickerson or not, had campaigned in Indian country north of Texas and had been promoted from private to lieutenant; Christian had campaigned in the Indian country and across the entire South, finally joining in the defense of Atlanta, Georgia.

The second witness called by the prosecution was Mack Norman, the man whom Otto Waerenskjold had been sent to arrest and secure by bond. Another eyewitness to the crime, Norman said he had been in the store only a few minutes when Wilhelm was stabbed, and that he was deeply agitated by the event—"much excited," in his words. The transcript records him further as saying he believed Wilhelm and Dickerson were six or eight feet from the exit door when "the lick was struck." On cross-examination Norman testified that he had not seen Dickerson's knife. Apparently in explanation, he repeated, "I was excited."[8]

J. Barnett, the first man to ride in pursuit of Dickerson, was called third by the prosecution. He testified that he had just left the store when he heard Bowlden's call. He turned and saw Wilhelm stagger through the door and pitch forward on his face. The transcript reads: "I took the defendant's track. Obe Erwin and I started and Oscar Rierson came on and overtook us, we pursued him ½ mile."

The matter of foreign nationality came up once more during Barnett's testimony. Apparently in response to a question from the defense, he said: "Prairieville was a small place, Norwegian settlement. Deceased was Norwegian, a leading man among them and stout built."

Although Barnett was a prosecution witness, he was the first to give favorable testimony concerning Dickerson's character. The defense must have asked how long he had known Dickerson and what people thought of him. He said: "I knew the def't before this he had been here 8 or 10 years

CHAPTER 11

—148—

before this, he was regarded by his neighbors as a quiet peaceable and inoffensive man."

Perhaps surprised by this testimony, the prosecution conducted a re-examination of Barnett, but he reiterated, "All gave defendant a good character."[9]

The prosecution next called John Cole, the blacksmith who had prepared Dickerson's weapons and was employed by Mr. Elliott. He said that he had known Dickerson for twenty-three years and lived three miles from him at the time of the murder. "I made a knife for Deft 6 or 7 inches long & one or one & ½ wide, made it from a cedar pattern he brought. I also put a mainspring in a six shooter for him. I think it was in Sept 1866 that I did this work. I think the knife was after the fashion of a Bowie knife, as well as I recollect. deft when he took the knife & pistol away said I will make them whoof for the landing without mentioning any name" (the transcript shows "whoop" in place of "whoof" in the next part of Cole's testimony).

On cross-examination the defense worked to counteract the impression that Dickerson had had the weapons made for his attack on Wilhelm. With recurrent misspelling of Dickerson's name, the text shows Cole testifying that the knife would be a "good knife for cutting corn." "Mr. Dickinson hunted a good deal. I know him to be frequently hunting. The knife was suitable knife for hunting. The term 'Whoop for the landing' was a term in common use amongst hunters, and could be applied to deer, turkeys, buffalo, or any other game."

Cole added: "I kept a book, and once a week went to Elliott & put the account on his book. The book I kept, was little book and was lost or mislaid, don't know what became of it. The charges for the knife was 75 cts & for the pistol $1."

After this testimony, Cole took up Dickerson's character and reputation (the transcript here misspells the word "peaceable" as well as Dickerson's name). "I was frequently at Dickenson's house. . . . I knew Dickinson in Augt. 1850 was intimate with him. He was known as a quiet peacable man. I know his character for peacable and inoffensive conduct. It was good. He was considered by the community as a peacable and inoffensive man."

The prosecution re-examined, evidently asking whether it was usual for a hunter to carry a pistol. Cole replied, "I have seen hunters carry six shooters. Mr. Dickenson farmed some, hunted some, and coopered some." Coopers were barrel-stave makers; the work was considered by some to be a lowly occupation.

Cole explained further that people often carried weapons during the troubled times following the Civil War. "The killing took place in 1866, something over a year after the war closed. It was the custom to carry pistols; there was a great deal of lawlessness; the country was unsettled. A great many people were driven from their homes, and frequently peaceable, quiet people were compelled to carry pistols for defense."[10]

T. M. Hoffman was the next witness called by the prosecution. A neighbor of Dickerson's, Hoffman had ridden home with him from Prairieville six weeks or so before the murder. The transcript shows him saying: "The deft and myself were leaving Prairieville for home, he said the Norwegians had changed their day for coming to town, and he must change his too that he had been there several times lately and that he wanted to see dec'd; and that when he did see him he was going to hurt him and hurt him bad, that he was prepared for him now, he threw back his coat & showed pistol on one side & knife on the other . . . he said he had had his knife & pistol fixed."

The matter of foreign nationality came up yet again. Presumably referring to a man he considered a home-grown American, Hoffman said, "J. R. Johnson and family lived at Prairieville," and then added, "dont know whether there were any others there who were not norwegians."

On cross-examination by the defense, Hoffman went into more detail about his ride with Dickerson. "We were near town when he told me. I saw him in town that day. he was not drinking, I never saw him drink. I did not ask him any questions, he voluntarily told me, he did not tell me why he wanted to hurt him & and I did not ask why. I think it was Mrs. Waerenskjold that I first told of this conversation. Nobody but Mrs. W. was present, it was at her house. I don't recollect of seeing Deft again until I saw him here in Court House. Deft & myself were not particularly friendly. He said he had knife and pistol fixed. Knife was in a scabbard. Can't describe it, am satisfied I saw it. . . . He did not carry them secretly, don't recollect seeing them in town. I did not tell dec'd about it. I heard that Mr. Cole had made a knife for him."[11]

Dr. Luce, a physician, was the last witness the prosecution called. His testimony was brief but significant. He said he had known Dickerson since 1857 and had practiced "in his family." He had looked on while Dr. Turgerson (Turgerson was brought over from Bosque County) examined Wilhelm's body and had also attended the coroner's jury hearing. He confirmed the previous testimony regarding the deadly wound, but then added information indicating that Dickerson felt he had been provoked by Wilhelm: "Sometime before the killing; deft told me that Dec'd had scandalized him & unless he made reparation he would hurt him bad."

CHAPTER 11

On cross-examination by the defense, Dr. Luce added more information that tended to show provocation by Wilhelm. "If I recollect right, Mr. D told me that he & Dec'd had had a conversation on the prairie, near Mr. Spikes', he said Dec'd had slandered him and talked about him, that dec'd had met him on the prairie and talked pretty rough, it was after this meeting on the prairie that I had my talk with him. I saw dec'd in town on the day of killing, saw deft & that he was armed, told dec'd to look out."[12]

At this point the prosecution rested its case and Dickerson's attorneys put on his defense. Five witnesses testified to Dickerson's good character, using terms like "reputation for peace," "peaceableness," "peaceable citizen," "inoffensive," "quiet," "good order," "good citizen and neighbor."[13] After presenting this character testimony, the defense offered a witness whose statements, through no fault of his own, open the way for profound and sober speculation.

This witness was Tom Spikes, a Negro and former slave. The transcript here reads: "(The entire testimony of Tom Spikes which follows was lined through and exed out.)" In spite of this parenthetical observation, Johnson was able to read some of Tom Spikes's testimony and recorded it as follows: "Was living at Mr. Warrenskjold's in 1866. he is dead. I lived with him before I was freed and afterwards. I heard him say the defendant will have to leave the country."

The last sentence was very helpful to the defense. From it the jury could infer that Wilhelm habitually told people about Dickerson's misconduct, and that, worse still, he did so in front of an individual who, having been in the menial status of a slave, should not have heard anything about it. By producing Tom Spikes's testimony, the defense aimed to show that Wilhelm had given Dickerson powerful provocation.

Upon cross-examination by the prosecutor, Spikes's testimony stood unchallenged. Spikes repeated: "He said he will have to leave the county." But then Spikes added something that could have proven explosive: "He said this to a lady." Following this the transcript reads: "(end of stricken testimony)."[14]

Who was the lady Spikes mentioned?

She was never identified. Why not? Spikes certainly knew Elise was the lady of the household. If she were the lady to whom he was referring, he would surely have named her. Most likely, therefore, he meant Mary Reagan. Spikes would have known who she was. He had been living with the Waerenskjolds during the time she and her mixed race baby were sheltering in their home.

Furthermore, it would have been reasonable for Wilhelm to tell Mary

Reagan that Dickerson would have to leave the country. He would have done so because Elise and he were protecting her from Dickerson as well as sheltering her until she was able to travel.

Speculation might lead one to assume that Spikes actually said the words "Mary Reagan" when he spoke of a "lady." This, however, may be too strong an assumption; one need not go that far to explain why his testimony was exed out. Had testimony about Mary Reagan come up, it would have opened a whole new subject in the trial. The prosecution would have had to elicit information about her, inquiring who she was, why the Waerenskjolds were sheltering her, who the father of her mixed race baby might be, and what contact Dickerson had had with her.

Questions like these would have blown the defense apart. Instead of leaving the impression that Wilhelm had provoked Dickerson, they would have shown exactly the opposite—Dickerson's behavior toward Mary had provoked Wilhelm to say that he would have to leave the country.

By bringing in Spikes's testimony, the defense was taking a great risk.

Why did the court order Spikes's testimony stricken, and which side made the request? Again, one has to speculate because the transcript does not recite motions made by the respective attorneys, or the court's rulings on orders in response, or the court's orders to jurors to disregard testimony.

Spikes's testimony may have been disqualified because he was deemed incompetent. But it is also possible that the attorneys made a deal to strike Spikes's testimony. Once the defense was satisfied that his testimony showed Wilhelm to have made a provocative statement, it needed nothing more from Spikes—in fact, anything else Spikes might have added could have counted heavily against Dickerson. For its part, the prosecution may have accepted this because striking part of the testimony would cut off, at least to some degree, the defense effort to prove provocation.

The court may have been persuaded to grant a joint motion to strike Spikes's testimony on the grounds that disputed evidence concerning Dickerson's misconduct toward Mary Reagan would have brought in collateral issues prolonging the trial. Moreover, considering sentiments in the South regarding sexual relations between a black man and a white woman, the evidence concerning Mary and her child might have inflamed the jury to such a degree that a mistrial would have to be ordered. Had this occurred, the final resolution of the charges against Dickerson would have been delayed, resulting in increased costs and lost time for the parties concerned.

The deletion of Spikes's testimony may provide one of the reasons that Dickerson's incriminating letters to Mary Reagan were never introduced into evidence—there was no reason to bring them into the trial. And there are other possibilities. The district attorney determined what evidence the prosecution should introduce, and he may have decided against using the letters. Or the judge may have ruled before the trial that they should not be produced.

It is also possible that Elise had destroyed Dickerson's letters, with the result that they were not available to demonstrate his misconduct. Or if she still had the letters, she may have withheld them, knowing that the subject of sexual relations between a white woman and a black man could result in public violence.

Whatever the reason, the court's order to strike Spikes's testimony probably benefited the defense. The jury would have been left with the impression that Wilhelm's statement about Dickerson—"he will have to leave the country"—had helped to provoke his murder.[15]

After Spikes left the witness stand the defense called M. L. Elliott, one of the previous character witnesses. This was to deal with the troublesome matter of the account book showing Dickerson's payment for the knife and pistol. Elliott explained, first, that it was his father rather than he who had employed Cole. "I had nothing to do with the books," he said. "I recognize this book as one of my father's books. Cole put down the work in a book and transferred it to my father's book."

Cole had previously testified that he had lost or mislaid his own record book. The defense, however, had possession of a book that it contended was Cole's and tried to get this introduced into evidence. The prosecution objected, and the judge sustained the objection.[16]

Having failed to get Cole's book into evidence, the defense turned to Elliott for testimony about Dickerson's character. The transcript shows Elliott repeating the familiar "he was considered a quiet & peaceable man."

Ole Olson, a Norwegian, was next called by the defense. Some time before the murder, he and John Reiersen had been out on the prairie looking for stock when the pair of them saw Wilhelm and two of his friends meeting with Dickerson. Olson testified that when he and Reiersen rode up, "Deft and Dec'd were off their horses talking. We stopped. They were not much friendly, they were angry. Dec'd said if you will take back what you said, this matter can be compromised. If you wont, you must abide by consequences. Deft said I will see you in Hell first."

Cross-examination by the prosecution elicited testimony that again showed Dickerson's violent reaction. Olson repeated: "Dec'd said if you will take back certain things this can be compromised if not you must abide by the consequences Deft said I will see you in Hell first. I have told what I heard. Dec'd was a Norwegian and so am I." Olson's testimony suggested that Wilhelm had outraged and perhaps provoked Dickerson when he said Dickerson "must abide by consequences."[17]

The defense apparently now claimed that the record of Dickerson's payment for the knife and pistol had been forged in the large ledger kept by Elliott's father. The blacksmith Cole was called back to examine this larger ledger. The transcript reads: "Deft's counsel asked the following question 'Look down pages 2 & 3 and see if anything is charged to deft.' Plffs [plaintiffs] objected & objection sustained to which Deft excepted." The defense failed to show a forgery of the payments for the weapons.[18]

Because of this failure, the defense now called another character witness, K. McKinney, who confirmed the previous testimony: "Defts reputation for peace and quiet was good." He then added, "He was a man of family."[19]

This last point, presumably mentioned to show that Dickerson had been a responsible head of household, served only to raise a new issue. It was well known that Dickerson had left his family behind when he fled to Arkansas. Furthermore, his statement to Dr. Luce about Wilhelm having "slandered" and "scandalized" him indicated that Dickerson's attempt to run off with Mary Reagan despite being married to her aunt was widely known.

M. L. Elliott was called on the subject of Dickerson's family relations, and testified: "I lived 3½ miles from Deft at time of killing. Mrs. Dickerson lived on his place after he left. I understand that she died on the place. She died in 67. She was buried at Stovers."

On cross-examination Elliott testified: "Deft left his daughter. She left soon after her mother's death. It was said he sent after her."[20] The defense presumably hoped Elliott's statement would show that Dickerson had concern for his family even though he had left them after the murder.

This being the final evidence submitted in the trial, the handwritten transcript was tendered to the prosecutor and to defense attorneys for examination. Perhaps Spikes's testimony was exed out at this point, but in any case the attorneys agreed that this transcript was "a full fair and complete statement of all the facts given in evidence at the trial of the above entitled cause of the State of Texas vs N. T. Dickerson." They signed and applied their seals.

The judge then added: "I, M. H. Bonner Judge Presiding on the trial of the above and foregoing case of the State of Texas v N. T. Dickerson do hereby approve the above and foregoing 17½ pages as a full fair and complete statement of all the facts in testimony on the trial of said cause, the same being approved as such in open court this 13 Febry 1875."[21]

He signed and sealed, but the proceedings were not yet over. With the case now about to go to the jury, the defense tried to bring Mary Reagan back into consideration without actually naming her. It asked the judge to instruct the jury that the murder was caused by "insulting words or conduct of the person killed towards a female relation of the party guilty of the homicide."

To make this request, the defense must have known the facts about Mary Reagan, including Dickerson's misconduct toward her. Not only this, but the defense was acting with flagrant cynicism, completely distorting Elise and Wilhelm's kindness toward Mary Reagan and her child. In place of their kindness, it was playing on southern prejudices, implying that gallantry had led Dickerson to defend a woman's inviolable honor and sacred reputation!

The judge, however, refused to give this requested instruction to the jury, there being no evidence to support it. Testimony about Mary, with or without her name, had never entered the case.[22]

With this last devious maneuver disposed of, Clerk Erwin was able to take charge of putting the transcript on file. The jury recessed and shortly came back with its verdict. (Derwood Johnson discovered this verdict glued to the back of the transcript document, with "assess" misspelled.) It read: "We the Jury find the defendant guilty of Murder in the Second degree and ascs his punishment in the State Penitentiary for the period of Ten Years of hard labor."[23]

The defense had beaten the prosecution's charge of "malice aforethought." Dickerson would not get death.

The sentence was read to Dickerson, and he was asked if "he had any thing to say why sentence of the Court should not be pronounced upon him in accordance with the judgment heretofore rendered on the verdict of the Jury and he having made answer that he had nothing to say." When he replied that he had nothing to add, the court directed that he be taken by the sheriff of Kaufman County and two guards to the penitentiary.[24]

Elise's letter to Madam Staack reports her disagreement with the verdict. She clearly understood the difference between first and second degree murder and the meaning of malice aforethought. With extraordinary reserve she commented: "a mild punishment, to be sure, for such a cold-blooded and long premeditated murder."

Dickerson was jailed, but Elise said she expected the defense to appeal the case to the state supreme court. Perhaps an appeal was started, but if so it was never heard by the appellate court. On August 7, 1875, nearly six months after the trial, Governor Coke issued a proclamation granting Dickerson a full pardon and ordering his release from custody.[25]

Elise must have been stunned by this action. How could the perpetrator of so heinous and public a murder be allowed to go free? The grounds, at least on the surface, were lawful. After the trial the prosecutor, District Attorney William H. Martin, proposed the pardon and sent the governor petitions with 681 signatures setting forth arguments for pardoning Dickerson.

The governor cited several of these in his decision: Dickerson's extreme age (he was actually sixty-one), his previous good character, and "the probability of the loss of his testimony by lapse of time."[26] Justice in so blatant a crime, however, was not reversed on legal grounds alone. Large forces were at work, some of them obvious and others dark and deep-seated yet profound in their influence. In issuing his decision the governor made a particular point of observing that the district attorney, together with a large number of "good citizens of Kaufman and other counties," had recommended the pardon. To put it plainly, votes were at stake.

Texas at the time was in the throes of a political upheaval, almost a revolution. The Republican Party had controlled state politics since the Reconstruction period began following the Confederate surrender in 1865. Former Confederate leaders had always opposed Reconstruction rule, and in 1870 when President Ulysses S. Grant declared Reconstruction in Texas over, the Republican Party was doomed—the former Confederates turned immediately to the Democratic Party to recapture control of the state.

Governor Coke was a leader in this restoration. In 1873 he won the first Democratic campaign for governor since the end of the Civil War. The next election was to take place in the fall of 1875—not a good time to alienate 681 potential voters who had just signed petitions for Dickerson's pardon. Responsive to voter sentiment and leading the effort to restore control by prewar political forces, Coke easily won reelection. Flushed with victory, he ran for election to the United States Senate in the spring of 1876 (at the time the state legislature elected U.S. senators). On winning, he resigned as governor and went to Washington. He was returned to the Senate at every election until he retired in 1894.[27]

The other leaders in the trial had their own political ambitions and rode the same political tide as Coke. Bonner, the judge, had been appointed to the Kaufman County District Court in 1873. Soon after presiding at the Dickerson trial he was elevated to the Texas Supreme Court and became its chief justice in 1878. District Attorney William Martin, prosecutor in the case, later won two terms in the U.S. House of Representatives. James Harrison, the Van Zandt County state legislator who had requested the governor to return Dickerson to Texas for trial, sought political office again after an interval of three terms and ran successfully in the 1883–84 election for the state house of representatives.

All the trial leaders had been supporters of the Confederacy and had been military officers in the war. Chilton, the defense attorney, was the most prominent in the Confederate cause. He had been a slave owner and a member of the notorious Knights of the Golden Circle, a militant organization that favored ownership of a slave by every white person so that the "master race" could engage in "self-improvement." In 1861 Chilton brought Governor Sam Houston the order of the Secession Convention requiring him to swear loyalty to the Confederacy; when Houston refused, Chilton brought back the news that resulted in Houston's removal as governor. During the war Chilton was a colonel in a Confederate battalion that campaigned in the Indian Territory north of Texas.[28]

James Harrison, the Van Zandt County state representative, had been a captain in Company E, 11th Texas Infantry, the unit in which Wilhelm had served at the beginning of the war. William Martin, the prosecutor, was a member of Hood's Brigade, which had fought desperate battles as part of General Robert E. Lee's army in the Virginia and Pennsylvania campaigns. A major at the end of the war, Martin led the surviving members of the brigade back to Texas. Bonner, the judge, was a colonel in the ordnance department and commander of the gun factory at Rusk. Before the war he had been an attorney in Tyler, and he was probably well acquainted with Chilton.[29]

These trial leaders undoubtedly shared the view that Wilhelm and the Norwegians were foreigners just as strongly as did the witnesses who spoke that word with apparent opprobrium during the trial. An attitude of hostility toward strangers had long been part of the "nativist" tradition in the United States. Before the Civil War nativism in the north found a home in the bigoted "Know-Nothing" Party with its hatred of Irish immigrants and Roman Catholics. In Texas there was endemic hostility toward any "foreign" element, whether Mexican, Indian, or the Germans massacred at the Nueces River early in the Civil War. In the post–Civil War period, the suppression of the former slaves was permeated with the same venomous spirit of hostile superiority present in nativism.[30]

Little wonder that Wilhelm's nationality and status as foreigner surfaced during the trial. Considered a Unionist, he had been arrested and nearly lynched by Confederate extremists near the end of the war. Dickerson, on the other hand, was an indigenous American from Tennessee, part of the influx into Van Zandt County that produced its majority vote for secession in the 1861 referendum. That he was seen as a homegrown American in a case involving foreigners probably contributed to his relatively light sentence and to his subsequent pardon by the governor.

Nor was the governor's reference to "loss of testimony" surprising. Dickerson's statements that Wilhelm had "slandered him," "talked about him," and "scandalized" him imply that his lying rumor campaign against the Waerenskjolds, carried on before he murdered Wilhelm, had reached and convinced a number of people. Some of them apparently had left the area; had they still been present, they would have provided additional character testimony on his behalf.

Dickerson's personality and character traits were never fully examined at the trial. In her 1866 *Aftenbladet* letter Elise called Dickerson a "contemptible assassin," and she obviously considered him a coward for attacking her husband, who was unarmed. By describing Dickerson's misconduct toward Mary Reagan alongside his role as a pastor, she also portrayed him as a corrupt and malevolent fraud. Yet witnesses to his character testified that Dickerson was a quiet and peaceable man.[31]

What was the truth? Evidence from tax records and other sources show Dickerson was a financial failure. He had started out with a 640-acre land grant in Van Zandt County and had also bought additional land. Through mismanagement and bad luck he lost his holdings, and by 1860 he was apparently completely landless. The witness Cole's characterization of Dickerson's occupations—he "farmed some, hunted some, and coopered some"— suggest an unstable, careless, and indifferent occupational life.

During the trial the defense never brought up his preaching activities, which suggests that they were too trifling and inconsequential to win him any respect. One would surmise that he was a jackleg preacher—an untrained, self-appointed gospel spouter, someone who traveled around to camp meetings ranting about perdition and hellfire. Judging by his references to hell in his threats to Mary Reagan as well as to Wilhelm, he appears to have been possessed with ideas about Hades and damnation.[32]

Nor could he claim the honor of having fought for Texas and the South in the Civil War. Even though he was forty-six in 1860 and not obliged to serve, he could have volunteered as many others of his age group had done.

Further, had his religious convictions been strong enough to prevent him from joining up, they would surely have been mentioned at the trial.[33]

His misconduct toward his niece Mary Reagan, in effect an attempted seduction, suggests some sort of midlife crisis—he was fifty-one when she came to live in his home. Whatever his compulsions, his unwanted advances and threats against her reveal grossly bad judgment on his part. This, his apparent failure, and his neighbors' testimony that he was "inoffensive," "quiet," and "peaceful" yield an image of a repressed and trivial person.

Given an inadequate personality, where did Dickerson find the resolve to murder Wilhelm? One might hazard that it rose from the Texan impulse to revenge, a quality Elise had identified years before when she replied to Tolmer's allegations against the state. Back then she had said that Texans "are much too prone to avenge every real or fancied insult with a bullet or a stab." She repeated this point in her Confession of Faith when she warned her sons against "false honor"—the error of conforming to customs and community attitudes rather than doing what is right. Probably it was this vainglorious impulse lying in Dickerson's sad being that led him to murder Wilhelm.[34] And, all in all, his later "mild" sentence and pardon are redolent of political collusion between former Confederates who were seizing the reins of power.

One might suppose that word of the governor's pardon would have destroyed Elise's spirit and thrust her back into mourning. Her letter to Madam Staack, however, exhibits the attitude she probably maintained. Instead of starting the letter by rendering a painful account of her own problems, she began by expressing sympathy for her friend: "Many thanks for your friendly letter. It pains me very much that you are neither in good spirits nor in good health—the former I could, of course, well imagine. It must be very unpleasant for you not to be able to be with Hans when he is sick. How far away is he? I hope that he is better now."

Then, in words tinged with humor, she described goings on around her: "Niels, Oscar Andersen (who works for Niels), and Rosell, the French tailor who traveled around here seven or eight years ago as a peddler and who now rooms at Niels's, keep up such a talkfest that I hardly know what I am writing."

Before long she wrote another letter, this time to Thomine Dannevig in Norway: "Here we live in the same old way and as usual enjoy good health. Otto's wife and youngest child, Florence Maud, were both baptized two weeks ago today by a Methodist minister. Ophelia's parents are Methodists, but she would have been willing to be baptized by our pastor [Estrem] if he had not demanded that she learn the catechism by heart. My two grandchildren are pretty youngsters. Lilli is very lively and impetuous, while Florence is very patient."

She told of having attended a party at the home of John Reiersen, the son of her former friend Johan Reinert Reiersen, and about visitors from California having been at the event. The close of the letter shows her mind idly drifting back to her first husband in Norway: "I understand that you have been in Tonsberg. Did you see Foyn? I have often read in the newspapers about his successful whaling."

Elise had to pay fees to the attorney who assisted the prosecutor at the trial of her husband's murderer. The trial was expensive for her as well as costly in emotional terms. The pardon notwithstanding, she sailed back unruffled into her ordinary world.[35]

BEATING HARD TIMES

B
Y THE MID-1870S drastic changes were coming to the world of Texas ranching. The once fertile land of the eastern counties was overgrazed and almost played out. Settlers in Central Texas were claiming the rich blackland soils that ran in a 350-mile swath from the Oklahoma border through Dallas to San Antonio. Even before the Civil War, cattlemen north of Dallas had been taking their stock over the Shawnee Trail into Oklahoma for sale in markets as far away as Illinois.

After the war, drovers started rounding up wild cattle from the mesquite deserts along the Mexican border, driving them in herds of three thousand up the Chisholm Trail to San Antonio. From there they walked the mavericks fifteen miles a day, letting them browse on the prairie grasses all the way to the railhead at Abilene, Kansas, where they were shipped to Chicago and the Midwest. Ex-Confederate soldiers—called "waddies," perhaps from an old word for a bludgeon used to prod animals—served as the trail hands. Plain saddle-busters doing dull, dusty work, they bore little resemblance to the cowboys of pulp fiction, but before long they and their drover bosses captured the cattle market from the smaller stockmen in East Texas.[1]

As early as 1870 Elise considered building up her orchard fruit production to reduce her dependence on livestock. In that year while counseling her sister-in-law Emilie Syvertsen in Denmark about immigrating to Four Mile Prairie, she wrote enthusiastically: "I would be very happy if you would bring a few trees with you. Of pear trees the following: empresses, bergamots, and gray pears. Of apples these: Gravensteins, glass apples, and pigeons. Of plums the following: green plums and St. Catherine plums; and some good cherry trees. Also bring some gooseberry and current bushes. It goes without saying that I will pay for the trees and for their transportation here, and I will give you a good cow for your trouble."

Unfortunately, Elise's lavish order for "a few trees" was never filled. Emilie's husband was unable to sell his farm, and only after being widowed in 1884 did she come to Four Mile Prairie. By then it was too late for Elise to start planting orchards.[2] From time to time Elise did speak of growing fruit from native stock—plums, cherries, and berries—but these were mostly for her personal use. By 1873 the decline of her ranch was becoming obvious. In that year she wrote to Thomine Dannevig telling her about severe livestock losses.

A dry summer and fall had withered the wild prairie grasses, the animals' natural forage. Winter came early with intense cold, and a ravaging equine disease (probably influenza or encephalitis) broke out among her horses. She bought hay and grain for feed, but even with the extra fodder the horses could not survive their sickness. Her other stock—the cattle, sheep, and hogs she had relied on for years—were wasted and could barely eat. Many just lay down and died. Her losses from starvation and disease were in excess of two hundred dollars. Otto and Niels lost stock they were keeping with hers, and to make matters worse, she was helping Otto with funds to set up on his own.

Elise confronted her declining fortunes with a confidence rooted in her strong religious faith. When the old log cabin church fell victim to termites in the early 1870s, she arranged to hold services at her home. Pastor Ole Estrem undoubtedly presided at weddings and other ceremonies whenever he was in Four Mile Prairie, but most of the time the residents used her house for Bible reading and prayers just as they had in the early pioneer days.[3]

In 1875 a second church was built to replace the old log cabin. Elise spoke of it as "a small new church," but she must have been comparing it to the fine edifices at her father's parishes in Norway. The new church was a wooden building, painted white, sizable and well built. Except for a large cross mounted on the roof over the main entry door, it could have been taken for a one-room country schoolhouse. The cross stood out against the sky, a solid timber and emblem of faith.

The church's board and batten siding may have been copied from Norway, where construction of this type was common. Unusual in America, this style of building appears in Grant Wood's painting *American Gothic,* in which a dour-looking farm couple stand in front of a house finished with board and batten walls. On the Four Mile Prairie church the plank boards,

Four Mile Prairie Lutheran Church as rebuilt in 1875.
Photo courtesy of Derwood Johnson, Waco.

probably eight-by-one-inch pine, were set vertically. Strips two inches wide, the battens, were nailed over the seams between the planks. The resulting up-and-down-striped effect gave the building its plain country look. A photograph made of this building in the 1900s shows that it was far more handsome than the rough log cabin church. Well suited for religious purposes, it had three six-foot windows on each side, double hung and set with eight-inch glass panes.[4]

In 1876, the year after the new church was built, Elise raised funds for additional improvements. She had previously worked to solicit pledges for the pastor's salary, but now she turned her efforts to completing the church cemetery. Writing to the wife of Carl Quaestad, whom she addressed respectfully as "Madam Quaestad," she said: "Excuse me for taking the liberty of asking you if you would be willing to contribute one dollar toward getting a board fence around the graveyard where your mother is buried. You know that our settlement is small and many of us are widows. I therefore hope that our friends in Bosque who have relatives buried here will not think of me too harshly for making this request."[5]

Appeals like this one, for all their modesty and benevolent purpose, helped her acquire the attitudes and skills she needed to earn income for herself. Later on, she applied what she had learned to door-to-door selling and to raising contributions for her own salary as a Sunday school teacher.

In 1879 Elise made a major donation to the church. The old log cabin with its cemetery was situated on two acres of land that she and Wilhelm had owned. With the new building in place, she realized she should make an official transfer of the property to the congregation. She had a survey made, recorded the metes and bounds in a deed, and assigned the land a value of eight dollars. With Otto and Niels as witnesses, she signed the deed in June, 1879. The exact date was omitted, but the main section read: "I do hereby bind myself my heirs or assigns to forever warrant and defend the title to same unto the said members of the Lutheran Church of Four Mile Prairie against myself my heirs or any person claiming or to claim the same or any part thereof."

The heavy tone of the words "any person claiming or to claim the same or any part thereof" may have reflected Elise and Wilhelm's transactions involving the land containing the small lot. Their descendant Clair Hines of Peaster, Texas, relates that it was part of a 536.8-acre parcel they had obtained from E. W. Wiley, a grantee under a Mercer Colony certificate, whose heirs they had to sue to get their title. Later Elise sold the parcel to Israel Spikes, father-in-law to her son Otto, but kept ownership of the portion she later deeded to the church. Considering both of these facts, the congregation may have wanted protection in the deed against any legal challenges that might arise.[6]

Elise tried to overcome the decline of her ranch by increasing cotton production. From 1866 to 1875 commercial cotton growing expanded rapidly in Texas—more than two million acres were brought under cultivation, and the statewide yield rose from 359,000 to 813,000 bales. This growth, however, occurred mainly in the blackland prairie.[7] When Elise wrote to Thomine Dannevig in 1877 she showed that adverse weather conditions were adding to the problem of depleted soils in east Texas: "This year our cotton yield will be unusually poor, scarcely one fifth of what we would get under normally good conditions. My sons planted a lot of cotton because that is the crop most likely to bring in money. We had too much rain in the spring and too little during the summer."[8]

No one had ever said that life in Texas would be smooth. News about the decline of Four Mile Prairie spread to the northern states, and in 1878 *Norden,* the Norwegian-language weekly published in Chicago, printed a letter alleging that "the Norwegian settlements in Texas have dwindled so much that within a not very remote future there will probably not be a trace of them left."

For Elise this was a raw challenge. Emigration from Norway had accelerated since the Civil War, and having herself contributed to the image of hope in America, she realized the traffic would continue. In fact, in 1880 annual departures from the country reached 11 percent of the population, rising to 15 percent in 1882. Negative stories about Texas could drive away potential colonists; Elise felt compelled to offer a rejoinder.

She started with a debater's sarcasm, dismissing the author's notion about dwindling Norwegian settlements: "The good man could easily convince himself of the opposite if he would visit the Norwegian colony in Bosque County." Furthermore, the author had apparently repeated the long-standing view that Texas was an unhealthy place to live. Against this she asserted: "(I) have been living here more than thirty years, and I can truthfully say that my health has been as good as I could expect it to be in the most wholesome places on our earth."

Quite a good harvest, she said, had been produced during the year, even though "the times are very hard, for the prices of agricultural products are lower than they have ever been. Besides, we have had the driest autumn I can recall; consequently, it was very late before people could sow their wheat. And no sooner had the wheat sprouted, shortly before Christmas, when we had severe frost, so I fear the crop has been ruined."

Although Four Mile Prairie itself might be in decline, she claimed that Texas was still a good place for settlers. The territory beyond Bosque now being free of marauding Indian bands, she recommended that "if anyone wants to come to Texas, I would advise him to go to the western part of the state." Someone must have accused her of being a paid publicist for the state, for she closed her letter with an emphatic denial of the charge: "In conclusion I merely wish to add that never, either directly or indirectly, have I profited in the slightest way by praising Texas. I have praised Texas because I found that she should be praised." The last emphatic statement, proclaimed in a letter to the editor, was obviously written without payment.[9]

The early 1880s brought a particular downturn in Elise's fortunes. Her son Otto decided to move west to escape the decline of Four Mile Prairie. As early as 1877 he had taken his family on a four-week trip to Hamilton, a town forty-five miles west of Bosque. When he decided to move there he suggested that Elise should come along, but she wrote to Thomine Dannevig: "In my old age it is not at all pleasant to think of starting over again with all the uncertainties of pioneer life." She did not record the exact date of Otto's departure, but it seems likely that it was in 1880. She was sixty-five years old.

By 1882 Otto had established himself in Hamilton and was running a sheep ranch. In February that year Elise wrote to Thomine saying she had made an initial visit and wanted to go again because Ophelia had just given birth to another grandchild. This second trip, however, was out of question—"such a journey would cost at least $15, and that I can not afford."[10]

In the same letter she reported that she had only fifty-eight cattle left and was planning to sell fifteen of them. This was almost the last time she ever mentioned personally owning large animals; she was shrinking the livestock enterprise she and Wilhelm had started when they settled in Four Mile Prairie. Besides that, she was engaged in door-to-door selling of seed packets shipped to her from a grower in New York State. "But," she told Thomine, "to get orders I have to walk many a mile since I have no horse." In an effort to help Niels with living expenses, she took him, his wife, and their two children into her home.

In November of 1882 she wrote to Thomine saying she had been able to go to Hamilton after all: train fares had been reduced to three cents per mile and the trip now cost only nine dollars. The route was long and circuitous, covering over three hundred miles. From Four Mile Prairie she went by wagon fourteen miles north to Wills Point, where she took the Texas and Pacific Railway to Dallas. In Dallas she changed trains and went south to Waco. From Waco it was ninety miles to Hamilton, a three-day trip by wagon. This last stage may have taken Elise even longer—the route was through Bosque, where she regularly stopped off to stay with friends.

During this second visit to Otto the idea of moving to Hamilton had taken on fresh appeal. Writing to Thomine in November, she said she had decided to leave Four Mile Prairie permanently the following summer. Wistfully she added, "But that is not God's will . . . there (is) no longer any occasion for me to think about moving." Otto's sheep had contracted disease and he was selling his flock and his ranch. He had decided to live in the town of Hamilton itself, where he would set up a small merchant business.[11]

In the same letter, Elise spoke once more about her growing financial embarrassment: "Here we are ruined by doctors and lawyers. The former very seldom receive much from me, but my children, on the other hand, have to 'shell out' liberally to them. The lawyers, however, are to blame for my being poor."[12]

She and Niels were now renting land to sharecroppers because it was impossible to hire ranch help at an affordable wage. Under this system they supplied the sharecropper with a house, food for him and his family—"yes, . . . often clothing as well," work animals together with their fodder, and equipment. In return, the sharecropper agreed to pay over part of his crop in addition to rent.

Problems arose, however: "Very often, when the time comes to pick cotton, the renter says he is so much in arrears that he needs the whole crop to pay . . . (the rent). Then, if he is dishonest, he goes his way and picks cotton for some other man to whom he is not indebted. Thus it went with Niels last year, and thus it goes this year also. One renter last year left with a debt of $75, another with $50. This year a family moved away owing $50 and another even more."

Despite her difficulties Elise had an agreeable experience while on her way to Hamilton. Staying with friends in Bosque, she heard that Halvard Hande, the editor of *Norden*, was in town. She looked him up, and they evidently struck it off. His dispatch about her shows that he took it for granted his readers knew who she was: "In Bosque I had the pleasure of meeting Mrs. Waerenskjold, who was passing through from eastern Texas to visit a son in Hamilton County and was kind enough to look me up. She is an especially lively and interesting old lady."

About two years after this meeting she turned over the operation of her ranch to Niels, keeping only the maintenance of her garden and a flock of chickens as her share of the work. Free of constant burdensome decisions and tasks, she was able to devote her time to the things she enjoyed most—friends, news about people, her literary interests, and writing.[13]

Her legion of friends alone provided a regular source of personal information to pack into her letters. Mother Pabst had invited her to dinner when she was in Wills Point waiting to take the train to Dallas. Julie Knudsen had recently married an American widower. Petrine had died. A Dane had come to Prairieville and gone into saddle making with Oscar Mjaaland. The Aanon Knudsen family sent greetings to Marie Staack in Bosque.

Elise told stories about ongoing events. The man who had bought Knud Hansen's place "fell out with his neighbor—an old man whose name, I believe, was Hart—and shot him three times." The neighbor was not dead, but he might not live. "It is terrible that such things happen so often," but she did not say then or later whether the man died.

A letter she wrote to Marie Staack posed questions together with news: "How is your old mother getting along? Greet her very warmly for me. Is Ericksen still with you? How are Ragnhild and old Wilsen now that the Wilsens have left them? I have still not received a letter from Berta, even though

I have written her twice. Hoff has been at Otto's, and he told that Wilsen had died; but Mrs. Spikes says it is not so. You may not have heard that Done Spikes is married to Standley, a farmer, and Fanny to an Adventist. I believe his name is McCutchen or something like that."

She went on to relate that she had had visits from Norwegian and Danish relatives who had immigrated to the United States. One was from Wilhelm's cousin Nils Waerenskjold, an engineer and "an exceptionally fine and pleasant man," who had spent a half year in Minnesota and had just moved to Texas, where he "immediately got a very good position in Dallas." Tony Meldahl, son of one of her mother's relatives, came to Four Mile Prairie from the Midwest. Emil, his father, was living in West Virginia, and Tony himself was a steamboat pilot on the Ohio River. "This pays well," she said, "but is very dangerous and strenuous. He liked Texas so well that it is possible he will return and buy a farm here."[14]

Soon after writing to Marie, she had to renew her defense of Texas. A certain "A.U." had written *Norden* criticizing the state and ridiculing its Norwegian residents. Elise knew that A.U. was actually Andreas Underthun, a theological student from Luther Seminary in Iowa who had come to Texas in hope of finding warm weather to improve his health. She used only his initials in her reply, holding him nameless as well as burning his ears: "Apparently Mr. A.U. has not only taken all possible pains to ferret out every shady aspect of life in Texas but has also exaggerated matters considerably. That a man who finds everything and everybody so worthy of censure still chooses to remain in Texas strikes me as peculiar, and I will give him the good advice to go back where he came from."

A.U. had complained that the winter weather was cold. To this Elise responded that the weather was usually mild—she had been living in the state thirty-seven years and knew it to be so. It was spring when she wrote, so she added: "By the end of January I had already planted peas, carrots, lettuce, etc., which we have now been eating for some time." Mulberries and cherries were maturing, and wild and cultivated fruit would be ripening until frost.

Underthun had said that the houses in Texas were inferior. Elise commented that he could only have seen homes belonging to poor people or to newcomers still getting settled. The native Texans "have good houses and are very fine neighbors—dependable and ready to help when needed." Apparently he alleged that Texans in the town of Manor were disreputable characters. About this she observed: "Manor is close to our capital, and if I had not read accounts by cultured Scandinavians who had lived in Austin for many years, namely Svante Palm, the consul, and Mr. Buaas—both of whom describe conditions quite otherwise—A. U. might have tempted me to believe that all the world's rogues must have congregated there. But I suppose this must be accepted merely as an outburst caused by his sour mood."

She took exception, too, to snide jokes he made about the names that Norwegian families in Bosque had given their children. "It is true," she said, "that some of them are odd and not happily chosen," but he had no business to expose them in a paper when his "countrymen had showed him all friendliness and hospitality." Too, he declared it was "not proper for the Norwegian women to be called 'madam,'" prompting Elise to mock, "whether he finds this to be too grand or too humble a title, I am unable to tell."

In her final paragraph she addressed A.U.'s assertion that some of the Norwegians were practicing a form of "slavery"—they were paying a person's passage across the Atlantic in exchange for a year of work at less than customary wages. About this, she said, "he approaches the shameless" because Norwegians who made these contracts did so at their risk; they paid in advance but the beneficiary might die or be dishonest and "skip out" on the arrangement. Were she in a position to do the same, "I would feel I was doing our poor countrymen in Norway a favor . . . to help them in this way."

All in all, she thought A.U.'s comments about his countrymen were absurd and his opinions of Texans equally so. "As for me," Elise proclaimed, "I am well satisfied with Texas and the Texans."[15]

Elise's increased opportunity to indulge her literary tastes brought her into contact with the Norwegian playwright Henrik Ibsen's drama *A Doll House* (*Et Dukkehjem* in Norwegian). Thomine Dannevig's second son, Nils, had sent it to her. Later, in a letter to his brother Commodore Thorvald Dannevig, Elise commented: "I have always enjoyed reading and still do. One of your most lauded writers does not appeal to me at all, however, and he is Ibsen. I suppose the fault is mine, since he is so generally admired."[16]

Going against the tide of opinion was nothing new for Elise, and certainly it was not the literary quality of Ibsen's work that alienated her. She respected good writing when she found it, and Ibsen was an enormously powerful dramatist. There is no way to know exactly why Elise felt as she did, but the fact that she objected to the play invites speculation about her reasons.

Superficially one might think Ibsen's harsh psychological realism, new to the theater and literature in those times, was what troubled her, except that nothing superficial ever fits with Elise. One needs to go deeper, to the idea that creative artists sense the winds, the emerging conditions of their times, like the Aeolian harp standing on a hillside in ancient Greece and breathing musical notes as the winds wafted through it. Ibsen knew the world that Elise knew; not only was he Norwegian but he grew up in the same part of Norway as she did and was her contemporary. His works repeatedly showed how the changes of the nineteenth century affected people's lives and cast them into moral dilemmas. Women's experiences and their relationships and attitudes within their families regularly entered his plays. A summary of *A Doll House*, a play about a woman who leaves her world, opens the way to deeper speculation about Elise's reaction to the play and playwright.

Ibsen used a soothing title to tell a grim story. Nora is a young woman who in the first act is warmhearted and living the expected life of her time—she is a loving mother and devoted wife. The play opens with Nora preparing a cozy family Christmas for her husband and their two children. Her husband enters as she is happily arranging gifts, but because their income has been limited, instead of respecting her efforts he calls her a featherbrain and spendthrift. She protests—he has recently been promoted to manager of his bank and soon will have a very good income.

In response he berates her with a harangue about thrift. Crestfallen, she quietly replies, "Whatever you say." Having established his domination, he turns patronizing—"the little lark's wings mustn't droop . . . don't be a sulky squirrel"—and presents her with a large sum of money. She is overjoyed and recovers her spirits at once. The money will not only bring them a wonderful Christmas but, more important, will help her to deal with a secret burden she has carried alone for years.

The truth is that Nora is not a spendthrift. She has carefully been using part of her slim household budget to repay a loan. A few years before, when her husband was suffering from a deadly winter illness, she borrowed a large sum from a man named Krogstad, an unscrupulous employee at her husband's bank, to take the family on a curative trip to Italy. Had her husband known the actual source of funds for the trip, he would have refused to go even at the risk of his life. Because she understood this, Nora resorted to deception—she told him the money was a gift from her father.

When Krogstad made the loan to her he insisted that her father co-sign the loan note, but her father was sick and so near death that it was impossible to tell him she needed the money or to get his signature. Desperate to have the money to save her husband's life, Nora committed a crime: she forged her father's name on the note.

Krogstad had a reputation for having lied at the bank and having forged documents, and Nora's husband knew it. Upon becoming manager of the bank he decides to fire Krogstad. Learning of his impending dismissal, Krogstad comes to Nora at her home and demands that she stop her husband from taking action. She refuses to do as he wishes, so Krogstad threatens to give her husband a letter exposing the loan and her criminal forgery of her father's signature.

When her husband comes home Nora, spurred by Krogstad's threat, begs him to reconsider the firing. He rejects her plea, becoming so provoked in his superior manner toward her that he orders their maid to take the dismissal letter out and mail it immediately.

Krogstad receives the letter and angrily decides to carry out his threat. He comes to Nora's home again, enters the living room, and shows her his disclosure letter. They argue. He finds out she has been considering suicide, but he tells her it will do no good—he will ruin her husband and children anyway. As he leaves the house he drops the letter through the slot in the mailbox outside the front door. The mailbox is locked, and her husband has the key. Nora cannot retrieve the letter.

While Nora and Krogstad have been arguing in the living room, her husband has been in his study talking with a visitor. He now enters the living room, opens the front door, and collects the mail. Nora frantically tries to stop him from reading Krogstad's letter, but he crossly brushes her aside. He reads the letter and realizes that exposure of the loan and Nora's forgery will result in his own dismissal and the destruction of his career. He must reinstate Krogstad.

He turns furiously on Nora. Thinking she squandered the money she borrowed on trifles, he rages that she has been deceiving him for years. She is a liar, a hypocrite, and a criminal by nature. Worse still, her corruption will infect their children.

She beseeches him to believe she borrowed the money out of love for him and their children, but he treats her pleas as deception. With that, he judges her guilty and gives her his decision about their future. She is unfit, but they will remain together in a loveless marriage to preserve his career. Furthermore, because she cannot be trusted to raise their children, he rules that someone else will bring the children up in their home while she remains there powerless.

At this point a maid enters with a new letter from Krogstad. The husband tears it open and finds Nora's note inside—Krogstad has decided to dismiss the loan and drop his threat to expose Nora's forgery. He no longer needs repayment because he is going to marry his long ago fiancée, who has been hired as his replacement at the bank.

Nora's husband shouts, "I'm saved!"

Nora responds, "And I?"

Mistaking her meaning, her husband says he forgives her and invites her to lean her feminine weakness on him.

Not at all. She is icy. She rejects his offer.

She tells him he has shown her that their stereotyped life was a fraud. She had believed they were equals sharing the work of their family, she raising their children while he earned their living. Now she sees he had been treating her just as her father did. Her father had called her "a doll-child" and played with her the way she played with her dolls. All her life she has been a beggar without rights in the home of her men, doing the tricks that they demanded she do.

She will not go on with her husband. It would require a miracle to change their unequal power while they are married. She no longer believes in miracles. She must break away and make a new life. She will leave him and their children.

As the play ends, her husband is begging her to stay. She exits. He babbles about a true marriage between equals, about a miracle happening. A door slams offstage.

So bitter was this ending that the play's publisher feared the audiences in a major market, Germany's middle-class theaters, would not tolerate it.[17] He asked Ibsen to write an alternative conclusion in which Nora retracts her fierce decision and stays with her husband and family. Ibsen did as requested, but he viewed the change, since called "the German ending," with contempt. Everyone has agreed with him—the middle-class public in Germany, theatergoers elsewhere, and the critics. The German ending is practically unknown and is not performed today.

Elise no doubt read the play in its original version, and it may well have been the harsh realism of its increasing agony that turned her away. Equally true, Nora's abandonment of her family was contrary to the values Elise lived by, and she may have been offended by the egotism involved in Nora's departure. Robert Ferguson, Ibsen's English biographer, has observed that Nora's decision to leave her family was a "hymn to individualism," drastic and self-seeking, an act "above the claims of conventional morality." Elise had no taste for such extreme individualism. In Texas she showed that she upheld family values, and she always identified strongly with others—her countrymen, her native land (despite distancing herself from Ibsen by speaking of him as one of "your" writers), her new homeland, and the Texans, all full in her embrace.[18]

And yet Elise herself had lived above the claims of conventional morality. Above all, one might speculate that Nora's story touched her sensibilities about her divorce from Sven Foyn and her departure from Norway. The play was too autobiographical; it struck too close to home.

Although not exactly like her own story, it was close enough for her to be unable to accept it even as a work of high literary quality written by a genius of the theater who belonged to the land she said she would never forget. Never mind that the play demonstrated the very conditions that she knew personally confronted women in Norway, the same conditions that had caused her to make her break for freedom. *A Doll House* cast a choice like her own in a perspective she did not want to see. For all her practical realism and commitment to truth, it offered too harsh an interpretation of her own actions. She had to reject Ibsen.

If there was a spokesperson for Elise's experience it was Camilla Collett, Elise's contemporary born in 1813 and, like her, the daughter of a Lutheran pastor. Elise read Collett's groundbreaking feminist novel *The District Governor's Daughters,* composed in 1854–55, and reported the fact in an 1887 letter to Thomine Dannevig. The book came far closer to the reality of her experience than did Ibsen's theatrical drama.

A pace setter like Elise, Collett in her book expresses the theme of denial of a woman's essential rights. The story plot builds around the romance of Sofie Ramm, the youngest daughter of a rural district governor. She is awakened to love when Georg Kold, a sophisticated university graduate who is her father's assistant, demonstrates sensitivity to her world of poetic dreams. After they have established an exquisitely chaste relationship and hope of a happy marriage, Georg quite unexpectedly puts his career aspirations above Sofie—he privately denies his love for her to his best friend because sentiment will inhibit his career. Sofie overhears his denial and decides to reject marriage with him; she realizes that what he has told his friend means he will disregard her individuality. In a loveless marriage the bliss she had envisioned with him will die—she will be dominated by him, doomed to live a submissive, deadening life.

Although Collett has Sofie eventually marry an older man who loves her deeply, the book caused a furor. It dared to challenge the sanctity of dutiful family obligations by saying a woman's marriage should be based on love and on her right to equality and respect. Collett registered one of the first expressions of protest against the social rules that governed women's lives, the rules that said a woman must marry and have children even if she has to do so with a man who is cold and indifferent to her. It was not a woman's lot to experience happiness.[19]

The District Governor's Daughters makes clear Elise's underlying reason for leaving her country. Like Sofie she was capable of love; once she reached Texas she willingly exercised the powers that were hers as a woman—to choose a man, marry him, and have children. That she did so shows that any personal differences she may have had with Sven Foyn were not the reason for their break. They were experiencing discontinuities rooted deep in the changes of the time, the same changes that prompted Camilla Collett to show through an enervating romance that women were stifled when they had no other choice and could do nothing else than marry, take on family duties, and submit to a loveless life with their husbands.

Ibsen and Collett were by no means the only authors Elise read. In her later years she named twenty other writers she was reading. In her Confession of Faith she had stated her canon of literary criticism—to read serious works—and generally she chose important writers.

She noted with satisfaction, also, that *Nylaende* (New frontiers), issued in Christiania by the Norwegian Society for Women's Rights, was edited by a woman, as was *Posten,* a newspaper published in the later 1880s and early 1890s in Norway. Because times were hard on her Texas ranch, many of the books she read were gifts from friends, and her copies of *Norden* and *Faedrelandet og Emigranten* were sent to her free by their editors in Chicago and La Crosse, Wisconsin.[20]

Elise's enthusiasm for reading helped her to rise above her near penniless situation but could not redress it. By the late 1880s she was virtually destitute of funds. In a letter to Marie Staack she wrote: "If I had not collected 15¢ yesterday I would not have had enough even to buy stamps for this letter. I do wish that Andreas would send the $1.50 he owes me." Andreas, Marie's brother, had bought an album (probably photographs) from Elise, and this was not the first time she had written to Marie about his debt. A few months earlier she had said, "He would do me a great service, because I am extremely hard up." She wrote, too, about a small income she derived from Sunday school teaching and her work as a sales agent for book publishers.

A letter she wrote to Madam Basberg, the wife of a chief customs officer in Christiania and a former good friend, was especially revealing. She told of an understanding she had reached with her sons: "Things are well with me now—yes, much better than I could expect and better than I deserve, and I cannot thank God enough, who arranges everything so well for me. From New Year's on I shall have $80 a year and a free house, garden, wood, and pork, and on that I can live quite well in my old age."

Following this highly personal disclosure she talked about her thrifty life:

"Since I have turned everything over to them, I now have nothing but an old cat, a few chickens, and some turkeys. I have a living room and a kitchen for myself, and the people who live in the other part of the house are kind and agreeable."

Her thoughts strayed back to her more affluent days in Norway: "At times I think how much fun it would be to spend a few months in Norway and stay with you in Christiania and have some of the good food you know so well how to prepare. I miss the delicious fish of Norway so much. I have not eaten fish cakes since we lay in Drobak, waiting for a favorable wind."[21]

The day after writing Madam Basberg she wrote to Thomine Dannevig, telling her quite extraordinary news:

> I had borrowed $150 to pay a debt but had more than that due me. Then my loan was unexpectedly called in while I could not collect what was owed me. I was forced to try to get the money from a bank with good security; but this was more difficult than I had thought. The guarantor demanded not only a mortgage on my sheep and cattle, but I had to promise him also to attempt to borrow the money in Norway.
>
> I then wrote to Foyn, briefly explaining my situation, and, just think, he was so extremely kind as to send me $400!
>
> There is perhaps not one man in a thousand—no hardly one in a million who would do as much for a divorced wife as Foyn has done for me.
>
> I was so happy that I slept very little that night.

"Things will be simple and frugal," she wrote in a separate crowning sentence, "as are my clothes, but you know that I have never been fond of luxury."[22]

Foyn's gift to her was equivalent to more than twelve thousand dollars in today's currency, and it bought her a measure of freedom that lasted the rest of her life. It was almost as if he had reentered her existence like a mythological *deus ex machina* of ancient Greek comedy, descending in the last act of a play to resolve the dilemmas assailing the protagonist and bring all to a happy ending.

Foyn could make this gift to her because he had become enormously wealthy, perhaps the richest man in Norway. Not long after he and Elise parted he had given up sailing in favor of commercial sealing and later whaling off the north coast of Norway. In those days no one looked on such an occupation as cruel and ravaging. Animal life seemed rich and plentiful, a limitless resource to be exploited for human sustenance and pleasure—seals yielded splendid furs as well as fine oil for emollients, and whales gave rich oil and bones for corset stays. The conquest of wildlife in the seas was considered one of the great accomplishments of economic development, a boon to humankind through increased production derived from presumably inexhaustible resources.

Foyn made his fortune by industrializing sea hunting. In the early 1870s he invented and patented a harpoon-firing canon and then a harpoon with an exploding head, known as the grenade-harpoon. His inventions were considered great innovations, heroic conquests flowing out of the splendid individualism and progress of the nineteenth century.[23]

On one occasion during these later years Elise told Thomine that she went on "apostles' steeds" to visit neighbors—this referring to the disciples of the Bible, who used their legs to get around on their missionary journeys. By this time she had deeded all her land to Niels, and when he was offered the huge sum of ten thousand dollars for it, he turned down the offer. The land never passed out of her family during her lifetime.

Elise's garden was providing her with a good source of sustenance. She managed it herself, successfully planting ordinary potatoes as well as sweet potatoes, digging asparagus for her table in the spring, and telling friends, "Yes, turnips and carrots can be had all winter long."

In one inspirational passage she wrote about her produce: "As for me, I am getting along quite well. I work every day in my garden and now have asparagus, peas, carrots, turnips, beets, and potatoes to eat, while the tomatoes, squash, and melons are in bloom and my first planting of sweet corn already has tassels. So you see I have a good garden, and we have had mulberries every day for a couple of weeks. I planted raspberry and blackberry bushes and we will get a few berries. I have forty-nine chickens and a hen that will set tomorrow; this will be all I need."[24]

CHAPTER 13

FINAL VICTORY

B USINESS STARTED into a severe decline in the early 1890s, and by 1893 the entire country had fallen into a profound depression. Elise's acute financial problems were now past, but she wrote to friends in Norway about the economic havoc. Prices for beef stock had become impossibly weak, and cotton fell from an already low six cents per pound down to four cents.

Now in her late seventies, she was obliged to write to her friends that her two sons and their families were struggling. Niels escaped total failure only because unlike other growers, he did not need to hire cotton pickers—five of his seven children were picking bolls for him. All the same, he had to work without letup even though sick with one of the local endemic diseases (probably dysentery). In Hamilton, Otto's wife Ophelia was weaving rugs for people to "earn a little bit."[1]

For her own part, Elise kept her small business transactions going, dealing with attendant complications as they came along. On one occasion she was in Hamilton visiting Otto and had bought an assortment of needles to send to Marie Staack over in Clifton forty-five miles away. She had to arrange to have their mutual friend Hansen take the needles over, and then she had to write Marie a letter explaining how to handle the payment: Marie was to give thirty cents to Gunild Andersen, and then tell Gunild to take twenty-five cents and pass it on to Hansen's mother. Elise's dealings with the book supplier Vickery were less complicated but more aggravating—"I got absolutely nothing for my work," she wrote to Marie, "not even reimbursement for the money orders I had bought and several little things I had ordered." She dropped Vickery from her list of suppliers.

Major changes, too, were taking place in Elise's community. With the land exhausted, rural decline hit Four Mile Prairie, and her friends, both American and Norwegian, were leaving. Houses were empty, fields untended, and everything was becoming dismal. Her hopes for starting another reading club fell apart when the last two knowledgeable Norwegian-speaking men moved away.

Political movements such as the Populist Party were spreading from farms in the North to the ranches of Texas. Otto, long active in the Democratic Party in Hamilton because of his job as a deputy sheriff, had many friends in the bellicose Populist Party.[2]

Although Elise reported on Otto's political participation, she had only a passing interest in political matters. Her general attitude first showed in a letter written to Thomine Dannevig back in 1871, when she commented on the end of the Franco-Prussian War. She expressed relief that the conflict was over and then remarked: "But I do not like either of them." Without pause she ended the paragraph with a seeming non sequitur—"We have read about the balloon and bazaar in Christiania"—a sudden change of subject that showed how little interest she actually had in the war.

She abandoned her usual disinterest in politics to say that she read "everything" about the debate between the Norwegian parliament and the Swedish king over which was to control appointment of ministers in charge of the government departments (education, defense, and so forth). She was taken by surprise, though, when the parliament won, and she could only express hope that things would settle down. That was not to be the case; from then on the parliament constantly agitated for and eventually won Norway's independence from Sweden.

In regard to America, Elise once mentioned the Whiskey Ring during President Grant's administration, and she described the 1880s star route frauds involving government contracts with private mail route operators, but she had little interest in national affairs. "I skip everything about elections in the Northern states and the religious controversies in the Lutheran Church in America," she declared.[3]

At times she used a sharp journalist's eye to favor her friends with sensational news that leaped over the wearisome distractions of economic and political events. In one such instance she wrote to Thomine Dannevig about the destruction of the Spring Palace in Fort Worth. The building, she wrote, was "very large and exceptionally beautiful," the whole of it, inside and out, "artistically decorated with things that grow in Texas."

Because the construction materials and displays were highly inflammable, smoking was prohibited inside, but "someone carelessly dropped a match on the floor, and when a little boy kicked it, a fire started and in no time the whole building was in flames." Seven thousand people were in the building, yet all got away except one man "who sacrificed his life . . . to save women and children by lowering them with a rope." When he tried to save himself, the rope was so badly burned that it broke; "his clothing caught fire, and he died shortly afterward."[4]

As usual, though, she was most eager to pass on cheerful news. In another letter to Thomine she reported: "At Bosque I attended an unusual wedding, unusual in that (the) son and two daughters of a wealthy widow were married at the same time. There were about five hundred guests. We met at the church and from there went to the house of the brides and had dinner. Many stayed there for the evening meal too, because there was to be dancing at night. I also went to another large wedding where we had a very nice time."

Other good news concerned the success of Norwegian settlers in Texas. Elise had made a trip to Tyler, where she stayed with two families whose parents had been "the poorest Norwegian couple ever to come to Texas, but honest and industrious. Now all of their six daughters have married well and the son married a daughter of Governor Roberts."

There were occasions, of course, when her thoughts turned to being old and to reflections on death. Just after her seventy-fifth birthday she wrote to Marie Staack saying she had to rest frequently when doing garden work. A short time later she received a letter from Thomine Dannevig's brother, who told her that his wife, formerly Elise's good friend back in Norway, had died.

Elise asked Thomine to thank her brother for conveying the news, adding: "It saddens me indeed, for I realize so well what a great loss it must be for him; but perhaps it will not be too long before he can join her. What a wonderful hope it is that we may gather with our loved ones in a better world where there is neither sickness nor sorrow nor parting! How dark and hopeless it would be to contemplate the grave without this blessed consolation."[5]

Amid all the events and thoughts of her senior years, Elise found time for a brisk new correspondence with Rasmus Anderson, the first professor of Scandinavian languages at the University of Wisconsin. Their exchange, which began in 1894 when she was seventy-nine, came about because he asked her to write the history of Norwegians in Texas. In effect, a request from so distinguished a writer was like a lifetime achievement award—it recognized her career as a writer.

Anderson was known for being cantankerous, extroverted, and a thoroughgoing curmudgeon, but he was a celebrity among Norwegian Americans. In addition to holding the professorship at the University of Wisconsin, he had been United States minister to Denmark, a post he won as a reward from the Democratic President Grover Cleveland for leaving the Republican Party and supporting Cleveland in the 1884 presidential election.[6]

Stories about Anderson abound, and it is helpful to know these to show the caliber of the man with whom Elise was corresponding at the end of her life. Two of the more instructive accounts about him concern his association first with Ole Bull and then with Henrik Ibsen. Anderson met Bull in Madison, Wisconsin, during the violinist's hugely successful post–Civil War American concert tour. He claimed to have introduced the violinist to Sara Thorp, the daughter of Joseph Thorp, a logging magnate and member of the Wisconsin senate. Because Bull and Sara later married, Anderson saw himself as something of a Cupid and felt a vested interest in them.

The couple went to live in Norway, but when Bull continually went off on prolonged European concert tours, Sara's mother urged her to return to Wisconsin. She did her mother's bidding, and when Bull took her absence amiss, she turned to Anderson for advice. Knowing that it would please Bull and take Sara's mind off her troubles, Anderson put her to work translating a Norwegian book into English. He wrote about this in his autobiography, not quite claiming full credit for the couple's reconciliation but certainly showing that he had a hand in it.[7]

Anderson's association with Ibsen discloses even more clearly the kind of character with whom Elise was dealing. Robert Ferguson's biography of Ibsen records that Anderson visited the playwright on two occasions, the first being in Copenhagen, Denmark, where they sat up drinking champagne until three in the morning. Anderson reported that during this bibulous session Ibsen held forth on the subject of present-day human society, proclaiming it was rotten to the core and that he intended to cleanse it by composing plays far more shocking than he had ever written before.

Several years later in Vienna, Anderson called on Ibsen without being given an invitation or even telling the playwright in advance that he was in the city. He arrived unannounced at Ibsen's apartment one day at 11:00 A.M., a rash act considering the playwright's well-known biting and haughty reserve. Somehow the maid showed him in, and when Anderson entered the parlor he saw cakes and decanters of sherry and port set on a round table in the middle of the room.

Fortunately Ibsen's wife Suzannah was present and pulled up a chair so that Anderson could join them. Once seated, Anderson had the temerity to ask, "Is this your daily custom to drink wine and eat cake at this time of day?"

Suzannah quickly replied that it was her husband's fifty-ninth birthday and that they were glad Anderson had come. Ferguson reported an agreeable celebration: "They drank wine, ate cake, and Anderson smoked."[8]

At the time that Anderson contacted Elise he was carrying on feuds and controversies with all sorts of people. Although aware of his combative reputation, Elise seemed not in the least bit cowed. In fact, she did not comply with his request for a new history of Norwegians in Texas—she simply referred him to her *Billed-magazin* articles written in 1870. She did, however, write him four letters over the next few months and also composed an article for *Amerika,* which by then had become one of the leading Norwegian-language weeklies in the country. Anderson presumably asked Elise to write the *Amerika* article; he was writing for the newspaper at the time and later became its editor.

In her first letter, dated May 10, 1894, Elise talked about her role as a book sales agent. She told Anderson that several people had asked for an English version of the history of Norway, and she suggested he write it "to awaken the interest of our countrymen in the old land of their forefathers." To nail down her point, she added: "I have two sons, both married to Americans, who, as well as my grandchildren, do not understand Norwegian."

At the end of this letter she made a statement that marked a striking change from her earlier days. In those days she had spoken her mind bluntly and without apology, but now she closed her letter to Anderson: "Please forgive an old woman for her ramblings, which perhaps bore you."[9]

In her second letter, written on July 3, she commented on a copy of an article he had sent her from *Billed-magazin.* It reported his supposed aristocratic lineage, and Elise's reservations about such matters came to the fore. She observed: "It amused me to think how much greater a man you are than your mother's proud relatives! That class pride in Norway is indeed insufferable; but I hope that in this respect matters have improved since I left there in 1847."

Elise's remark about Anderson's mother's claim to noble antecedents was as kind as it could get: the noble heritage had been diluted because both his mother and grandmother had married men who could make no claim to aristocratic rank. Anderson might have been miffed at Elise's comment—he freely used his presumed aristocratic ancestry to advance himself—but he seemed not to take offense at it. Perhaps he was mollified because she again wrote a self-effacing close to her letter: "Pardon, dear professor, if I have tired you with my long letter."[10]

Strangely enough, when she gave him historical facts in this letter, she did something she had never really done before: she wrote about herself. She began by saying her parents were Danes, that her father had been a pastor, and that in 1839 she had married Sven Foyn. This was where she remarked that she and Foyn had been divorced "due to incompatibility—absolutely nothing else—we agreed to a friendly separation." In support of this she added: "He has truly proved to be a friend by sending me money several times after my second husband was murdered by a scoundrel of a Methodist preacher in 1866."

Another personal disclosure concerned her reticence about writing in English. She told Anderson she had contacted a Norwegian who had done a book on the success of Scandinavians in America, and she had asked that man if he would like her to do a biography of Johan Reinert Reiersen together with an article on Texas. Apparently the man was considering her offer, but in telling Anderson about it, she said, "I cannot write it in English, but I suppose it could be translated. I write letters in English, but it is another matter with things that are to be published."[11]

In the letter she wrote Anderson on December 26, 1894, she reminisced. She recalled her early years, how she and Wilhelm had married in Buffalo, Texas, in the fall of 1848, how they had settled in Four Mile Prairie "where I purchased land," how they had been visited by Johannes Nordboe and Cleng Peerson, and how many of the first arrivals had come from Hamar. She related that the early colonists had performed lay baptisms and funerals during their first years in Four Mile Prairie and that they had built a log cabin church.

When telling that their first pastor, Anders Emil Fridrichsen, had consecrated their modest church building, she reported that he was the son of the man who had succeeded her own father as pastor at West Moland (Lillesand). She had been exchanging letters with Fridrichsen's mother, and it was from her that Elise learned about young Fridrichsen wishing to be their pastor at Four Mile Prairie. Elise did not mention that Fridrichsen "considered himself better than others," nor did she say that he left after only three years.

She related also that she had met Andreas Gjestvang in Norway after Reiersen had turned the editorship of *Norge og Amerika* over to her. It was on this occasion that she said she had taken on the publication when Reiersen left because "no one wanted to put out such a dangerous sheet, that might lure people into migrating."

Gjestvang, she wrote, had started the Captain Tolmer contretemps by asking if the slurs against Texas published in *Hamars budstikken* were true. Her reply, along with letters written by Wilhelm, Nordboe, and Cleng Peerson, appeared first in that paper and then were issued as a pamphlet. Both the newspaper items and the pamphlet, she observed, had "contributed not a little to the emigration to Texas. All the newcomers came directly to our house and stopped several days, or weeks, with us—one family even stayed six months."[12]

She had written in her letter of July 3 that in addition to the role of Cleng Peerson, "it seems to me that Johan Reinert Reiersen . . . deserves special mention because of his influence on immigration," and this was the subject she addressed in her article for *Amerika*. She was ready for another good fight, and Reiersen's reputation was worth it—by the time she got through she had composed nearly two thousand words.

The reason she needed to do battle for Reiersen arose because the title of founder of Norwegian immigration to Texas had been usurped by people who favored Cleng Peerson. Peerson, after all, was considered the pathfinder for modern Norwegian emigration to America—he had persuaded a boat-load, the "Sloopers," to leave Norway in 1825 and had led them first to land in Orleans County, New York, and later to Fox River, Illinois. He had come from Fox River to Texas, and his reputation came with him. Besides, he was the one who had located the land in Bosque County, and when the colony around Clifton flourished (Elise claimed there were two thousand Norwegians in Texas by the 1890s, most of them in Bosque), the Bosque folk looked to him as their founder. To celebrate this role, in 1885 they had raised a nine-foot monument over his grave at Our Savior's Lutheran Church cemetery.

Elise countered Peerson's reputation by making a case for Reiersen. She reviewed Reiersen's career in Norway, stressed his farsighted idea favoring emigration as a way to help the poor, described his visit to Texas in the early 1840s (long before Peerson ever came), and told about his publication in 1844 of the *Pathfinder* for Norwegian emigrants with its advocacy for emigration to Texas.

Knowing that Peerson had faced no great perils in reaching Bosque, she told about Reiersen's valiant pioneer struggles. She described his near dis-aster when his raft capsized, dumping his vital goods into the Red River and nearly killing him and his family. (Reiersen's son Oscar, a former Confed-erate soldier and one of those who had ridden in pursuit of Dickerson, by then a bank cashier in Key West, Florida, had described the river scene in a letter to Elise.) She reported further on the diseases and hardships Reiersen had confronted in setting up the original colony in Brownsboro and how he had led the way to Four Mile Prairie and Prairieville. With this she stopped—she had said enough to show that Reiersen, not Peerson, had been the pathfinder for Norwegian Texans. It was due to Reiersen alone, she asserted, "that Norwegian settlements were founded in Texas."[13]

Perhaps Elise's critique of Peerson's role in Texas planted doubt in Anderson's mind, because some years later he got into a fracas over the much bigger issue of whether Peerson even deserved credit for having prompted the 1825 Slooper emigration. Peerson was supposed to have written a letter that had played a crucial part in the Slooper passengers' departure, but the letter itself was missing. It was supposed to have existed because a copy of it had appeared in another letter written by someone else. Anderson claimed Peerson had never written the original letter and implied that if the letter existed at all, it may have been a forgery.

Along with other arguments to make the case, Anderson said Peerson may not even have been able to write! The proof for this, he claimed, was a letter attributed to Peerson when he was living in Texas but known to have been prepared by a scribe. The words "by guided pen" (*paaholden pen* in Norwegian) written under Peerson's signature meant that the entire letter had been written for him and that he even had to be helped in writing his name.

Anderson's main adversary in the fracas was the distinguished Norwegian-American historian Theodore Blegen, who wrote two articles in reply, one of them filled with detailed facts, running to nearly five thousand words. Anderson, however, coolly dropped the subject. He went on to other matters that interested him more, one of these being the discovery of America by the Norwegian Viking Leif Eriksson five hundred years before Columbus sailed into the Caribbean. Though even more ready to engage in controversy and more contentious, Anderson had a great deal in common with Elise.[14]

She wrote her third letter to Anderson on the day after Christmas in 1894. Now she set the record straight on two other matters that had rankled her for years. The first concerned the temperance society that she and Wilhelm had tried to establish. It operated in Four Mile Prairie and Brownsboro, especially in the latter, where she said there was "a disgusting amount of drinking." The Lutheran organization with authority over her church got involved, and with that, "our temperance society died (because) the Synod told us that it was a sin for us to join such an organization—something that they certainly can never make me believe."

She wrote forcefully too about Pastor Elling Eielsen's mission to Four Mile Prairie, perhaps because she knew Anderson was personally acquainted with Eielsen and had written about him. She started by saying her community had been very pleased with Eielsen—"I wish that all our pastors were as zealous for a practical, working Christianity as he was." From there she went on to criticize a controversial autobiography Eielsen had written after he left Texas, one that she had addressed before. In 1886 she had written *Faedrelandet og emigranten,* denouncing Eielsen's statement "that we had no divine services in Texas till (he) arrived here." Now in writing to Anderson she put the libel away with sarcasm: "We were no more godless then, nor did we lead more unchristian lives at that time than we do now when we have three pastors."[15]

As she was busy corresponding with Anderson, Elise was working on her future living arrangements. It was late 1894 and she was almost eighty. In mid-November she wrote to Thomine Dannevig:

> I have decided to move to my son Otto's and to settle down peacefully with him for the rest of my days. My health is still good, but I am not nearly so strong as I used to be and it is quite difficult for me to carry on my work in the house and garden as I have done up to now. I am going to have a room to myself at Otto's and take my meals with the family. Life will be easier for me; but it will be very hard to leave my dear old home where I have now lived for forty-six years. It is sad to think that I may never see Niels and the dear children or my other relatives, and my kind old neighbors, for I shall be too old to take trips alone. As you know, I shall be eighty in February.

On a previous occasion she had told Thomine, "I have always been fortunate enough to have good friends wherever I have been, and that is a great blessing." Now she wrote to Marie Staack about how friends would help her make the move. A new rail connection to Hamilton had just been established, but she had decided to take the old route through Clifton because "it is very difficult for one as old as I am to go to a strange place."

She did not mention that Niels would be taking her on their last wagon ride to the Wills Point train station; perhaps she assumed Marie would know Niels would be her driver, and she may deliberately have said nothing about it out of sadness. She told Marie that her old friend Olsen would meet her in Dallas and that (presumably after she stayed at his home overnight) he would bring her back to the railroad station to continue her trip the next day. On reaching Clifton another friend would meet her and take her over to Hansen's. She would wait at Hansen's until Otto could get away from his

Photo of Elise imprinted on her calling card in 1894, when she was
corresponding with the prominent Norwegian American Rasmus Anderson.
On the back of the card was an inscription to her grandson.
Courtesy of the University of Texas Institute of Texan Cultures at San Antonio.

work and travel from Hamilton to pick her up. She hoped it would not be
too long before Otto could come.[16]

With the help of her friends her trip to Hamilton went smoothly, and she
settled in with Otto, expecting to be with him quite a while. She needed a
card to leave with people when she made social calls and perhaps too for her

latest enterprise—selling sets of silver tableware door to door. She had a card made with her photo imprinted on the back, and she gave one of these to Otto's son. On the back she wrote: "To my dear grandson, William Edward Waerenskjold."

On the day after Christmas she wrote to Rasmus Anderson saying, "I arrived in Hamilton last week, and it is my intention to remain here until God calls me away."

It was not her last letter to him. She wrote one more on January 10, giving the year in error as 1894. The last paragraph read: "Yes, Svend Foyn is dead. I received the account of his grand funeral from a friend in Tonsberg." She observed that he had left nothing of his huge fortune to his birthplace and native land, but in this she was mistaken. He left his property to his wife Lena, the woman he married after he and Elise parted, and on Lena's death most of his fortune would go to charitable and religious organizations in his hometown and his country.

The slight bitterness of Elise's last remark about Foyn may have been caused by the illness that was about to lead to her death, for God soon called her away.[17] She died on January 22, 1895. Anderson wrote a personal tribute to her: "My correspondence with her caused me to esteem most highly this gifted, scholarly, brave and noble woman."

Otto reported her death in a letter to his brother Niels back in Four Mile Prairie, presented verbatim:

Der Brother

I wright you this fue lines with a sad hart to let you know that ower dear Mother is no moar hur spearit took it flight yesterday evening a bought 6 O.clock P.M. she passed away wery easey. She has bin poarly since the 26 day of Dec but have bin up the moast of the time but hald a very bad coaf and no appetite. I got hure every thing that she wanted the Docter said that she was woaren ought she wanted to die! I am sad

Well Niels I will close for this time as I do not feal like wrighting this leaves all up but not well. Closing with love to you all I remain your brother thil deth

O. T. WARENSKJOLD

Because schools were closed during the Civil War, Otto never learned correct spelling, but in its rough-hewn yet tenderly loving way, his letter is

Elise's ultimate tribute. She was confident in her faith—she wanted to die. It was time for the next journey, where she would find Thorvald and everyone she held in her heart.[19]

The epitaph over her grave at the Howard Street Cemetery in Hamilton is carved on one side in Norwegian and on the other in English.[19] It says (erroneously) she was born in West Moland, the area where the Lillesand church is located even now. She was actually born in Dypvaag on a rugged but lovely fjord on the Skagerrak coast leading to Oslo.

ELISE	ELISE
KONE AF	WIFE OF
WILHELM	WILHELM
WAERENSKJOLD	WAERENSKJOLD
FOEDT I VESTRE	BORN IN WEST
MOLAND NORGE	MOLAND NORWAY
FEB. 19, 1815	FEB. 19, 1815
DOEDE I	DIED IN
HAMILTON	HAMILTON
JAN. 22 1895	JAN. 22 1895

CHAPTER 14

DEPARTURE

ELISE LEFT A GREAT GAP in the life history she told Rasmus Anderson—she never explained under what circumstances she left Norway. To be sure, she wrote about the insufferable snobbery of the Norwegian upper classes and the attractions of Texas, but these observations disclosed little about her immediate motives for departure. Perhaps she thought neither Anderson nor anyone else would understand her decision. Perhaps, too, she thought her journey belonged to her alone and that she was under no obligation to explain it.

At one point, though, she did write to Andreas Gjestvang saying she would give him her reasons for leaving Norway. This was in a letter dated October 4, 1846, when she invited him to join her emigration party. First she told him why she saw him as a candidate: "It would please me a great deal if you decided to accompany me to Texas because I am convinced that I would enjoy your company from the opinion I have made of you based on your letters, and I also share the political viewpoints you have written to Reiersen."

Her words in translation seem quite coquettish, and perhaps they were so, but in Norwegian they come across as pleasantly polite, a promise of agreeable company meant to persuade Gjestvang to take on the risky business of emigration. She knew Gjestvang was married, and she told him about her own marriage and her separation from Sven Foyn. From there she went on to say: "Why I have decided to go to America would be too farfetched to explain or to put in writing to a stranger, but if I am going to have the pleasure of getting to know you . . . I will explain it to you. Also, I will have the opportunity to give you proof that the separation (from Foyn) was not caused by bad conduct on my part."[1]

Because Gjestvang did not join her emigration group she apparently never followed up on this promise, and as best one can tell from her letters and other writings, she never offered to explain her departure to anyone else. All the same, she was right in saying her decision to leave Norway for Texas was "far-fetched." No one who knew anything about her beginnings would have dreamed she would ever do anything so bizarre. The idea was too rash, a gross violation of her social origins. She had grown up in the secure upper class of Norway and it made no sense for her to desert that setting.

In her last letter to Rasmus Anderson, Elise wrote that she "had not the slightest interest in emigration" when she was married to Sven Foyn, but after her separation from him she served a preparatory apprenticeship by joining progressive causes that moved her steadily toward a deeper sense of the limitations she faced as a woman in Norway. Collett and Ibsen's treatment of women's lives were splendid literary achievements, but they were screams of desperation. For Elise there was another possibility—action.

Her association with the progressive group and Reiersen showed her that emigration might offer an escape from the confining world she knew. At the same time, she was well aware that public officials and the *embets* class considered emigrants "egotists and traitors to Norway." She needed time to reach a decision to leave, and when she accepted Reiersen's offer to take over *Norge og Amerika* she took a major step in that direction.[2]

The catalyst for her final decision to emigrate seems to have been an angry newspaper exchange she had with War Commissioner Johan Broch, commander of the military district at Larvik near Tonsberg, a prominent man in political as well as military affairs. Their clash started when Elise published a letter she had received from Hans Gasmann, a large landowner and former member of the Norwegian parliament whose departure for Wisconsin had provoked a firestorm of criticism from the governing classes in 1842.

Broch evidently took Elise's publication of Gasmann's letter as an act of political defiance. Without knowing the details of his outraged commentary, one can imagine what he had to say: this presumptuous woman ought to be attending to a husband and bevy of children rather than using her social standing to promote emigration by publishing the words of Gasmann, that despised emigrant.

Elise's letter to Gjestvang shows she was operating at a high level in this exchange. She pointed out that War Commissioner Broch was father-in-law to J. W. C. Dietrichson, a major figure in the Norwegian Lutheran Church. In 1844 Dietrichson had been sent to the northern plains states to ensure that the immigrant churches were following orthodox Lutheran doctrine

Painting of a ship in Lillesand harbor made about the time Elise was
active in reform in Norway. She brought the painting to Texas.
Photo by Charles H. Russell, courtesy of Sue Ann Trammel, Cleburne, Texas.

and practice. Among other things, he was charged with fighting the influence
of Haugeans, people like the pastor Elling Eielsen, whom Elise would later
praise for his missionary work in Texas.

Furthermore, even though Dietrichson had been sent to America, he
shared in the official opposition to emigration, and he sent home numerous
accounts of the hardships faced by the settlers who had allowed themselves
to be "enticed over here." Trying to stem the growing tide of departures from
Norway, he addressed people "infected with the desire to emigrate" like this:
"Where can the Christian life be better developed than in the peaceful, dear
fatherland . . . where is there more law-bound liberty than in fortunate Norway . . . [and] . . . where will the Lord to whom the silver and gold belong,
bless your industry more than in that circle where he has placed you!"

Given this background of attack on emigration, Elise found no pleasure
in her dispute with War Commissioner Broch. She described the exchange
as "quite nasty" and told Gjestvang that others had joined in the attack on
her: "Several embetsmen have accused me of being smitten by Reiersen's
basic principles, and I am not ashamed to admit that it's true. Rather, I am
proud of it, and truly feel honored to have Reiersen's friendship, no matter
how much the Norwegian aristocracy hates him and tries to mock him."[3]

Her final words in this letter told Gjestvang that the controversies had "strengthened my courage to act as publisher of *Norge og Amerika.*" She moved to Christiania, a more central place from which to promote emigration through the magazine. There she established herself at the Captain Stolt building in Lillevognmandsgade, a street now overlaid by the Oslo Central Railway Station and the Sonia Hennie Plass honoring the famous Norwegian Olympic figure skating champion who starred in 1930s Hollywood movies.[4]

From her residence she could reach the Christiania Tugthus, the jail where serious offenders served their sentences. She chose it as a place for a new personal mission to help the poor and unfortunate. She began visiting the convicts in the prison workhouse.

It was there that she discovered Wilhelm Waerenskjold, one of the incarcerated. Because he had served most of his jail sentence by the time she met him, the record of his case had been placed on permanent file at Akershus Festning, the nearly mile-long fortress guarding Christiania harbor. The prison section of that fortress, then called Agerhuus Slaverie, served as the central storage warehouse for criminal case documents. Today these records reside in the vaults of the Norwegian National Archives, and there one can find Wilhelm's dossier. Akershus Festning remains a looming eminence overlooking the Oslo harbor, a training place for military officers and a home to Norway's World War II Resistance Museum.

To Elise, Wilhelm must have seemed like a good candidate for emigration to America. He was a rogue, an aristocrat who had gone wrong, an adventurer. His family were military aristocrats descended from an early eighteenth-century Danish noble, but they had been deprived of their military rank soon after Norway was taken from Denmark and unified with Sweden. His father, Lieutenant Otto Christian Waerenskjold, the last in the family's military tradition, was pensioned off from the fortress at Frederikshald (Wilhelm's birthplace, now called Halden) when the stronghold was decommissioned in 1818. His mother was Caroline Paulsen.

Lieutenant Otto Christian Waerenskjold is believed by some to have been a notorious rake and seducer, and perhaps it was for this reason that he and Caroline never married. The certificate remanding Wilhelm to jail (the *jurisprotokol*) identified him as illegitimate. His sisters Ottilde and Emilie, both of whom came to Texas after Wilhelm died, were likewise illegitimate.

Wilhelm had been convicted of stealing from the goldsmith Kjaernaas (Kyarnahs), for whom he worked as an apprentice in Frederikshald. Kjaernaas had him prosecuted and imprisoned there, but after being released Wilhelm became involved in two other crimes. An innkeeper accused him of carrying off a pillowcase with towels and other minor items, and civil authorities charged him with forging and altering a travel pass he had been issued. Regarding the pass, the archives held in the Norwegian government's vaults show that he was charged with changing his travel destination from Copenhagen, the capital of Denmark, to Sweden. Together with his other wrongdoings, forgery of a government document was considered a gross violation of the law. He was prosecuted a second time, and in May of 1843 he was sentenced to a three-and-a-half year term in the Christiania Tugthus, where he was obliged to wear leg irons at all times.[5]

As he had finished his sentence Elise wanted him along because she could use an adventurous young man (he was seven years her junior) in her small emigrant company. Years later when she wrote her genealogy in English for her children, she said his last name meant "protective shield." This was probably the way she felt about him, and it was the translation of his name that she meant to have go down in the family history.

By the time Elise found Wilhelm she had already signed on Torger Andersen and "student" Buch. As an ex-convict Wilhelm would do well to travel to an unsettled territory where no one would know or care about his record for excessively resourceful opportunism exhibited by his criminal career. The four emigrants set out for Drobak to board *Ygdrasil* and start on their journey.[6]

Ygdrasil, named as it was for the mythic world ash tree of Viking times, brings to mind the adventures of Odin, the chief god of that pagan religion. A shamanistic figure, Odin went on many journeys, some of them occult. Before men were created he hung himself on the guardian tree Ygdrasil, sacrificing himself so that he could sojourn in the underworld to gather wisdom.

In another legend he drank from Mimir's spring at the foot of Ygdrasil, and from this he learned runes, letter symbols that gave him power to work charms and exercise enormous sagacity. Most of the magic of the runes was benevolent, such as the power he claimed to say, "If hatred takes root in men's minds, I can uproot it." His victories in gaining knowledge and wisdom for mankind had a cost. He had to give up an eye for what he learned, and he came back half blind.

Elise's bold journey had a similar mythic quality. Supported by her powerful religious faith, she paid a heavy price on her way—the death of her youngest son, the murder of her husband, and her descent into near poverty—but she found the runes that told of women's future. Like her, women would remain all they ever had been while taking on tasks called up by the ever-changing world.

If a traveler had passed by Elise's empty cottage soon after she left Lille-sand, he might have asked, as Frederick Law Olmsted did on his journey through the Nacogdoches Wold, "Where is the person that once occupied this home?"

The reply would have come—"Gone to Texas."[7]

APPENDIX

DICKERSON INDICTMENT
THE STATE OF TEXAS, COUNTY OF KAUFMAN
IN THE DISTRICT COURT FEBRUARY TERM, 1867

N. T. Dickerson late of the County and State aforesaid, on the 17th Day of November, 1866, with force of arms, in the County aforesaid, in and upon one William Warenskgold, in the peace of God and of the State, then and there being, feloniously, willfully, and of his Malice aforethought, did make an assault, and that he the said N. T. Dickerson with a certain knife, which he the said N. T. Dickerson, in his hand, then and there had and held, the said William Warenskgold, in and upon the left side of the body between the ribs of him the said William Warenskgold, then and there feloniously willfully, and with Malice aforethought, did strike and thrust, giving to the said William Warenskgold then and there with the knife aforesaid in and upon the aforesaid left side between the ribs of him the said William Warenskgold, one mortal wound of the breadth of three inches and in the depth of six inches, penetrating the heart of him the said William Warenskgold, of which said mortal wound, the said William Warenskgold did then and there instantly die. And so the jurors aforesaid, upon their oaths aforesaid do say that the said N. T. Dickerson, him the said William Warenskgold, in the manner and by the means aforesaid, feloniously, willfully and of his malice aforethought did then and there kill and murder contrary to the form of the Statute in such case made and provided, and against the peace and dignity of the State.

J. W. JOHNSON
FOREMAN OF THE GRAND JURY

NOTES

CHAPTER 1

1. On elements of myth see Campbell, *Hero with a Thousand Faces*, 3.

2. Elise's family history and education are in Clausen, *Lady with the Pen*, 4–6. On parish registers as statistics see Nedrebo et al., *How to Trace Your Ancestors*, 6, 11. The youthful portrait appears in Higley, "Elise Tvede," 5. Elise's bible citations, Russell, *Confession of Faith*, 127–29. On the *embets* as an elite corps, clergy within the *embets* class, and the state church, see Derry, *History of Modern Norway*, 9, 27; Kirsten Seaver's introduction to Collett, *District Governor's Daughters*, 13. Discussion of the state church now is from Losneslokken interview, May 8, 2003.

3. For Elise's perspectives on human freedom and the value of practical work see Russell, *Confession of Faith*, 27, 28. Paul Johnson addresses agitated times and change for women in *Birth of the Modern*, 482–89. On the industrial revolution see *Encyclopedia Britannica*, 15th ed., 6:304–305; cast-iron stoves treble Nes exports, Hamran letter, March 1, 2003, p. 1; birth rate change in Norway, Thorvald Moe, *Demographic Developments*, 19.

4. Clausen, *Lady with the Pen*, 7, 10–12, 153, 156.

5. Clausen, *Lady with the Pen*, 8–10, quote, 156. Drunkenness reached a peak in 1833–77 due to invention of the still; Blegen, *Norwegian Migration*, 172.

6. Reiersen was a respected progressive editor in Norway; Nelson, "Introduction," 14. He was described as the ablest editor in Norway; Clausen, *Lady with the Pen*, 158. See chapter on Texas in Reiersen, *Pathfinder*, 184–94.

7. Elise quote on taking over *Norge og Amerika* is in Clausen, *Lady with the Pen*, 170. Elise letters to Gjestvang, October 4, 1846, December 5, 1846, January 29, 1847, are in Overland, *Fra Amerika til Norge*. This multivolume work is the source for a collection of letters by Elise and many other Norwegian immigrants; the nineteenth-century letters cited in these notes without publication detail are either from *Fra Amerika* or in the document section of the bibliography.

CHAPTER 2

1. For Drobak departure date and travel companions Wilhelm, Andersen, and Buch, see Elise Waerenskold, dispatch, *Norge og Amerika*, April 10, 1847. Elise letter to Gjestvang, October 4, 1846, p. 2; rumor that Wilhelm was Foyn's bookkeeper, Higley telephone interview, May 20, 2003; Clausen, *Lady with the Pen*, 11n.

2. Name of ship *Ygdrasil,* Elise dispatch April 10, 1847, p. 2. Description of Ygdrasil in Norse mythology, Crossley-Holland, *Norse Myths,* xxiii–xxiv, 6, 15, 62, 123, 182.

3. Specifications and description of ship *Ygdrasil,* Austheim email, January 20, 2000.

4. Account of Kock experience, Elise dispatch, April 10, 1847, *Norge og Amerika,* p. 2. Kirkgaard of Trondheim *Norge og Amerika* editor, Syversen and Johnson, *Norge i Texas,* 164n.

5. Quote on leaving Norway, Elise dispatch April 10, 1847, p. 2.

6. Arrival Havre de Grace (Le Havre), Elise dispatch April 10, 1847, *Norge og Amerika,* p. 2; *Ygdrasil* stop at Deal, Austheim email, January 21, 2000.

7. List of market prices and customs check, Elise dispatch April 10, 1847.

8. Comment on Consul Clausen, same letter.

9. Description of sailing ship passenger quarters and travel, berths, hatches, and sources of water are in Guillet, *Great Migration,* 66–123, drawing of mess table and berths 100. Description of bunks, DeYbañez interview, October 15, 2000. Quote on separation in bunks, Elise dispatch, *Norge og Amerika,* July 12, 1847, p. 3; hanging smoked meat and bread, p. 4. Fare prices, Elise dispatch April 10, 1847, p. 1.

Bathing took place in seawater-filled wooden tubs—men out on the main deck, depending on the weather and ship's rules. Wooden buckets, the best made of cedar, served as toilets and were dumped overboard. For women the buckets would be set in a private area on the passenger deck. At night the men would resort to the buckets, but during the day they would relieve themselves at outhouse-type privies located forward ahead of the forecastle. Called "the head," these facilities had outlets to the sea so that passing waves occasionally washed them clean.

Water for drinking and laundering was stored in casks and five-gallon kegs filled from springs, ponds, and lakes near the shore; sometimes the water was simply dipped up from harbor rivers, polluted or pure, where ships lay at anchor. At sea rain was caught in vats or bailed from the scuppers specially blocked during storms; drinking water taken from the scuppers tasted of varnish. Clothing, diapers, sanitary napkins, and menstrual sponges were washed in seawater then rinsed in rainwater to get rid of the ocean salt residue. ("Head" defined, Benke, "Stories and History." Sanitation, laundry, and personal care aboard ships, Druett, *Hen Frigates,* 29, 95–96.)

10. Start of clipper ship building in Bath, Maine, in 1849, Fairburn and Ritchie, *Merchant Sail,* p. 3197; index of vessels showing *New England* built in Bath 1834 and rebuilt 1846, p. 4079. Identification of the ship with particulars, Arrison email, March 6, 2000 (author assumes responsibility for interpretation that this is Elise's ship). Square footage of sails on *New England* compared to *Ygdrasil,* DeYbañez interview. Sickness, uncleanliness, and length of journey, Elise dispatch July 12, 1847, p. 1. *Billet bow* was the term used when a ship had no carved figurehead mounted on its bow timber.

11. Length of journey and food supplies, Lovoll, *Promise of America,* 21. Length of Columbus voyage, "Columbus," Goetz, *Encyclopedia,* vol. 16, 656–57.

12. Distances across Atlantic from Le Havre to New Orleans, description of best route across Atlantic, Jeremy Hood interview, October 15, 2000. Wind velocity and direction charts, knots of Gulf Stream current north along Florida, Janet Hood interview, October 15, 2000.

13. Sailing conditions, Elise dispatch July 12, 1847, p. 5. "Slatting" defined, Jeremy Hood interview; Druett, *Hen Frigates,* 58, 59 (forty-five-degree list on tacks). Name of captain as Robinson, captain not a "real man," Elise dispatch April 10, 1847, p. 2. Arrison email, March 5, 2000.

14. Atlantic ocean distances and latitudes, *Hammond's World Atlas,* 6; Jeremy Hood interview.

15. Sickness and deaths, German and French passengers, passengers sing but lose hope, lice, diarrhea (dysentery), Elise dispatch July 12, 1847, pp. 1, 5.

16. Dates of deaths, National Archives Resources, *Passenger Lists,* New England ship's manifest for arrival July 10, 1847, Passenger Microcopy M259 Row 27. Cause of death of Jewish man, Elise dispatch July 12, 1847, p. 3.

17. Deaths and burials at sea, Druett, *Hen Frigates,* 175–76.

18. Mainland sighting date, old German singing, Elise dispatch July 12, 1847, p. 5. Cross currents at Key West, DeYbañez interview.

19. Food, drink, near starvation, batch foods, Elise dispatch July 12, 1847, pp. 1–5. Food from barrels, Guillet, *Great Migration,* 72.

20. Captain flees, "bad for us," Elise dispatch July 12, 1847, p. 3.

21. Beauty of Mississippi, Elise dispatch July 12, 1847, p. 5.

22. English Turn described, Owen telephone interview, October 18, 2000.

23. Arrival in New Orleans on July 10, 1847, Elise dispatch July 12, 1847, p. 1.

24. Advice to emigrants, Elise dispatch July 12, 1847, pp. 1–4. Drawing of cooking in buckets over brazier in the forecastle, Conrad, *Last Essays,* 225.

25. Diarrhea attack due to bad New Orleans water, Elise dispatch July 12, 1847, p. 5.

26. Buch departure, Elise dispatch July 12, 1847, p. 5.

27. National Archives Resources, *Passenger Lists,* New England ship's manifest for arrival July 10, 1847, Passenger Microcopy M259 Row 27.

CHAPTER 3

1. Sickness quote, Elise dispatch, *Norge og Amerika,* July 12, 1847, p. 5. Boredom and date left New Orleans, Elise dispatch, *Norge og Amerika,* August 15, 1847, p. 1. Map showing Red River flowing into Mississippi, Hunter, *Steamboats,* 50. Map (1895) owned by Pointe Couppe Parish police, Louisiana, shows Red River flowed into Mississippi at Lettsworth, Pointe Couppe Parish, Cifreo telephone interview, November 15, 2000.

2. Transfer at Alexandria, low fares, quote on heat and being sick, Elise dispatch August 15, 1847, p. 2. *St. Helena* particulars based on low-water steamboat designs, river hazards and their names, Hunter, *Steamboats,* 75–100, 119, 102, 232. Stilts, Olmsted, *Journey,* 29–30.

3. On Red River "Great Raft," see Vaughn-Roberson, "Red River Raft." For reproduction of "Carte de L'etablissement Francois sur la Riviere Rouge," French map showing "Embarras d'Arbres," see Seale, French Village to American Town, 6. On Rigolette de Bon Dieu, Cane River Lake, see the report *El Camino Real,* 14. Red River jumps channel, "About Historic Natchitoches"; beer suds quote, Hunter, *Steamboats,* 84.

4. Descriptions of river steamboats, Hunter, *Steamboats,* 75–100; Elise quotes on deck just above waterline, American steamers built differently, engine, deck passengers, hammocks, Elise dispatch August 15, 1847, p. 1. The modified hull made *St. Helena* frail. She risked going hogback—arching up amidships—if she rammed too hard against a sandbar, ledge, or riverbank. Special iron rods called "hog chains" were set between her decks to help prevent upward thrusts. She could break her spine if the hogs were disconnected or gave way.

Rear Admiral David Potter remarked in general that America's southwestern river vessels "would not live ten minutes in [an ocean] seaway made by a top-gallant breeze. . . . The first roll—everything on them above deck would go overboard, and the first time they pitched they would break in two." Potter knew what he was talking about: during the Civil War he commanded the Union Navy riverboat squadrons that controlled the Mississippi from St. Louis to New Orleans and helped cut the Confederate states in half. Potter quoted in Hunter, *Steamboats,* 82.

Elise was in no mood to admire the ship's versatility, but the winding Red River course and her comments on the journey indicate how the pilot steered *St. Helena*. He controlled the engines to bring the ship around sharp bends, navigate currents, and snake by shoals and snags. At times he shut down one engine to bring the ship's nose around into its own wake. At landings with no docks he slowed the engines and gently set the prow against the riverbank. If necessary, he had the ship tied by rope to a tree for loading or overnight anchorage. To back away from moorings he simply put the engines in reverse.

At the time that Elise and her friends were sailing, sidewheelers were the most common type of steamboat on western rivers. The two paddlewheels could operate independently. Each one had its own boiler and steam engine, an arrangement that made the ship highly maneuverable. The buckets scooped only as deep as the ship's keel, so they had to be wide and massive to drive the ship. On the largest vessels the paddlewheels might reach forty feet high; on the much smaller *St. Helena* models they still measured ten feet at least. Although a marvel of nineteenth-century mechanical technology, their noise and endless splashing added to the main deck din. The paddlewheels added to the low-fare passengers' discomfort.

Although the engines reverberated through the whole ship, the main deck vibrated most heavily. *St. Helena* and her relatives revolutionized inland water travel, but anyone living down below like Elise and her friends simply had to bear the throbbing. (Grim life for deck passengers, deckers' quarters like a stable, Hunter, *Steamboats*, 419–41; quote on cabin passengers, Elise dispatch August 15, 1847, p. 3.)

5. Description of travel on Red River, affront and transfer at Alexandria for Grand Ecore, Elise dispatch August 15, 1847, p. 3.

6. Grand Ecore a main crossing point, *El Camino Real*, 15.

7. Description of Great Bank and Nacogdoches Wold, Johnson and Yodis, *Geography of Louisiana*, 45. For the route map of Grand Ecore and west, see Confederate Civil War Map.

8. For description of El Camino Real in Louisiana, see *El Camino Real*. Description of Old San Antonio Road, McGraw et al., *Texas Legacy:* Reiersen river sinking, Clausen, *Lady with the Pen,* 161.

9. Friendly German and slave guide in Grand Ecore, journey across the Nacogdoches Wold, Elise dispatch August 15, 1847, pp. 3–7.

10. Quotes on protest and sleepless night by swamp, *kondisjonert* family, Elise dispatch August 15, 1847, pp. 3–4.

11. Olmsted and his career, *Encyclopaedia Britannica*, 15th ed., 8:921.

12. Olmsted's journey through Nacogdoches Wold, Olmsted, *Journey*, 42–82; "Gone to Texas," quote 62. Elise's account of her journey through Nacogdoches Wold, Elise dispatch August 15, 1847, pp. 3–6.

13. Elise dispatch August 15, 1847.

CHAPTER 4

1. Description of Nacogdoches, Olmsted, *Journey*, 78–79. Anonymous, *Handbook of Texas Online* (hereafter cited as HTO), "Cherokee War."

2. On Thomine Grogard, see Elise dispatch, *Norge og Amerika*, August 15, 1847, pp. 6–7.

3. Friends of Grogard quote, Elise dispatch August 15, 1847; pp. 6–7.

4. Descriptions of cabins, Bealer and Ellis, *Log Cabin*, 1–25; quote on quite poor cabin, Elise dispatch August 15, 1847, p. 5.

5. On organization of Henderson County, Normandy original name of Brownsboro, see HTO, Hudson, "Henderson County," 1–2.

6. Most horses kept for riding, Elise dispatch, *Norge og Amerika,* January 14, 1848, p. 10.

7. Elise's sickness and quotes, Elise dispatch August 15, 1847, p. 6.

8. Mosquitoes, ticks, and ants, Elise dispatch January 14, 1848, p. 11. Some Texas bound emigrants go north, Clausen, *Lady with the Pen,* 82 (hereafter cited by title alone).

9. Debate with Lindberg, Elise dispatch August 15, 1847, p. 8.

10. Statements about Olsen, and Gregers and Jens Jensen, quotes, Elise dispatches August 15, 1848, p. 8; January 14, 1848, pp. 3, 5.

11. Difficulties in acquiring horse and wagon, quotes, Elise dispatches August 15, 1847, p. 10; January 14, 1848, pp. 1, 10–11.

12. Account of trip and rough route to Brownsboro (arrival date inferred by author), quotes, Elise dispatch January 14, 1848, pp. 2, 10; quote on attractiveness of prairie, p. 1. HTO, Anonymous, "Cherokee War," p. 1; Comanche on frontier to the west, Fehrenbach, *Comanches,* 349–61; HTO, Kleiner, "Jordan's Saline," 1.

13. The landlord Cook, Norwegian sharecroppers, illnesses, Elise dispatch January 14, 1848, p. 3; *Lady with the Pen,* 83–84, 162.

14. Grogard death and dissatisfaction over lack of pastor, Elise dispatch January 14, 1848, p. 4; *Lady with the Pen,* 81.

15. Brownsboro as town name, L. M. Davis, "Brownsboro, Texas," 1. Johnson notes that the Norwegian Brown came to Texas after 1850; email, August 14, 2004.

16. Detail on Ole Reiersen donation of cemetery land in Brownsboro and carving of brownstone grave markers is from historical marker on Route 31 in Brownsboro; Russell site visit, Old Norwegian Cemetery, Brownsboro, October 20, 1999.

17. Elise accounts about Brownsboro residents, Reiersen, Elise dispatch January 14, 1848, pp. 6–10.

18. Advice to newcomers, Elise dispatch January 14, 1848, pp. 6–10; Mr. B, p. 7.

19. Promise to Kirkgaard, expected manuscript not coming from Reiersen, Elise dispatch January 14, 1848, pp. 1, 10. *Norge og Amerika* only regularly published source, author's observation based on *Pathfinder* discussion in Blegen, *Norwegian Migration,* 243–48.

20. Gjestvang postmaster at Loiten (near Hamar), *Lady with the Pen,* 27; Elise quote on meeting Gjestvang, 170.

21. Johan Reiersen letter to Gjestvang, February 2, 1848, Elise Waerenskjold, April 1, 1848, postscript to Reiersen letter to Gjestvang, 1–3. Elise handy with epithets, *Lady with the Pen,* ix.

22. Elise flank attack on Reiersen, Reiersen letter/Elise postscript to Gjestvang, February 2, 1848, 1–3.

23. Elise staying in Texas and considering buying land, Reiersen letter/Elise postscript to Gjestvang, February 2, 1848, 1–4.

24. Elise's ideals like de Tocqueville's, *Democracy in America,* 1:48–56, 2:99–104, 349–52; Elise quote on equality, Elise dispatch January 14, 1848, p. 8.

25. Quote on slavery, Elise dispatch August 15, 1847, p. 8.

26. Return to Nacogdoches, Elise dispatch January 14, 1848, p.11; Noreodegaard, Elise letter to Gjestvang, October 4, 1846, p. 3. Anderson to bring family, Elise dispatch January 14, 1848, p. 6. Freeholder a small landowner, Blegen, *Norwegian Migration,* 5, 8, 170–72.

27. Thomine Grogard death, *Lady with the Pen,* 82.

CHAPTER 5

1. Quote on prairie land, Elise dispatch, *Norge og Amerika,* January 14, 1848, p. 1; empresario grants, Fehrenbach, *Lone Star,* 132–51, 284, 138–46 on Austin; HTO, Ericson, "Mercer, Charles Fenton," p. 1.

2. For Sam Houston award to Mercer and empresario controversy see HTO, Ericson, "Mercer Colony," 1–3. Texas fever, Gray, *History of Agriculture,* 1:907;

3. Annexation, Haley, *Sam Houston,* 284–94

4. Continuing litigation furor, HTO, Ericson, "Mercer Colony," 2; Fehrenbach, *Lone Star,* 282–84; Gray, *History of Agriculture,* 1:637–38.

5. Elise quote on Mercer allocation, Elise dispatch January 14, 1848, p. 1.

6. Texas land distribution policy, Hibbard, *History of Public Land Policies,* 18; HTO, Lang and Long, "Land Grants," 3.

7. Mercer Colony litigation continues to 1936, HTO, Ericson, "Mercer Colony," 2. Reiersen meets Houston, Nelson, "Introduction," 37; *Lady with the Pen,* 79.

8. Legislature creates counties and settles Mercer issue 1850, HTO, Ericson, "Mercer Colony," 2.

9. Reiersen in Four Mile Prairie February, 1848, Reiersen letter to Gjestvang, February 2, 1848. Wilhelm to Four Mile in June, *Lady with the Pen,* 84.

10. Elise's old house, *Lady with the Pen,* 42.

11. Marriage license and certificate of marriage, Henderson County, *Marriage Records 1847–1854.*

12. Foyn divorce date; Elise unaware that divorce action not final, *Lady with the Pen,* 11n.

13. Sexual desire, cup of sensuality, Russell, *Confession of Faith,* 54, 55.

14. Gulf Coastal Plain, Stephens et al., "4. Physiographic Regions," in *Historical Atlas of Texas.* Soil and grass types, Cummins email, June 25, 2001. Buffalo, Pearce, *Bobby Pearce's Field Guide,* 2. Fertile soil, Elise dispatch January 14, 1848, p. 1; *Lady with the Pen,* 28 (cattle as principal livelihood, 45).

15. Elise description of products, Elise letter to Gjestvang, December 16, 1860, 2.

16. Cows, barter, Elise dispatch January 14, 1848, p. 11; black cow, Gray, *History of Agriculture,* 2:846. Dallas a trading post, HTO, McElhaney and Hazel, "Dallas, Texas," 1; people coming, Elise letter to Gjestvang, February 30, 1851. Cattle trail to Shreveport, Kownslar, 421.

17. Round of work, Kownslar, *The Texans,* 263; *Lady with the Pen,* 93–95.

18. Elise home photo, Derwood Johnson; fire irons, rail splitter, Elise letter to Gjestvang, February 20, 1851, 1. Pig-tight fence quote, barbed wire, HTO, McCallum and Owens, "Barbed Wire," 1.

19. Women's clothing, Druett, *Hen Frigates,* 44–47. Only showgirls and prostitutes painted their faces, Stewart, "Home on the Range," 40–50.

20. Beer at Christmas, wine, July 4 celebration, fourteen families arrive, *Lady with the Pen,* 41, 44, 83.

21. Land claim dates, Texas General Land Office, "Name Search Results."

22. Cleng Peerson visit, *Lady with the Pen,* 38, 169–70. Peerson travels, Hauge, *Cleng Peerson,* 61–107, 357–65. Sources differ on Peerson's role in finding the Bosque land. The inferences in the present volume rely on Elise's letters and the Hauge account.

23. On Nordboe, see *Lady with the Pen,* 38, 168–70; Johnsen, "Johannes Nordboe," 23–24; HTO, Hewitt, "Norwegians," 3; Ibsen, *Peer Gynt,* 42–49; Johnson, email, August 14, 2004.

24. Otto's birth, *Lady with the Pen,* 13n.

25. Otto quotations, *Lady with the Pen,* 41–42.

CHAPTER 6

1. Tolmer articles, *Lady with the Pen,* 27n.

2. Tolmer, *Scènes,* 25–36; the section on Texas (pp. 25–40) was translated by Charles H. Russell; Elise quote, *Lady with the Pen,* 33.

3. Tolmer spurious, Jordan, "J. Tolmer—Spurious Traveler"; Dumas linked to *Journal des Debats,* Schopp, *Alexander Dumas,* 226.

4. Tolmer, *Scènes,* 25.

5. Elise quote, *Lady with the Pen,* 27.

6. Elise quotes, *Lady with the Pen,* 28–30 (horseback travel New Orleans to Galveston, route impossible, 33). On *cravache, mastingo,* and *metiz,* see Tolmer, *Scènes,* 28, 36, 37.

7. Quotes and Elise replies to Tolmer, *Lady with the Pen,* 28–38 (*Hamars Budstikken* and *Morgenbladet,* 27; Texans quick to avenge, 31; Elise quote on slavery, 33).

8. Ole Bull Oleana Colony, Haugen and Cai, *Ole Bull,* 115–37.

9. Elise letters to Gjestvang, December 16, 1850, February 20, 1851, November 21, 1852 (see Waerenskjold in bibliography); Nordboe letter to Gjestvang March 2, 1852 (see Nordboe); Orbeck to Gjestvang February 13, 1850 (see Reiersen); all are in Overland, *Fra Amerika.* Gjestvang correspondence dwindles, arrival and bad report, *Lady with the Pen,* 44, 86.

CHAPTER 7

1. Reiersen's view that religion builds colony, author's inference based on Nelson, "Introduction," 41–43; *Lady with the Pen,* 86, 158; Elise dispatch, *Norge og Amerika,* January 14, 1848, p. 4. Services held in homes, Elise dispatch January 14, 1848, p. 4; *Lady with the Pen,* 17, 89, 101, 111, 167 (friends slipping from Lutheran Church, 43–44).

2. Camp meetings and Elise quotes, *Lady with the Pen,* 38–44.

3. Log church built, *Lady with the Pen,* 47. Log church drawing, *Monitor,* 3b–5b. Drawing of log church was produced by McFarland for the 1970s anniversary celebration, Trednick telephone interview, February 26, 2003.

4. Niels's birth, *Lady with the Pen,* 44.

5. Thought self superior, *Lady with the Pen,* 50, 53, (quote "no temporal gain," 53; Fridrichsen a theological candidate, 167).

6. Eielsen in Texas and temperance society, *Lady with the Pen,* 45, 47–50, 87.

7. Warenskjold, portrait of Jesus embroidery, photo. Patten observation on Elise eye condition.

8. Elise's father influenced by Rationalist philosophy, *Lady with the Pen,* 5–6.

9. Elise's concept of God, belief that salvation was open to all religions, and doubts about the Trinity are in Russell, *Confession of Faith,* 26–29, 38 (hereafter cited simply as *Confession*); Melancthon, *Encyclopedia Brittanica,* 15th ed., 7:1024–25.

10. Immaculate Mary, *Confession,* 30–31.

11. On Norwegian Mormons see Blegen, *Norwegian Migration,* 181, 371, and his *Land of Their Choice,* 178, 182, 185.

12. Elise quotes on polygyny, *Confession,* 31–32.

13. Advice to sons, *Confession,* 54–59.

14. Evidence that "Confession of Faith" document was written on the eve of the Civil War is that all three sons had been born and Darwin's theory of Evolution was not available to Elise until late 1860; Elise critique of evolution theory, *Confession,* 71, 45–46, 64. Wilberforce-Huxley debate, *Encyclopedia Brittanica,* 15th ed., *Macropedia,* 16:1028.

15. Spiritualism, *Confession,* 36.

16. Phrenology and free will, *Confession,* 46.

17. Animal souls, *Confession,* 66.

18. Slavery quotations, tolerate Negro daughter-in-law, lecherous person, *Confession,* 56, 62–65.

19. Finding intellectual stimulation, *Confession,* 46, 48.

20. Post office in Prairieville, daguerreotype, *Lady with the Pen,* third photo. Census data for Texas is from HTO, Anonymous, "Census and Census Records," Van Zandt County, Carol Wiede, June 10, 2003.

21. Elise quotes and data, *Lady with the Pen,* 48, 51, 53, 87; Property tax records, Van Zandt County, *Tax Rolls,* 1859, 1861.

22. Houston opposes secession, Haley, *Sam Houston,* 380–91; free Negroes unwelcome, Campbell, *A Southern Community,* 110–14; letter to Thomine Dannevig, *Lady with the Pen,* 49n. 51.

CHAPTER 8

1. Elise quote, slavery leading to war, *Confession,* 62, 64. Right to secede, Divine et al., *America,* 296–99. European abolition of slavery, Johnson, *Birth of the Modern,* 240, 322–36. In 1859 violent northern abolitionists under John Brown attacked the United States arsenal at Harpers Ferry, Virginia, hoping to secure arms to begin a war for emancipation. Although Federal troops retook the arsenal and Brown was tried and executed, the event threw the southern states into frenzy. The Democratic Party—a fragile coalition of politicians from both regions—fractured. When the party met to nominate a candidate for the 1860 presidential election, it broke into two blocs—Deep South and North—each choosing to run their own candidate. The Constitutional Union Party, with a middle-of-the-road platform, also ran a candidate.

The Republican Party, just organized in 1854 and strong in California and Oregon as well as the North, nominated Abraham Lincoln. With the opposition divided, the Republicans won handily. It took slightly less than 40 percent of the popular vote, but the count in the Electoral College was 180 for Lincoln to 123 for the other three candidates.

2. Election of 1860, outbreak of Civil War, Lincoln declares insurrection, Divine et al., *America,* 416–31. On secession in Texas see HTO, Buenger, "Secession," 1–4, and HTO, Wooster, "Civil War," 1–6 (Texas joins Confederacy, 1–2); Houston opposes secession, Haley, *Sam Houston,* 387–400. For secession votes see Buenger, *Secession and the Union,* 39, 65.

3. Elise and Wilhelm own a slave, Van Zandt County, *Tax Rolls,* 1861, 1862.

4. Free Negroes must leave state, number of free Negroes, HTO, Hales, "Free Blacks," 1; property owning freemen, Schweninger, "Prosperous Blacks," 39.

5. No Waerenskjold slave 1851–60, Van Zandt County, *Tax Rolls,* 1850–60. Slaves in Van Zandt and Harrison counties, Silverthorne, *Plantation Life,* map on distribution of slaves, 214. Value of slaves on Elise and Wilhelm tax pages, Van Zandt County, *Tax Rolls,* 1861, 1862.

6. No Waerenskjold slave 1863–65, Van Zandt County, *Tax Rolls,* 1863–65. Juneteenth, Campbell, *Grass Roots Reconstruction,* 3. Houston freed his slaves, Haley, *Sam Houston,* 407. One other explanation for the disappearance of the record of a slave from the Waerenskjolds' tax records is possible: perhaps the record was no longer necessary because the person had left the state. Unlikely as it may seem, Elise and Wilhelm may have been offering the person listed as their property a way to comply with the law until he or she could get away. As shown by events related to Wilhelm's murder after the war, Norwegian and other neighbors knew that he and Elise were generous and sympathetic to the unfortunate. Might not the person listed as their slave in the tax register even have been a fugitive, someone using Elise and Wilhelm's home as a kind of underground railway stop on the way to freedom?

Bands of Confederate enforcers were constantly roaming the countryside in search of fugitive slaves as well as food, horses, and conscripted men who had not reported for their military duty. If Elise and Wilhelm were sheltering a freeman—or woman—over a two-year period, the individual's presence would have become known. Having that person recorded as a slave with a nominal value in the tax records would have been a logical subterfuge, a sensible thing to do. Considering the heated sentiments of the time, the less said about it the better, even in correspondence. Besides, Elise and Wilhelm were not the sort of people to boast about doing good deeds.

7. On Committee of Public Safety, Confederate Texas successes, and Twiggs see Fehrenbach, *Lone Star,* 351–53, and three HTO sources: Wooster, "Civil War," 1–3; Smith, "Twiggs," 1–2; Ward, "Dowling," 1. For Confederate enforcers see HTO, Smith "Quantrill," 1. Germans massacred, HTO, Buenger, "Unionism," 2.

8. Sources on Wilhelm's three Texas Confederate Army tours are Fitzgerald letter to Betty Freeman, September 4, 1995, p. 2, and Henry B. Simpson History Center, military records for Wilhelm Waerenskjold (also named as William Van Shaw). Massacre of Germans, Marten, *Texas Divided,* 121. Wilhelm's father a military officer, *Lady with the Pen,* 13–14n. Evangeline at Bayou Teche, Longfellow, *Evangeline,* 82.

9. Norwegians in Union forces, Ager, *Colonel Heg,* xiii, 3–10, 199–204 (Union Norwegians knew of Confederate Norwegians, 132, 135); Jenson, *History of Four Mile Settlement,* 74–77; Johnson and Clausen, "Norwegian Soldiers," 1–5.

10. Elise Civil War account, *Lady with the Pen,* 57–60.

11. United States Congress, *Red River Expedition,* 213–14, 383–97; HTO, Leatherwood, "Red River Campaign," 1–2.

12. HTO, Smith, "Quantrill," and Metz, "Belle Starr."

13. Elise interrupted, arrests and hangings, *Lady with the Pen,* 57–58, Hines, "Personal Civil War," 57–58.

14. Johnson, *History of the American People,* 156.

CHAPTER 9

1. Elise quotes on Thorvald's death, *Lady with the Pen,* 64–67.

2. Patten emails, September 13, 1999; October 13, 2002. Calomel causes loose teeth, Stevens, *Rebirth of the Nation,* 69.

3. One last kiss, *Confession,* 66; think too much of earthly things, *Lady with the Pen,* 65

4. Betty Trednick interview, August 26, 1999; Four Mile Prairie church site visit, October 27, 1999; Four Mile Prairie Ministerial Records, 96.

5. Report of Wilhelm death, *Lady with the Pen,* 67–69; *Aftenbladet* report with Mary Reagan account, Forrest Brown (trans.), 1–2.

6. Lord Fafnir quote, Crossley-Holland, *Norse Myths,* 134; Wilhelm's wound, Derwood Johnson, Transcript of Dickerson Trial, 6 (hereafter Johnson Transcript).

7. *Aftenbladet* report, Forrest Brown (trans.), 2; *Lady with the Pen,* 69.

8. Four Mile Prairie Ministerial Records, 96. Reiersen and Peerson deaths, *Lady with the Pen,* 38n, 60, Elise quote 73.

CHAPTER 10

1. Livestock deaths and drought, *Lady with the Pen,* 60, 63.

2. Widow Bache, Elise quote "only God knows which one next," *Lady with the Pen,* 67–68; Elise quote about stepmother, in Norway friends would care for her boys, *Lady with the Pen,* 48.

3. Request to Thorvald Dannevig for pictures, Ole Nystel report and quote, *Lady with the*

Pen, 67–68; Nystel's own account, Nystel, *Three Months,* 5–15. Nystel was forced onto a horse and kept prisoner by the Indians during their three-week trek to their encampment in Kansas. According to their custom for young captives they offered to adopt him into their tribe; when he repeatedly tried to flee they ransomed him to the owner of a trading post at the Big Bend of the Arkansas River. Once free he worked his way back to Bosque County, where he later wrote an account of his experience and the brutality of his captors. On the trail to Kansas they had tortured him, twisting and wrenching his wounded leg, kicking, striking, and whipping him, firing pistols near his head, forcing him to ride naked except for a loose coat and bare legged on a fresh calf hide, flesh side up, so that his skin ripped off when he dismounted. They wantonly killed a defenseless Negro, driving a spear through the man's chest as he begged for mercy, forcing Nystel to watch and to laugh.

4. Grasshoppers, *Lady with the Pen,* 71–72.

5. Elise in widow's weeds, *Lady with the Pen,* photo set p. 5; Tomasi, "Widow's Weeds." Elise daguerreotype some ten years earlier, *Lady with the Pen,* photo set p. 3.

6. Pastor fund-raising, Prairieville party, borrows money, help with milking, leisurely life, many freed Negroes lazy, sale of plums, quote on sadness, good fruit, and hog production, Estrem coming, *Lady with the Pen,* 67–75, 102.

7. *Billed-magazin* assignment, Elise quotes on request to Quaestad, *Lady with the Pen,* 75–76.

8. Quaestad to do separate account, Elise urging Quaestad to do account, *Lady with the Pen,* 87, 156; no evidence in Norwegian-American Historical Association archives that Quaestad ever wrote the account, Forrest Brown, telephone interview, February 8, 2003.

9. Reiersen's ideas, Nelson, "Introduction," 14–20. Elise *Billed-magazin* article, *Lady with the Pen,* 76–90.

10. Nelson's World War II career in Norway, Mrs. Frank G. Nelson, telephone interview, December 16, 2002. On Knudsen memoirs see Nelson, "Introduction," 11–12. Nelson knew that Knudsen's memoirs had been published (Knudsen, *Livsminner; barneaar og ungdomsaar* [Oslo, Norway: Aschehoug, 1937]) but evidently used the original documents in the Norwegian National Library.

11. Reiersen early career, Nelson, "Introduction," 3–26.

12. Elise support of Reiersen trip, three hundred specie daler contributed, departure and return dates, *Lady with the Pen,* 76–77. On Gasmann see Blegen, *Land of Their Choice,* 65.

13. For Reiersen on Norwegian colonies, conditions in America, and route to Texas, see Nelson, "Introduction," 20, 25–39; on Bryan as Texas consul in New Orleans see HTO, Kesting, "Bryan," 1; Haley, *Sam Houston,* 265. Nelson (37) states that Reiersen met Houston in Austin, but according to Haley (252–54), at the time Houston was maintaining his presidential office in Washington-on-the-Brazos, where he received visitors on his front porch.

14. Reiersen, *Pathfinder,* chapter on Texas, 184–95; Blegen, *Land of Their Choice,* 118–19. Reiersen is also valuable on emigration.

15. Quotations, *Lady with the Pen,* 79–80; HTO, Benham, "Rusk, Thomas Jefferson," 1.

16. Elise hint that Reiersen was disappointed over limited immigration, *Lady with the Pen,* 82–83; Reiersen zeal of public causes ebbs, quote on Elise attitude to slavery, Nelson, "Introduction," 41–49, 51.

17. Spirit of the industrial revolution, Johnson, *Birth of the Modern.* Reiersen a Rationalist in religion, Elise letter to Gjestvang, September 26, 1852, 2. Reiersen's enterprises, Nelson, "Introduction," 50.

18. Elise quote on materialistic life, *Lady with the Pen,* 65.

19. Elise on people, Nielsen changes name, *Lady with the Pen,* 281–89, 80.

20. Elise discourse on Texas and quote, *Lady with the Pen,* 86–90.

21. Elise's article for *Faedrelandet og emigranten,* Otto and Niels confirmed, Otto engaged, wedding and reception quote, *Lady with the Pen,* 91, 97, 99–101.

CHAPTER 11

1. Dickerson found 1874 in Arkansas, Governor Coke involved, Hines, "Personal Civil War," 71–72; Elise letter to Governor Coke.

2. Christian Reiersen writes State Representative Harrison, Harrison writes governor, Christian Reiersen brings Dickerson back, Dickerson in sheriff's custody, Hines, "Personal Civil War," 73–74 (notice in *Galveston Daily News* and *Tyler Democrat,* 71–72).

3. Subpoenas for Dickerson trial, no bond, date of indictment, Johnson, Transcript, 1–2.

4. Cutrer, "Chilton." Elise present and estimate of length her stay for trial, Elise to Kaufman, *Lady with the Pen,* 103, 104.

5. Length of the trial, figures in the trial, quote from indictment, Johnson Transcript, 2.

6. The Statement of Facts was filed by Erwin, Johnson Transcript, 3; finding of transcript, Johnson interview, April 4, 2003. Abbreviations in transcript, Johnson Transcript, 4–13.

7. Bowlden testimony, Barnett on pursuers, Johnson Transcript, 4–7, 8.

8. Mack Norman testimony, Johnson Transcript, 7.

9. A. J. Barnett testimony, Johnson Transcript, 7.

10. Cole first testimony, Johnson Transcript, 7–8.

11. Hoffman testimony, Johnson Transcript, 8–9.

12. Dr. Luce testimony, Johnson Transcript, 9. This person was Israel Spikes, known as "Big Swede" because of his friendship with the Norwegians. Elise's son Otto was married to his daughter Ophelia. Israel Spikes was subpoenaed as a witness for the prosecution at the trial but evidently was not called; *Lady with the Pen,* 99n.

13. Character witnesses, Johnson Transcript, 9–10.

14. Tom Spikes testimony, Johnson Transcript, 10.

15. Analysis of Tom Spikes testimony, Dahle letter, March 14, 2003. Although it seems unlikely because of Mary Reagan's careless behavior, she may have taken the letters with her when she left the Waerenskjolds. She evidently had planned to go to relatives in Tennessee, and if she took the letters when she did so, she could not have been recalled to produce them at Dickerson's trial without special legal proceedings.

16. Elliott testimony, Johnson Transcript, 10.

17. Olson testimony, Johnson Transcript, 10–11.

18. Elliott and Cole recalled, Johnson Transcript, 11

19. McKinney character witness, Johnson Transcript, 11.

20. Elliott recalled, Johnson Transcript, 11.

21. Attorneys and judge sign off on transcript, Johnson Transcript, 11–12.

22. Insulting words or conduct, Johnson brief notes following Transcript, 2.

23. Jury verdict glued to back of transcript, Johnson Transcript, 2.

24. Sentence read to Dickerson; see Featherstone, copy of Sheriff Boggess order.

25. Elise disagreement with verdict, *Lady with the Pen,* 103; Kaufman County District Court order to jail Dickerson; Governor Richard Coke, Pardon Document, supplied by Elvis Allen.

26. Governor's pardon for Dickerson based on district attorney's recommendation, Governor's pardon document, Hines, " Personal Civil War," 75.

27. On political considerations in pardon, Coke defeats Republicans, see HTO, Moneyhon, "Reconstruction," 5–7; Coke U.S. Senator, Payne, "Coke," 1–2.

28. See HTO for political careers: Flachmeier, "Bonner," 1; Walkup, "Martin," 1; and

Bryan, "Harrison," 1. On Chilton in Knights of Golden Circle, delivers oath of loyalty to Houston, Confederate military officer, see HTO, Cutrer, "Chilton," 1; Haley, *Sam Houston,* 388; Long, "Knights of the Golden Circle," 1–2.

29. See HTO for Confederate military career: Bryan, "Harrison," 1; Walkup, "Martin," 1. On Bonner Confederate military career, see Frank Johnson et al., *History of Texas,* 2487.

30. Nativism, Divine et al., *America,* 405–407.

31. Dickerson's statements, Johnson Transcript, 9; Elise's report of Wilhelm death *Aftenbladet,* p. 1.

32. Dickerson improvident, Hines, p. 42; hunted some, Johnson Transcript, p. 8; "hell," Elise report of Wilhelm death *Aftenbladet,* p. 2.

33. No record on Dickerson in Confederate forces, Fox interview; Hewett, *Norwegian Texans,* 216.

34. Elise quote on bullet or stab, *Lady with the Pen,* 31.

35. Elise quotes, *Lady with the Pen,* 103–105. Elise paid fees to assist in prosecution, Johnson interview, April 4, 2003.

Chapter 12

1. On cattle driving, Shawnee trail, waddies, see HTO, Skaggs, "Cattle Trailing," 1–2, and Worcester, "Chisholm Trail," 1–2; waddies from wad, *Roget's International Thesaurus,* 508.

2. Fruit trees, Emilie in Texas, *Lady with the Pen,* 98, 125.

3. Decline of ranch, church services at Elise home, *Lady with the Pen,* 102–103, 111. Log cabin church destroyed by termites, *Monitor,* May 14, 1998, p. 5B.

4. New church, Derwood Johnson photo, *Lady with the Pen,* 111. Art Institute of Chicago, "Grant Wood: *American Gothic.*"

5. Fund raising appeal, *Lady with the Pen,* 112.

6. Deed for land donation to church, Trednick interview and document, October 27, 1999, document, Elvis Allen letter; on Wiley see Hines, "Personal Civil War," 44.

7. Cotton production, *Lady with the Pen,* 113. Cotton acreage and bales, Texas Agricultural Statistics Service, *1867–1889 Texas Historical Crop Statistics,* 12.

8. Elise quote on poor cotton yield, *Lady with the Pen,* 113.

9. Elise's *Norden* letter, *Lady with the Pen,* 113–15; emigration from Norway, Nedrebo et al., *How to Trace Your Ancestors,* 19.

10. Otto wants to move west, Elise reluctant, Otto moves to Hamilton 1882, Elise wants to visit but can't afford it, *Lady with the Pen,* 113, 115.

11. Door-to-door selling, lowered train fare enables a visit to Otto, but sheep disease prevents Elise move to Hamilton, *Lady with the Pen,* 115–17.

12. Elise quotes on doctors and lawyers, financial embarrassment, sharecropper problems, *Lady with the Pen,* 116–17.

13. Hande encounter, ranch belongs to Niels, *Lady with the Pen,* 116, 125.

14. Exchanges with friends, *Lady with the Pen,* 117–26.

15. A.U. reply in *Norden, Lady with the Pen,* 121–23.

16. Niels Dannevig sends *The Doll House,* Elise dislikes Ibsen, *Lady with the Pen,* 118, 124.

17. Summary of *The Doll House,* Ibsen (Fjelde translation), 120–96.

18. Hymn to individualism (offensive to Elise), the "German ending," Ferguson, *Henrik Ibsen,* 244, 245–47. Johnson, *Intellectuals,* chapter 4, p. 84 is on Ibsen.

19. Summary, Collett, *District Governor's Daughters;* Elise's reading, *Lady with the Pen,* 124, 129, 136.

Ibsen, who knew and respected Collett, admitted his debt to her in developing the theme that women, denied any opportunity other than family life, were forced to subjugate their individuality to the will of others no matter how unsatisfactory or even repugnant the circumstances. Not only did he portray Nora walking out on her family, but Hedda Gabler in his most famous play heroically blasts herself in the temple with a pistol as her husband stands by in their living room blustering about his future.

20. Elise's reading, *Lady with the Pen,* 124, 129, 136.

21. Acute financial hardships, Basberg quotes, *Lady with the Pen,* 130–35.

22. Recovery due to Foyn gift, quotes on simple and frugal life, never fond of luxury, *Lady with the Pen,* 136.

23. Foyn history, Olsen, *Vestfold Minne,* 8–97.

24. "Apostles' steeds," getting along well quote, *Lady with the Pen,* 141, 143.

CHAPTER 13

1. National economic depression, Divine et al., *America,* 588–89, 598–99; cotton and beef prices, family financial hardship, *Lady with the Pen,* 165.

2. Needles payment complication, houses empty, reading club failure, Otto's Populist Party friends, *Lady with the Pen,* 148–54, 165. Niels was adding to the difficulties of these later years. A long section from the opening of Elise's July 7, 1890, letter to Thomine Dannevig (omitted from the version on p. 145 of *Lady with the Pen*) reads as follows:

I have had such a bad time since Christmas that I have not had the heart to write. My son Niels has, since then, kept a mistress. That is such a sin and shame that it causes me more sorrow than anything else in my whole life. The relationship between him and his wife is very bad you may understand, but she is not without fault either as she is quarrelsome and uses foul language when she is angry. It is all so terrible for the poor children as the three older ones know as much about their father's indecent relationship as the rest of us. She, Niels's mistress, was a beautiful and, I believe, decent girl when she came here with her father who rented land from Niels last year and lived in my house. When her mother died in 1888 Niels immediately started courting her, and I soon saw that she liked him as much as he liked her. I warned both her and her father because Niels had had an illicit love affair before, but it was soon over. . . . But this one ran away from her father for Niels's sake, and since Christmas he is supposed to have used $300 or more on her. There are six children [Niels and his wife's] and soon will be seven. He should save what he has for them rather than throwing it away on this seductress. Alas, there is nothing to show he will give her up. I'd rather this stays between us, but you can tell your brother.

Translated by Inger Russell, from a copy of the letter supplied to the author by Orm Overland; the full text of the letter will appear in the forthcoming volume 5 of Overland's series, *Fra Amerika til Norge.*

3. Elise's political attitude, *Lady with the Pen,* 165, 102, 117, 123. Grant's administration was rocked by political scandals during his two terms as president. The "Whiskey Ring" was the label assigned to federal revenue officials who had conspired with distillers to swindle millions of dollars in liquor taxes. Grant's private secretary was indicted in the case but acquitted in part because Grant filed a deposition on his behalf.

4. Fort Worth Spring Palace fire, *Lady with the Pen,* 150.

5. Wedding quote, success of Norwegians in Texas, reflections on death, *Lady with the Pen*, 135, 165, 145.

6. Elise letters to Anderson, *Lady with the Pen*, 154–70. Rasmus Anderson first professor, cantankerous, change from Republican to Democratic Party, Knaplund, "Rasmus B. Anderson," 1, 3–4, 5, 7.

7. On Anderson and Ole Bull see Haugen and Cai, *Ole Bull*, 161–62, 166, 168–69, 184; Knaplund, 4.

8. Anderson and Ibsen, Ferguson, *Henrik Ibsen*, 312, 322.

9. Elise first Anderson letter, refers Anderson to *Billed-magazin*, *Lady with the Pen*, 154, 155.

10. Elise second Anderson letter, *Lady with the Pen*, 155. Anderson's tenuous claim to aristocracy, Knaplund, 1.

11. Elise's account of herself, reluctance to write in English, *Lady with the Pen*, 156.

12. Fridrichsen, Gjestvang, Elise quote on *Norge og Amerika*, *Lady with the Pen*, 167–70.

13. Elise's defense of Reiersen as pathfinder for Texas, quote on newcomers, *Lady with the Pen*, 156, 157–62, 170.

14. Anderson's doubts about Peerson's "Slooper" role, Blegen, *Norwegian Migration*, 381–96; Anderson turns to Vinland, Knaplund, "Rasmus B. Anderson," 7.

15. Elise and Lutheran synod on temperance society membership, Elling Eielsen's biography, *Lady with the Pen*, 168.

16. Quote from Thomine Dannevig letter; fortunate to have good friends; friends to help with trip to Hamilton, *Lady with the Pen*, 130, 163–64, 168.

17. Business card, Institute of Texan Cultures vertical file; fourth and fifth letters to Anderson, *Lady with the Pen*, 166–68.

18. Date of death, Anderson tribute, Clausen, introduction, *Lady with the Pen*, 23–24. Otto letter to Niels, Institute of Texan Cultures vertical file. Elise's close friend Ouline Reiersen (Johan Reinert Reiersen's wife, whom he married after his first wife died and Ouline was widowed by his brother's death), wrote to Lovise Seeberg, one of Elise's dearest friends in Norway, observing that Elise and Foyn, "such wonderful Natures who could not live in harmony in this life, should have been called together to the throne of the Almighty. Elise had been so faithful a friend to all whom she knew in Norway, and they all loved her so much, that word of her death should be published." (Inger Russell, trans., from copy of the letter supplied to the author by Orm Overland; the full text of the letter will appear in the forthcoming volume 5 of Overland's series, *Fra Amerika til Norge*.)

19. Norwegian and English epitaph, Howard Street Cemetery, Hamilton, Texas.

CHAPTER 14

1. Quotes, Elise letter to Gjestvang, October 4, 1846, 1, 2.

2. No interest in emigration when married to Foyn, *Lady with the Pen*, 169. Official opposition to emigration, statement on traitors and egotists, Blegen, *Norwegian Migration*, 154–76, 157.

3. Broch exchange, Elise letter to Gjestvang, October 4, 1846, 1, 3; quote from Dietrichsen, Blegen, *Norwegian Migration*, 155.

4. Christiania move and residence, Elise letter to Gjestvang, December 5, 1846, 2; *Lady with the Pen*, 12.

5. Visits prisoners, Haugland translation of *Norwegian Biographic Lexicon,* vol. 4, p. 215. On Wilhelm a prisoner in Christiania Tugthus, illegitimate, see Inger Russell, trans., Wilhelm's jail sentence, "Jurisprotokol, May 1843"; Haugland trans. Wilhelm family history,

Clausen, *Lady with the Pen,* 13–14n. For a record of Wilhelm crimes see Riksarkiv, Oslo, Inventory. Wilhelm's younger sister Otilde, married to Adolph Wattner, came to Texas in 1871. His sister Emilie came to Texas in 1884 as a widow.

6. Waerenskjold means "protective shield," Elise Waerenskjold family history, 10. Emigration group and departure date, Elise letter to Gjestvang, April 10, 1847, 3.

7. Ygdrasil and Odin myths, Crossley-Holland, *Norse Myths,* 16; Thorisson, *Viking Gods,* 55. "Gone to Texas," Olmsted, *Journey,* 62.

BIBLIOGRAPHY

Published sources given in the opening section of this bibliography include material accessed on the Internet except items from the *Handbook of Texas Online,* which appear in a section of their own. Original documents and translations follow, and the final section consists of personal communications with the author.

"About Historic Natchitoches." http://www.natchitchestimes.com/ aboutnat (accessed February 19, 2000).

Ager, Waldemar. *Colonel Heg and His Boys.* Trans. Della Kittleson Catuna and Clarence A. Clausen. Northfield, Minn.: Norwegian-American Historical Association, 2001.

Albertson, Dorothy. *Four Mile Prairie Lutheran Church: Prairieville, Texas.* Tyler, Tex.: D. E. Anderson, 1964.

Allen, William W. *Texas in 1840; or the Emigrant's Guide to the New Republic.* New York: Arno Press, 1973. (Originally published 1840 by William Allen, sold at Booksellers on Wall Street, New York.)

Anderson, Rasmus. *The First Chapter of Norwegian Immigration (1821–1840).* Madison, Wis.: Published by the author, 1895.

Art Institute of Chicago. "Grant Wood: *American Gothic.*" http://www.artic .edu/aic/collections/modern/7pc wood (accessed June 11, 2003).

Bakken, Asbjorn. "One Hundred Years of Norwegian Whaling: The Start and the First Year." *Norsk Hvalfangst-Tidende,* no. 5 (1964): 122–37.

Bealer, Alex, and John Ellis. *The Log Cabin of the North American Wilderness.* Barre, Mass.: Barre Publishing, 1978.

Benke, Clifton. "The Stories and History behind Nautical Terms." http:// www.geocities.com/venturenewport/terms (accessed July 18, 1998).

Beyer, Harald. *A History of Norwegian Literature.* New York: New York University Press, 1956.

Blegen, Theodore. *Land of Their Choice.* Minneapolis: University of Minnesota Press, 1955.

———. *Norwegian Migration to America, 1825–1860.* American Immigration Collection. New York: Arno Press and New York Times, 1969.

Buenger, Walter L. *Secession and the Union in Texas.* Austin: University of Texas Press, 1984.

Campbell, Randolph. *A Southern Community in Crisis: Harrison County, Texas, 1850–1880.* Austin: State Historical Association, 1983.

———. *Grass-roots Reconstruction in Texas, 1865–1880.* Baton Rouge: Louisiana State University Press, 1997.

Campbell, Joseph. *The Hero with a Thousand Faces.* Bollingen Series 17. Princeton, N.J.: Princeton University Press, 1948.

Carter, Hodding, and Betty Carter. *Doomed Road of Empire: The Spanish Trail of Conquest.* New York: McGraw-Hill, 1963.

Chapelle, Howard, George Wales, and Henry Rusk. *The History of American Sailing Ships.* New York: Bonanza Books. 1935.

Clausen, C. A. *The Lady with the Pen.* Northfield, Minn.: Norwegian-American Historical Association, 1961.

Collett, Camilla. *The District Governor's Daughters.* Trans. Kirsten Seaver. Chester Springs, Pa.: Dufour Editions, 1992.

Connor, Seymour. *Texas: A History.* New York: Thomas Y. Crowell, 1971.

Conrad, Joseph. *Last Essays.* London: J. M. Dent and Sons, 1926.

Creasy, Sibyl. *Van Zandt County Abstracts.* http://www.rootsweb.com/~tvvanzan/abstractdg (accessed January 28, 2003).

Crossley-Holland, Kevin. *The Penguin Book of Norse Myths.* London: Penguin Books, 1980.

Davis, Charles. *American Sailing Ships: Their Plans and Histories.* New York: Dover Publications, 1984.

Derks, Scott. *The Value of the Dollar 1860–1989.* Washington, D.C.: Gale Research, 1994.

Derry, T. K. *A History of Modern Norway.* Oxford, England: Clarendon Press, 1973.

de Tocqueville, Alexis. *Democracy in America.* 2 vols. Trans. Henry Reeve. New York: Vintage Books, 1945.

Divine, Robert A., T. H. Breen, George M. Frederickson, and R. Hal Williams. *America: Past and Present.* 3rd ed. New York: HarperCollins, 1991.

Drake, Michael. *Population and Society in Norway, 1735–1865.* London: Cambridge University Press, 1969.

Druett, Joan. *Hen Frigates: Passion and Peril, Nineteenth Century Women at Sea.* New York: Touchstone (Simon and Schuster), 1998.

Fairburn, William, and Ethel Ritchie. *Merchant Sail.* 6 vols. Salem, Mass.: Higginson Book Company, 1992.

Fehrenbach, T. R. *Comanches.* New York: Da Capo Press, 1994.

———. *Lone Star: A History of Texas and Texans.* New York: Wings Books, 1968.

Ferguson, Robert. *Henrik Ibsen: A New Biography.* New York: Dorset Press, 1996.

Fjelde, Rolf (trans.). *Henrik Ibsen: The Complete Prose Plays.* New York: Penguin Books, 1978.

Flachmeier, W. A. "Elise Amalie Tvede Waerenskjold (1815–1895)." In *Legendary Ladies of Texas,* ed. Francis E. Abernethy, 263–69. Dallas, Tex.: E-Heart Press, 1981.

Gayarré, Charles. *History of Louisiana.* 5th ed. 4 vols. New Orleans, La.: Pelican Press, 1965.

General Land Office, State of Texas. "Van Zandt County. May 29, 1972." Austin: General Land Office, State of Texas, 1972.

"Glossary of Nautical Terms." http://www.execpc.com/~reva/terms (accessed February 9, 2000).

Goldsmith, Barbara. *Other Powers.* New York: Alfred A. Knopf, 1998.

Goodspeed, Weston. *The Provinces and the States: A History of the Province of Louisiana under France and Spain.* Madison, Wis.: Western Historical Association, 1904.

Gould, Florence C., and Patricia N. Pando. *Claiming Their Land.* El Paso: Texas Western Press, 1991.

Gray, L. *History of Agriculture in the Southern United States to 1860.* 2 vols. New York: Peter Smith, 1941.

Greenhill, Basil, and Ann Gifford. *Women under Sail.* Newton Abbot, Devon, England: David and Charles, 1968.

Guillet, Edwin C. *The Great Migration: The Atlantic Crossing by Sailing-Ship since 1770.* New York: Thomas Nelson and Sons, 1937.

Haley, James. *Sam Houston.* Norman: University of Oklahoma Press, 2002.

Hall, Margaret. *A History of Van Zandt County.* Austin, Tex.: Jenkins Publishing Company, 1976.

Hammond's World Atlas: Classics Edition. Maplewood, N.J.: C. S. Hammond and Company, 1962.

Hauge, Alfred. *Cleng Peerson*. 2 vols. Trans. Erik J. Friis. Boston: Twayne Publishers, 1975

Haugen, Einar, and Camilla Cai. *Ole Bull: Norway's Romantic Musician and Cosmopolitan Patriot*. Madison, Wis.: University of Wisconsin Press, 1993.

Hays, Neill S. *History of Four Mile Prairie Church*. Edom, Tex.: Neill S. Hays, 1998.

Hewitt, W. Phil. *The Norwegian Texans*. San Antonio: Institute of Texan Cultures, 1971.

Hibbard, Benjamin. *A History of Public Land Policies*. New York: Peter Smith, 1939.

Higley, Lisbeth. "Elise Tvede: Svend Foyn's Foerste Kone." In *Njortaroey*, 3–10. Tonsberg, Norway: Tonsberg Sparebank, 1995.

Hill, Dennis. *Norwegian Local History*. Jefferson, N.C.: MacFarland, 1989.

Hines, Clair. "A Personal Civil War: The Murder of Wilhelm Waerenskjold." *Norwegian-American Studies* (Norwegian-American Historical Association, Northfield, Minn.) 35 (2000): 37–89.

Hunter, Louis. *Steamboats on the Western Rivers*. New York: Octagon Books, 1969.

Ibsen, Henrik. *Hedda Gabler*. Trans. Rolf Fjelde. In *Henrik Ibsen: The Complete Major Prose Plays*. New York: Penguin Books, 1978.

———. *A Doll House*. Trans. Rolf Fjelde. In *Henrik Ibsen: The Complete Major Prose Plays*. New York: Penguin Books, 1978.

———. *Peer Gynt*. Trans. John Northam, 42–49. Oslo, Norway: Scandinavian University Press, 1995.

Institute of Texan Cultures Library. Waerenskjold vertical file. San Antonio.

Jenson, Martin T. *History of Four Mile Settlement and Church Established 1848*. Four Mile, Tex.: Four Mile Lutheran Church Roberts Printing, Dallas, [1972?].

Johnsen, Arne Odd (ed.). "Johannes Nordboe and Norwegian Immigration: An American Letter of 1837." *Norwegian-American Studies* (Norwegian-American Historical Association, Northfield, Minn.) 8 (1934): 23–39.

Johnson, David C., and Elaine C. Yodis. *Geography of Louisiana*. New York: McGraw Hill, 1998.

Johnson, Derwood, and C. A. Clausen. "Norwegian Soldiers in the Confederate Forces." *Norwegian-American Studies* (Norwegian-American Historical Association, Northfield, Minn.) 25 (1972): 105–33.

Johnson, Frank W., Eugene Barker, and Ernest W. Winkler (eds.). *A History of Texas and Texans.* Chicago: American Historical Society, 1914.

Johnson, Paul. *The Birth of the Modern: World Society, 1815–1830.* New York: HarperCollins, 1991.

———. *A History of the American People.* New York: Harper Perennial, 1999.

———. *Intellectuals.* New York: Harper and Row, 1988.

Jordan, Philip D. "J. Tolmer: Spurious Traveler." *Southwestern Historical Quarterly* 65 (April, 1962): 475–79

Kilcoyne, Jim (Tiger). *The Red River Campaign: March–May, 1864.* http://www.civilwarhome.com/tigerredriver.htm (accessed January 18, 2002).

Knaplund, Paul. "Rasmus B. Anderson, Pioneer and Crusader." *Norwegian-American Studies* (Norwegian-American Historical Association, Northfield, Minn.) 18: 23–31.

Koezler, Mary. *Immigrant Ships Transcribers Guild.* http://rootsweb.com.

Kownslar, Allan O. *The Texans: Their Land and History.* New York: McGraw-Hill, 1978.

Larsen, Karen. *A History of Norway.* Princeton, N.J.: Princeton University Press for the American Scandinavian Foundation, 1948.

Longfellow, H. W. *Evangeline.* New York: Penguin Books, 1964.

Lovoll, Odd S. *The Promise of America.* Minneapolis: University of Minnesota Press, 1984.

Lowe, Richard. *Planters and Plain Folk: Agriculture in Antebellum Texas.* Dallas: Southern Methodist University Press, 1987.

MacGregor, David. *Merchant Sailing Ships 1815–1850.* Annapolis, Md.: Naval Institute Press, 1984.

Macaulay, Carol. Sparta, Texas: Traditions of Self-sufficiency and Community Solidarity. Master's thesis, Texas A & M University, 1998.

Malone, Ann. *Women on the Texas Frontier: A Cross-Cultural Perspective.* El Paso: Texas Western Press, 1983.

Marten, James. *Texas Divided: Loyalty and Dissent in the Lone Star State 1856–1874.* Lexington: University of Kentucky Press, 1990.

McGraw, A. Joachim, John W. Clark Jr., and Elizabeth A. Robbins (eds.). *A Texas Legacy: The Old San Antonio Road and Caminos Reales—A Tricentennial History, 1691–1991.* Austin: State Department of Highways and Public Transportation, Highway Design Division, 1991.

Mills, W. S. *History of Van Zandt County.* Canton, Tex.: I. Mills, 1950.

Moe, Thorvald. *Demographic Developments and Economic Growth in Norway, 1740–1940.* New York: Arno Press, 1977.

MSN. *Find a Map.* http://www.maps.expedia.com/pub/agent.dll (accessed November 10, 2000).

Murr, Erika. *A Rebel Wife in Texas: The Diary and Letters of Elizabeth Scott Neblett, 1852–1864.* Baton Rouge: Louisiana State University Press, 2001.

Mykland, Knut (ed.). *Norges Historie.* 13 vols. Oslo: J. W. Cappelens Forlag A.S., 1978.

National Archives Resources. *Passenger Lists of Vessels Arriving at New Orleans 1820–1902.* Microcopy M259 Row 27.

Nedrebo, Yngve, Gunvald Boe, and Jan H. Olstad. *How to Trace Your Ancestors in Norway.* Trans. Eriksen Translations. Oslo, Norway: Royal Ministry of Foreign Affairs, 1996.

Nelson, E. Clifford (ed.). *A Pioneer Churchman: J. W. C. Dietrichson in Wisconsin 1844–1850.* Trans. Malcolm Roshort and Harris E. Kaasa. New York: Twayne Publishers, 1973.

Nelson, Frank G. "Introduction," in Johan Reiersen, *Pathfinder for Norwegian Emigrants to the United North American States and Texas,* trans. Frank G. Nelson. Northfield, Minn.: Norwegian-American Historical Association, 1980.

The New Encyclopedia Brittanica. 15th ed. Goetz, Philip, W. (editor in chief). Chicago: University of Chicago Press, 1987.

Nilsen, Sigrid. *Dypvaag Kirke,* brochure. Tvedestrand, Aust-Agder, Norway: Tvedestrand Boktrykkeri (printer), [1995?].

Nordboe, Johannes. Letter to Andreas Gjestvang, March 2, 1852. In *Fra Amerika til Norge,* ed. Orm Overland. 4 vols. Oslo, Norway: Norwegian Archives, 1992–2003.

Norlie, O. M. *History of the Norwegian People in America.* Minneapolis, Minn.: Augsburg Publishing House, 1925.

Nygaard, W. (ed.). *Aschehougs Konversasjon leksikon.* 2 vols. Oslo, Norway: H. Aschenhoug and Company, 1971–75.

Nystel, Ole. *Three Months with the Wild Indians.* Clifton, Tex.: Bosque Memorial Museum, 1994.

Olmsted, Frederick. *A Journey through Texas.* Austin: University of Texas Press, 1978.

Olsen, Jan H. T. (ed.). *Vestfold Minne, 1995.* Tonsberg, Norway: Vestfold Historielag, 1995.

Overland, Orm. *The Western Home: A Literary History of Norwegian America.* Northfield, Minn.: Norwegian-American Historical Association, 1996.

Overland, Orm (ed.). *Fra Amerika til Norge.* 4 vols. Oslo, Norway: Norwegian Archives, 1992–2003.

Pearce, Bobby (ed.) *Bobby Pearce's Field Guide of Historical Sites in Van Zandt County.* Austin, Tex.: TXGenWeb/USGenWeb Project. http://www.rootsweb.com/~txvanzan/vzhist (accessed March 30, 2002, June 6, 2003).

Peterson, William. *Steamboating on the Mississippi.* Iowa City: State Historical Society, 1937.

Ramsdell, Charles. *Reconstruction in Texas.* Austin: University of Texas Press, 1970.

Reiersen, Johan. *Pathfinder for Norwegian Emigrants to the United North American States and Texas.* Trans. Frank G. Nelson. Northfield, Minn.: Norwegian-American Historical Association, 1980.

Richardson, R. N. *Texas: The Lone Star State.* New York: Prentice Hall, 1970.

Roget's International Thesaurus. New York: Thomas Y. Crowell, 1946.

Roper, Laura Wood. *FLO: A Biography of Frederick Law Olmsted.* Baltimore, Md.: Johns Hopkins University Press, 1973.

Rosenberg, Kjell. *Lillesand Historie.* Lillesand, Norway: Mennesker, By og Boliger, 1990.

Russell, Charles H. *Confession of Faith.* Houston, Tex.: Published by author, 2001.

Schopp, Claude. *Alexander Dumas: Genius of Life.* New York: Franklin Watts, 1988.

Schweninger, Leon. "Prosperous Blacks in the South, 1790–1880." *American Historical Review* 95, no. 1 (February, 1990): 31–56.

Scott, Stanley. Angry Agrarian: The Texas Farmer, 1875–1896. Ph.D. diss., Texas Christian University, 1973.

Seale, Richard. From French Village to American Town: The Development of Natchitoches, Louisiana, 1788–1818. Master's thesis, Northwestern State University of Louisiana, 1995.

Silverthorne, Elizabeth. *Plantation Life in Texas.* College Station: Texas A&M University Press, 1986.

Starling, Susanne. *Land Is the Cry.* Austin, Tex.: State Historical Association, 1998.

Stephens, Ray, William Holmes, and Phyllis McCaffrey (consultant). *Historical Atlas of Texas.* Norman: University of Oklahoma Press, 1989.

Stevens, Joseph. *1863: The Rebirth of the Nation.* New York: Bantam Books, 1999.

Stewart, Doug. "Home on the Range." *Smithsonian,* May, 2002, pp. 40–50.

Storing, James. *Norwegian Democracy.* Boston, Mass.: Houghton Mifflin, 1963.

Surdam, David G. "The Antebellum Texas Cattle Trade across the Gulf of Mexico." *Southwestern Historical Quarterly* 100, no. 4 (1997): 477–92.

Surface Pressure and Winds. http://www.magma.mines.edu/fs_home/jsneed/courses/LISS389–83/LISS.380/syllabus/ . . . /fig.1.1.2 (accessed February 7, 2000).

Syversen, Odd Magnar, and Derwood Johnson. *Norge i Texas.* Stange, Norway: Stange Historielag, 1982.

Texas Agricultural Statistics Service. *1867–1990 Texas Historical Livestock Statistics.* Austin: Agricultural Statistics Service, 1990.

————. *1866–1989 Texas Historical Crop Statistics.* Austin: Agricultural Statistics Service, 1991.

Tolmer, J. *Scènes de l'Amerique du Nord 1849.* Leipzig, Germany: Avenarius and Mendelssohn, 1850.

Tomasi, Stephanie. "Widow's Weeds." http://www.mourningmatters.com/mourningmatters-artcle (accessed January 16, 2003).

Tyler, Ron (ed.). *The New Handbook of Texas.* Austin: Texas State Historical Association.

Thoresen, Per, and Erik Gessner. *Vestfold Minne, 1995.* Tonsberg, Norway: Vestfold Historielag, 1995.

Thorisson, Jon (ed.) *The Viking Gods.* Trans. Jean A. Young. Olso, Norway: Gudrun Publishing, 1995.

United States. Congress, Joint Committee on the Conduct of the War. *Red River Expedition.* Millwood, N.Y.: Kraus Reprint Company, 1977.

Unstad, Lyder. "Norwegian Migration to Texas." *Southwestern Historical Quarterly* 43 (October, 1939): 176–95.

Vaughn-Roberson, Glen. "Red River Raft." *Encyclopedia of Oklahoma:* Oklahoma Historical Society. http://www.ok-history.mus.ok.us/enc/rdrivrft.htm (accessed June 1, 2003).

Wagner-Martin, Linda. *Telling Women's Lives: The New Biography.* New Brunswick, N.J.: Rutgers University Press, 1994.

Way, Frederick. *Way's Packet Directory 1848–1894: Passenger Steamboats on the Mississippi River System since the Advent of Photography in Mid-Continental America.* Athens: Ohio University Press, 1994.

Webster's Third New International Dictionary. 3rd ed. 3 vols. Chicago: Encyclopedia Brittanica, 1981.

Wilson, David M. *The Vikings and Their Origins.* London: Thames and Hudson, 1991.

Handbook of Texas Online

All references can be accessed at http://www.tsha.utexas.edu/handbook/ onlinearticles/view. Following each title are its precise location at that online site and the date it was accessed.

Anonymous. "Census and Census Records." /CC/ulc1 (06/16/03).

———. "Cherokee War." /CC/qdcl1 (06/02/03).

———. "Old San Antonio Road." /OO/ex04 (10/18/03).

Benham, Priscilla Myers. "Rusk, Thomas Jefferson." /RR/fru16 (09/25/04).

Biesele, Rudolph. "German Attitude toward the Civil War." /GG/png1 (06/28/04).

Britton, Karen Gerhardt, Fred C. Eliott, and E. A. Miller. "Cotton Culture." /CC/afc3 (02/12/02).

Bryan, J. L. "Harrison, James Marshall." /HH/fhagp (01/29/03).

Buenger, Walter L. "Secession." /SS/mgs2 (08/26/00).

———. "Unionism" /UU/Umzu1 (06/28/04).

Campbell, Ralph S. "Slavery." /SS/yps (06/27/02).

Carlson, Paul H. "Sheep Ranching." /SS/aus.1 (5/28/01).

Cutrer, Thomas W. "Chilton, George Washington." CC/fch.29 (01/29/03).

———. "Twiggs, David Emanual." /TT/ftw3 (06/09/03).

Davis, L. Michael. "Brownsboro, Texas." /BB/hlb5 (06/04/03).

Dethloff, Henry C., and Gary L. Nall. "Agriculture." /AA/ama1 (02/12/02).

Ericson, Joe E. "Mercer Colony." /MM/uem2 (09/25/00).

———. "Mercer, Charles Fenton." /MM/fme23 (09/28/04).

Flachmeier, Jeanette H. "Bonner, Micajah Hubbard." /BB/fbo19 (01/29/03).

Hales, Douglas. "Free Blacks." /FF/pkfbs (06/09/03).

Harper, Cecil, and Dale E. Odom. "Farm Tenancy." /FF/aefmu (02/12/02).

Hewitt, W. Phil. "Norwegians." /NN/ptn1 (06/07/03).

Hudson, Lynda Sybert. "Henderson County." /HH/hch13 (06/02/03).

Kesting, Robert W. "Bryan, William." /BB/fbras (05/06/03).

Kleiner, Diana J. "Jordan's Saline, Texas." /JJ/hvj18 (06/02/03).

———. "Grand Saline, Texas." /SS/dks1 (05/28/01).

Kozlowski, Gerald F. "Van Zandt County." /VV/hcv2 (02/12/02).

Kreneck, Thomas H. "Houston, Samuel." /Hhfh073 (05/26/03).

Lang, Aldon S., and Christopher Long. "Land Grants." /MM/mpī1 (02/10/04).

Lang, Aldon S., and Berie R. Haigh. "Public Lands." /PP/gzp2 (02/23/03).

Leatherwood, Art. "Red River Campaign." /RR/qdr1 (06/09/03).

Long, Christopher. "Rusk, Texas." /RR/hcr12 (02/12/02).

———. "Killough Massacre." /KK/htk1 (02/12/02).

———. "Knights of the Golden Circle." /KK/vbk1 (01/30/03).

McCallum, Frances T., and James Mulkey Owens. "Barbed Wire." /BB/aob1 (06/07/03).

McElhaney, Jackie, and Michael V. Hazel. "Dallas, TX." /DD/hdd1 (06/06/03).

McKay, S. S. "Constitution of 1845." /CC/mhc3 (26/03/02).

Metz, Leon. "Starr, Myra Maybelle Shirley." /SS/fstbl (05/26/03).

Moneyhon, Carl H. "Reconstruction." /RR/mzrl (02/11/03).

Newton, L. W. "Olmsted, Frederick Law." /OO/for5 (06/02/03).

Payne, John W. "Coke, Richard." /CC/fco15 (01/30/03).

Ragsdale, Crystal S. "Waerenskjold, Elise Amalie Tvede." /WW/fwa5 (05/24/03).

Regenbrecht, E. M., and Chris Cravens. "Swine Raising." /SS/ags1 (5/28/01).

Ross, John R. "Cherokee County." /CC/hcc10 (02/12/02).

Skaggs, Jimmy M. "Cattle Trailing." /CC/ayc1 (06/11/03).

Smith, David Paul. "Quantrill, William Clark." /QQ/fqu3/ (06/09/03).

Stoltz, Jack. "Four Mile Prairie, Texas." /FF/hvf36 (02/12/02).

Walkup, David S. "Martin, William Harrison." /MM/fma62 (01/29/03).

Ward, James R. "Dowling, Richard William." /DD/fdo28 (06/09/03).

Werner, George C. "Texas and Pacific Railway." /TT/eqt8 (02/12/02).

Wilson, Stephen G. "Railroad Construction, Public Aid to." /RR/mpr1 (02/12/02).

Wooster, Ralph A. "Civil War." /CC/qdc2 (08/22/02).

Worcester, Donald C. "Chisholm Trail." /CC/ayc2 (02/12/02).

Documents, Translations, Maps, and Photographs

Confederate Civil War Map: Grand Ecore and west. Cammie G. Henry Research Center, Watson Memorial Library, Northwestern State University, Natchitoches, La.

El Camino Real. (Preliminary Draft, condensation of a report by: Kisatchie Delta Regional Planning Commission, Louisiana). Photocopy.

Engen, Gunnar, et al. Commemorative Program prepared for Olav V of Norway Visit to Texas, October 9–12, 1982. Dallas: Norwegian Society of Texas. 1982.

Featherstone, Sandra, District Clerk, Kaufman County, Tex. Copy of Kaufman County Sheriff Bennet Boggess order, dated Monday, June 21, 1875, 8 O'Clock a.m., to convey N. T. Dickerson to the State Penitentiary at Huntsville. Supplied to the author November 15, 1999.

Fitzgerald, Mary Ann. Letter to Betty Freeman, September 4, 1995, enclosing English language copy of "Our Heritage," attributed to Elise Waerenskjold.

Four Mile Prairie Documents supplied by Betty Trednick and Helen Wisdom. Centennial. Typed two-page history of Four Mile Prairie Lutheran Church and events at 1937 celebration of church founding, no date.

————. Elise Waerenskjold deed to Four Mile Prairie Lutheran Church land, June, 1879. Photocopy.

————. History of Four Mile Lutheran Church by Betty Ann Gunderson Vowell Freeman Trednick, March 22, 1998.

————. Ministerial Record Book, Four Mile Prairie Lutheran Church, July 4, 1964.

————. Photo of 1937 church Centennial celebration. Photocopy.

————. Photo of oak tree in center of the Four Mile Prairie Church cemetery, no date. Photocopy.

————. Late nineteenth-century photo of George Taylor home on Reiersen survey 1870–1880. Photocopy.

————. Plan of Town of Prairieville, September 18, 1867. Photocopy.

————. Photo of Prairieville School pupils and school about 1900. Photocopy.

————. Photo of Stagecoach Hotel, Prairieville. Late nineteenth-century photo scanned on computer by Jean Carruthers Old.

Four Mile Prairie Lutheran Church. "150th Year Celebration. Four Mile Prairie Lutheran Church. May 17, 1998." Mabank, Tex.: Monitor (Mabank newspaper printer), 1998.

Governor Richard Coke, undated Pardon Document for N. T. Dickerson. Copy supplied to author by Elvis Allen, Van Zandt County, at request of Sybil Creasey, Canton, Tex.

Gulbrandson, Alvhild. *Carl Knudsen-Gaarden: Lillesand By og Sjofarts-museum,* brochure. Lillesand, Aust-Agder, Norway: Terjes Trykkeri (printer), June, 1999.

Henderson County. *Marriage Records, 1847–1854.* Microfilm Reels: 1481017 1847–1854, 1578917 vol. A 1848–1864. Texas State Library and Archives Commission. Regional Historical Resource Depository at Texas A&M University–Commerce. Producer: Genealogical Society of Utah.

Henry B. Simpson History Center, Hillsboro, Texas. Texas Military Records Archive. Records for Wilhelm Waerenskjold (also listed as William Van Shaw), Christian Reiersen, Oscar Reiersen, Judge Bonner. (N. T. Dickerson not listed as Confederate soldier.)

Holt meninghetsraad (Holt Church Vestry). *Holt Kirke,* brochure. Tvedes-trand Kommun, Aust-Agder, Norway: Tvedestrandspostens (printer), no date.

Johnson, Derwood. Transcript of Dickerson Trial, with closing notes. Copy sent to author. Unpublished.

———. Photo of Elise's Four Mile Prairie home.

———. Photo of Four Mile Prairie Lutheran Church built in 1875.

Kaufman County District Court. *Minutes.* Microfilm reels: 1875 1305368, 1305369. Texas State Library and Archives Commission. Regional Historical Resource Depository at Texas A&M University–Commerce. Producer: Genealogical Society of Utah.

Orbaeck, Andreas, trans. Anne Saglokken: letter, February 13, 1850; thank you note, April 18, 1850. In *Fra Amerika til Norge,* ed. Orm Overland, 4 vols. Oslo, Norway: Norwegian Archives, 1992–2003.

"Prestegaard" (Priest's Farm), Vestre Moland, circa 1820. Photo of oil painting owned by the Sjofartsmuseum, Lillesand, Norway. Permission to publish: Alvhild Gulbrandson.

Reiersen, Johan/postscript Elise Waerenskjold, trans. Anne Saglokken: letter, February 2, 1848, to Andreas Gjestvang. In *Fra Amerika til Norge,* ed. Orm Overland, 4 vols. Oslo, Norway: Norwegian Archives, 1992–2003.

Reiersen, Ouline, trans. Inger Russell: Froeken (Lovise) Seeberg, March 3, 1895, supplied to author by Orm Overland, full text in *Fra Amerika til Norge,* vol. 5, forthcoming.

Riksarkiv, Oslo. Inventory of Persons Who Have Been under Justice, but Not in Akerhus Slaveri (trans. of *Fortegnelse over Personer der have vaeret under Justisens Tiltale, men ikke senere avlevent til Akerhus Slaveri*), Domsakter 1838–1862, arkivboks 139 and Kristiania Tukthus.

Russell, Inger, trans. Wilhelm's jail sentence, "Jurisprotokol, May 1843."
Copy from Norwegian State Archives in Oslo (Statsarkiv I Oslo), with
letter from Lisbeth Higley, May 21, 2003.

Sandefjord, Museum of. *Museum Sandefjord,* brochure. Sandefjord, Vestfold, Norway: Sandefjordmuseene, [1995?].

Ship *New England.* Alan Stewart, Research Assistant, at the Maine Maritime Museum, Bath, Maine, supplied information and a photo of an
oil painting of *The New England.*

"Termites destroy log church." *Monitor,* May 14, 1998, p. 5B.

Texas General Land Office, Archives and Records Division. "Name Search
Results." (Record of Elise and Wilhelm Waerenskjold land grants)
Customer ID 8119, Order ID 99–359.

Van Zandt County, Office of the Tax-Assessor-Collector. *Tax Rolls, 1848–
1886.* Microfilm reel 123401. *Tax Rolls 1848–1910,* Microfilm reel 123401,
1848–1886. Texas State Library and Archives Commission. Regional
Historical Resource Depository at Texas A&M University–Commerce.
Producer: Genealogical Society of Utah.

Waerenskjold, Elise. Dispatches to *Norge og Amerika.* Trans. Inger Russell:
April 10, 1847; April 16, 1847; July 12, 1847; August 15, 1847; January 14,
1848. In Odd Magnar Syverson and Derwood Johnson, *Norge i Texas.*
Stange, Norway: Stange Historielag, 1982.

———. Family history (handwritten). Copy from Archives, Norwegian-
American Historical Association.

———. Letters, in *Fra Amerika til Norge,* ed. Orm Overland, 4 vols. Oslo,
Norway: Norwegian Archives, 1992–2003. Various translators:

Letters trans. Randi Jahnsen: Thomine Dannevig, March 25, 1860;
Lillesand Friends, March 24, 1860; Thomine Dannevig, Spring or
Summer (?), 1865.

Letters trans. Astrid Mosvold: Andreas Gjestvang: February 20, 1851;
September 26, 1852.

Letters trans. Sidsel Roemer: Thomine Dannevig, October 16, 1858;
Andreas Gjestvang, November 21, 1852.

Letters trans. Inger Russell: Andreas Gjestvang, October 4, 1846; December 5, 1846; January 29, 1847. Addition to July 7, 1890, letter to Thomine Dannevig (see p. 145, *Lady with the Pen*) supplied to author by
Orm Overland, full text in *Fra Amerika til Norge,* vol. 5, forthcoming.

Letters trans. Ingelin Saethre: Andreas Gjestvang, January 20, 1847;
March 14, 1847; June 2, 1849; December 16, 1850.

―――. Letter to Governor Coke. Author's Dickerson trial file, copy owned by Elvis Allen, Kaufman County, sent by Sybil Creasey, Canton, Tex., March, 2003.

―――. Portrait, age 15, oil. Appears in Lisbeth Higley, "Elise Tvede: Svend Foyn's Foerste Kone," p. 5 in *Njortaroey.* Tonsberg, Norway: Tonsberg Sparebank, 1995. Provenance: portrait owned by Lillemor Strom, Stabekk, Norway. Permission to publish obtained.

―――. Portrait, age 43(?), daguerreotype enlargement. Institute of Texan Cultures, San Antonio, photo file. Permission to publish: Institute of Texan Cultures.

―――. Portrait, age 55(?), photo in widow's weeds. State Historical Society of Wisconsin.

―――. Portrait of Jesus, embroidery made at age thirteen in Norway. Owned by William Van Shaw, Dallas, Tex. Charles Russell photo. Permission to publish: William Van Shaw.

―――. Report of Wilhelm's Murder with Mary Reagan account. *Aftenbladet,* February 14, 1867. Trans. Forrest Brown. Sent to author.

―――. *Summons to All Noble Men and Women to Unite in Temperance Societies for the Purpose of Eradicating Drunkenness and the Use of Brandy Together with a Brief Exposition of the Deleterious Effects of Brandy Drinking.* Temperance pamphlet (Norwegian language handwritten edition). Copy from Archives, Norwegian-American Historical Association.

Waerenskjold vertical file documents. San Antonio: Institute of Texan-Cultures, 1999.

Ygdrasil. Specifications and a photo of the oil painting supplied by Else Marie Thorstvedt, Librarian, Norsk Sjofartsmuseum, Oslo, Norway. *Ygdrasil.* Permission to publish: by Elise Maria Thorstvevt, fax, November 3, 2000.

Interviews, Letters to Author, Emails, and Site Visits

Allen, Elvis. Stovers Cemetery location. Letter, March 2, 2003.

Anderson, George, Immigrant Ships Transcribers Guild. Email from gwa@ccnet.com, February 26, 2000.

Anderson, Victor, pastor, Four Mile Prairie Lutheran Church. Interview on church history, guided tour of cemetery, August 29, 1998.

Arrison, John G., Stephen Phillips Memorial Library, Penobscot Marine

Museum, Searsport, Maine. Emails from library@penobscotmarine-museum.org, February 26, March 6, May 26, 2000.

Austheim, Trond, researcher, Oslo, Norway. Data on barque *Ygdrasil* from Norsk Sjofartsmuseum. Emails January 20, 21, February 10, 2000.

Berge, Anne Britt, executive director, Norwegian-American Chamber of Commerce, Houston. Interviews on Norwegians in Texas, August 22, September 3, 1995.

Bertelsen, Janice Linberg, great-granddaughter of Erik Linberg, Civil War veteran CSA, Clifton, Texas. Interviews on Linberg's Civil War service, July 5, 12, 1995.

Brown, Forrest, archivist, Norwegian-American Historical Association. Emails, April 23, August 30, 1999.

———. Letters, August 8, 2000; May 22, June 5, June 29, November 2, 27, 2001; October 24, 2002; January 28, 2003.

———. Telephone interviews, February 8, March 19, May 5, 2003.

Cifreo, David, Pointe Couppe Parish Police Jury Office, Pointe Couppe, Louisiana. Map (1895) in the Jury Room shows Red River flowing into the Mississippi at Lettsworth. Telephone interview, November 15, 2000.

Cummins, Brian. "Soil and grass types Van Zandt County." Van Zandt County Agricultural Extension Agent, Canton, Texas. Email, June 25, 2001.

Dahle, John, attorney, Denver, Colorado. Review of Charles Russell chapter 9, Dickerson trial manuscript. Letter, March 14, 2003.

Delaney, Roxanne, volunteer seaman, *Elissa,* Galveston. Description of sailing *Elissa, Bounty* (for the film *Mutiny on the Bounty*), and *Niagara.* Interview, October 15, 2000.

DeYbañez, Alexandro, bosun's mate, *Elissa,* Galveston. General sailing ship information and estimate of square feet of sail canvas on *Ygdrasil* and *New England.* Interview, October 15, 2000.

Fox, Peggy, assistant director, Harold B. Simpson Research Center, Hill College, Hillsboro, Texas. Interview on CSA service records and CSA military organization, August 22, 1995.

Freeman, Betty. Interview, August 26, 1999.

Gill, Donald, U.S. Merchant Marine Academy. Referral to sources on the ship *New England.* Telephone interview February 3, 2003.

Gulbrandson, Alvhild, Lillesand, Norway, By-og Sjofartsmuseum. Tour of Lillesand to Elise/Foyn apartment building and Elise home. Interview on Vestre Moland Church, Elise activities, and Foyn marriage, July 15, 1999.

Hamran, Ulf. Referral to *Norwegian Biographic Lexicon,* vol. 4, p. 215, trans. Tor Haugland. Letter, May 17, 2003.

———. Meldahl family history. Letter, March 1, 2003.

Higley, Lisbeth, historian and author, Tonsberg, Norway. Wilhelm's release from jail and false rumor that he was Foyn's bookkeeper. Telephone interview, May 20, 2003.

Hoel, Martin, Clifton, Texas. Farmer and grandson of Christopher Mikel Hoel, Norwegian 1870s immigrant to Clifton. Interview on ranch life and tour of ranch, August 12, 1995.

Hood, Janet, Blue Water Cruising, Seabrook, Texas. Atlantic wind charts, Norfolk, Virginia, to Caracas, Venezuela, with emphasis on Turks Island Pass to New Orleans. Interview, October 15, 2000.

Hood, Jeremy, Blue Water Cruising, Seabrook, Texas. Description of sailing across the Atlantic, from Le Havre, France, to New Orleans; definitions of sailing terms, routes, wind velocities, days required. Interview, October 15, 2000.

Jensen, Lawrence, retired pastor, Our Savior Church, Norse (Clifton), Texas; great-grandson of Chris Jensen, CSA in Civil War; brother of Martin Jensen, former pastor, Four Mile Prairie Lutheran Church and author of church history. Interview, March 10, 1995.

Johnson, Derwood, Justice, 74th State District Court, McLennan County (Waco). Interview, April 4, 2003.

———. Manuscript review email, August 14, 2004.

Kirkeby-Moe, Wenche, Hamar, Norway. Norwegian Consul-General in Houston, 1999–2003. Interview, March 3, 2003.

Lipfert, Nathan, Maine Maritime Museum, Bath. Emails from lipfert@bathmaine.com, March 29, May 23, 2000.

Losneslokken, Auge, pastor, Norwegian Seamans Church. History of Norwegian religious thought. Interview, May 8, 2003.

Nelson, Mrs. Frank G., Hilo, Hawaii. Description of her husband's work on Johan Reinert Reiersen for the introduction to Reiersen's *Pathfinder for Norwegian Emigrants.* Telephone interview, December 16, 2002.

Orbeck, Mary, Clifton, Texas, great-granddaughter of Ovee Colwick, Norwegian immigrant. Interviews on Bosque colony, August 9, September 19, 1995.

Owen, Kenneth, Louisiana Collections, Tulane University Library. Description of sailing ships getting past English Turn on Mississippi below New Orleans. Telephone interview, October 18, 2000.

Patten, Bernard, MD, retired vice chairman of the Department of Neurology, and chief of the Neuromuscular Disease Division, Baylor College of Medicine, Houston. Diagnosis of Torvald death, Elise eye condition. Emails, September 13, 1999; October 13, 2002.

———. Diagnosis of Elise eye injury, Bay Area Writers' League meeting, June 5, 2003.

Russell, Charles. Notes on visit to Four Mile Prairie Lutheran Church, August 27–29, 1998.

Russell, Inger, and Charles Russell. Notes on visit to Howard Street Cemetery, Hamilton, Texas, summer, 2001.

———. Notes on visit to Old Norwegian Cemetery, Brownsboro, October 20, 1999.

———. Notes on visits guided by others: see entries for Polly Wattner, J. C. Sapp, Alvhild Gulbrandson, Doranne Stansell.

Sapp, J. C. Four Mile Prairie retired rancher (age 80). Guided visit to Elise's land and home site, October 27, 1999.

Sparks, Ophelia, great-granddaughter of Elise Waerenskjold. Interview and examination of daguerreotypes, March 5, 2001.

Stansell, Doranne, curator, Bosque Memorial Museum, Clifton, Texas. Interview and museum tours March 10, June 2, 1995.

Stewart, Alan, Maine Maritime Museum, Bath. Letter with attachment: Copy of *Shipping and Commercial News,* New York, Saturday, July 24, 1847 (recording arrivals in New Orleans), March 13, 2000.

Trammel, Sue Ann, great-granddaughter of Elise Waerenskjold. Permission to photograph three paintings Elise brought from Norway and photo portrait of Otto. Interview, summer, 2001.

Trednick, Betty Ann, historian, Four Mile Prairie Lutheran Church. Interview and study of church documents, including Elise land deed to the church, October 27, 1999.

———. McFarland drawing of log church produced for 1970s anniversary celebration. Telephone interview, February 26, 2003.

———. Property deeded to church included church and cemetery. Telephone interview, March 9, 2003.

Van Shaw, William, and Mary Margaret Van Shaw. Permission to photograph Elise Waerenskjold's Jesus embroidery and color tintype of Wilhelm; display of Elise's bonnet and veil. Interview, July 21, 1999.

Wainwright, Ilene, Louisiana Division, New Orleans Public Library. Description of steamship *St. Helena.* Telephone interview. March 15, 2002.

Wattner, Polly. Loan of Wilhelm Waerenskjold letters; guided visit with J. C. Sapp to Elise's Four Mile Prairie land and home site, October 27, 1999.

Weide, Carol. Van Zandt County population, 1850, 1860. Email from txsdc.tamu.edu, June 10, 2003.

Wernet, Mary Linn, head archivist, Cammie G. Henry Research Center, Watson Memorial Library, Northwestern State University, Natchitoches, Louisiana. Interview on resources on Natchitoches–Grand Ecore, February 28, 2000.

INDEX

ISBN 1-58544-453-7

52995

9 781585 444533